FIGURES, FACES & FOLDS

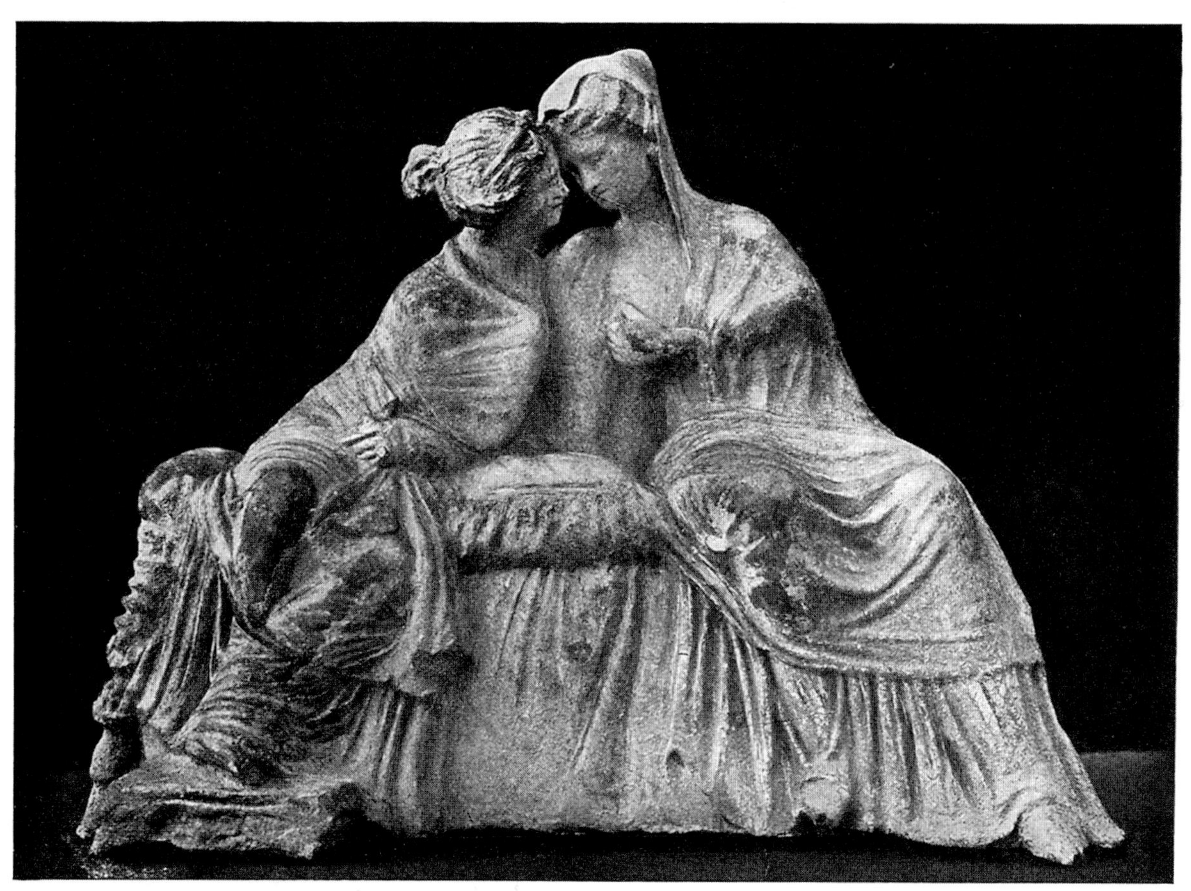

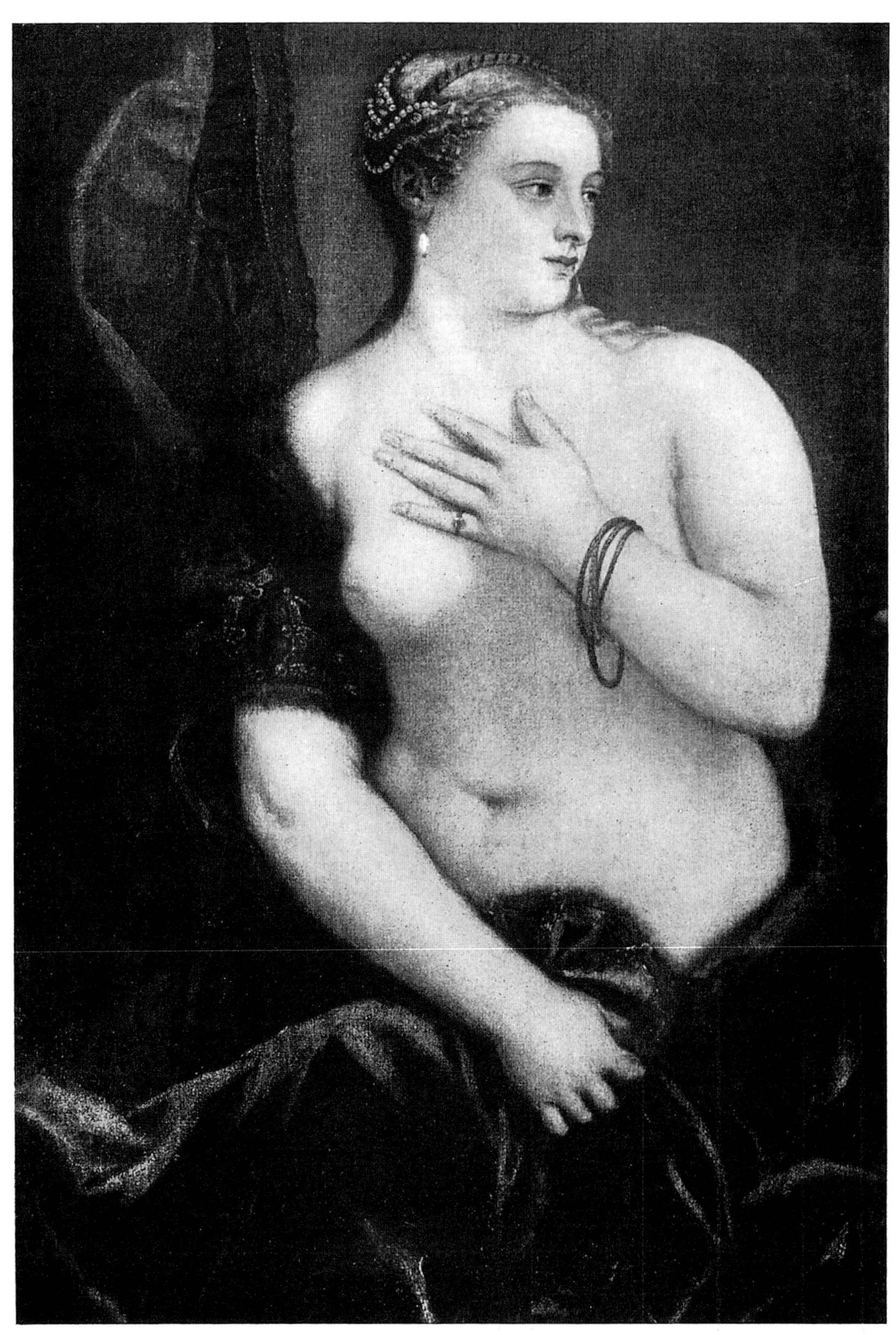

Venus, by TITIAN.

FIGURES, FACES & FOLDS

Women's Form and Dress for Artists, Students and Designers

ADOLPHE ARMAND BRAUN

DOVER PUBLICATIONS, INC.
Mineola, New York

Bibliographical Note

This Dover edition, first published in 2017, is an unabridged republication of the work originally published by Bridgman Publishers, Inc., Pelham, New York, in 1928.

Names: Braun, Adolphe Armand, 1869– author.
Title: Figures, faces & folds : women's form and dress for artists, students and designers / Adolphe Armand Braun.
Other titles: Figures, faces and folds
Description: Mineola, New York : Dover Publications, 2017. | "This Dover edition, first published in 2017, is an unabridged republication of the work originally published by Bridgman Publishers, Inc., Pelham, New York, in 1928."
Identifiers: LCCN 2016043660| ISBN 9780486815923 (paperback) | ISBN 0486815927
Subjects: LCSH: Human figure in art. | Women in art. | Drapery in art. | Clothing and dress in art. | BISAC: ART / Techniques / Life Drawing.
Classification: LCC NC765 .B74 2017 | DDC 700/.4561—dc23 LC record available at https://lccn.loc.gov/2016043660

Manufactured in the United States by LSC Communications
81592701 2017
www.doverpublications.com

PREFACE

THE object of this work is to provide a reference-work and compendium useful for art-workers of every kind who, in the ordinary course of their practice, employ the human figure, with or without its costume and drapery, for purposes of commercial art, illustration, fashion drawing, dress design, and the like. In the series of Standard Poses (114 in number) I have attempted to present as complete a collection as possible of the more graceful attitudes into which the female form naturally falls, graded according to standing, reclining, kneeling, sitting, and various "action" poses. At the same time it has been my endeavour to correlate with these the underlying principles of dress design and construction, and to show the fundamental poses which the female form assumes in wearing stately or beautiful garments.

The Standard Poses have been carefully planned to be of the greatest practical value possible to artists of all sorts, and my models have been chosen with equal care to express what is at the present day considered most beautiful in the types of the female figure. Every century has had its ideals and its "type" in this respect, as a glance at the Historical plates will show, and it has been my aim in producing the series to typify in form, pose, and gesture, the naturally graceful woman of the present day.

In compiling the series of Historical plates I have been at pains to select from the work of great artists and sculptors, from ancient times to the close of the nineteenth century, a series of examples of diverse periods, and schools to demonstrate not only the fairest types of these periods but also correlate them with the contemporary ideas of dress, and show the poses which such dress types evolved. I deal first with full-length figures, after which comes a study of faces graded according to full-face, three-quarter, and profile views, followed by a series of drapery examples. It is to be hoped that much will be gained from the study of these, as from the treatment of hands, draperies, anatomy, and the like which the examples reveal, as do the Standard Poses that follow.

The letterpress includes sections in Drawing the Figure and Face, Drapery, the Principles and Construction of Dress Forms, Practical Anatomy with special reference to the Poses, Notes on the Poses, etc. For the benefit of students and others, I have included a series of plates of large-scale features to show the construction of Shoulders, Necks, Torsos, Thighs, Legs, Feet, etc., and their response to movement. I have also dealt fully with Hands (including Gloves) —perhaps the most difficult of all to draw.

It is my hope that my work on this book has produced something not without originality and interest, expressing the trend of my ideas since the publication of my *Hieroglyphic or Greek Method of Life Drawing*, to which the present volume may be considered as a sequel and companion. In that work I sought to identify the main principles of Anatomy as it concerned Artists, and to incorporate them in a system of Life Drawing. In the present work I go a step further and treat with the natural attitudes of the female form, the principles underlying its clothing, and its response to the wearing of beautiful attire. If I have been in any way successful in achieving these objects, or even in revealing to the artist something additional of the beauty of the human form and its artistic presentation, I shall feel satisfied.

Finally, I must express my thanks to those artists and experts who have given me the benefit of their advice in preparing this book, and collaborated in the production of the drawings and various of the letterpress sections. Although I have not always shared their opinions, I have carefully thought them over, and utilized them as far as was compatible with my scheme, and I am duly grateful for the help I have received from these competent hands. To the collaboration of my models I wish to give particular praise and thanks. Their keenness and enthusiasm have been of inestimable aid and service in the preparation of the photographic poses.

LONDON, *November* 1928. A. A. B.

CONTENTS

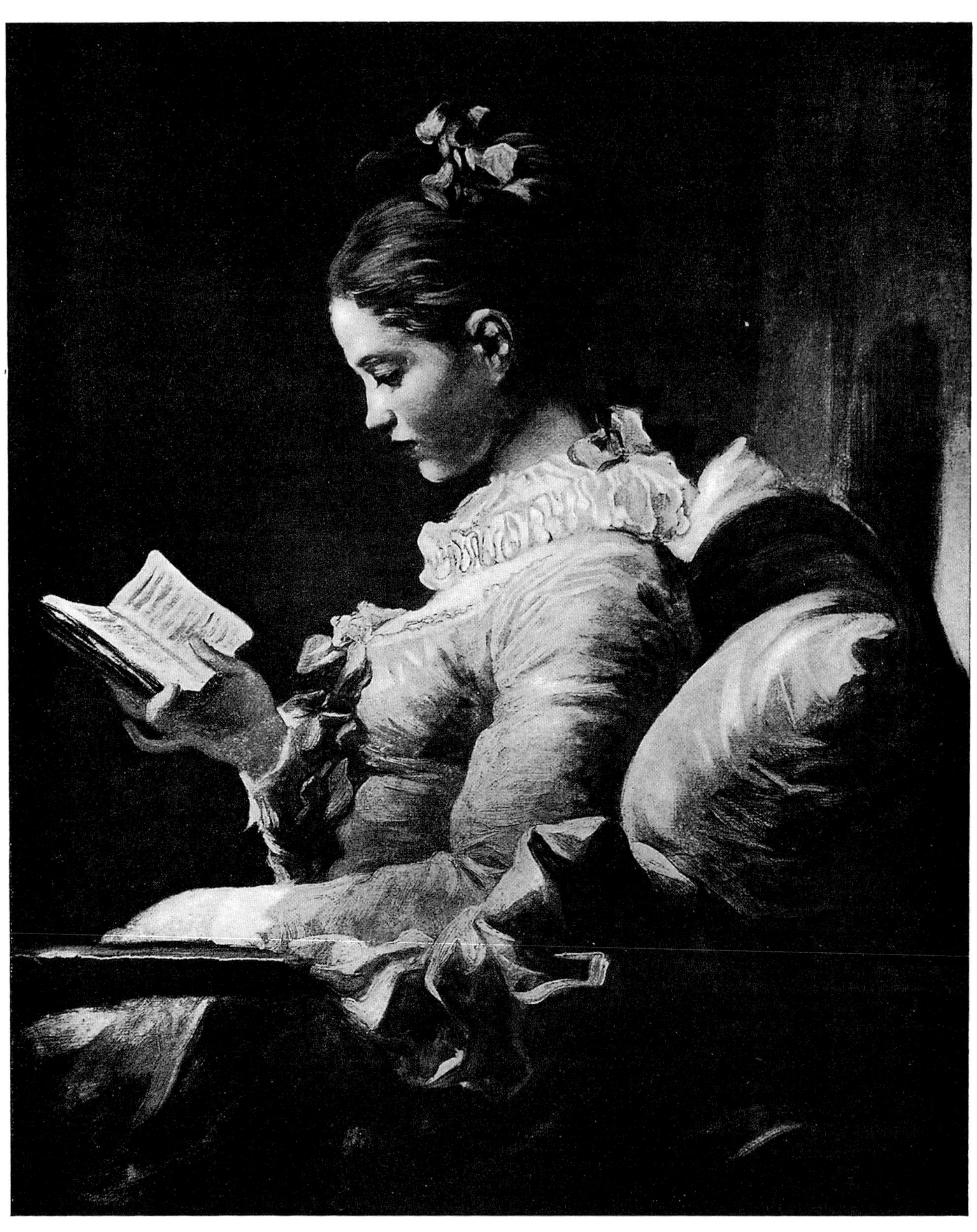

"The Reader," by FRAGONARD.

FIGURES, FACES, AND FOLDS

INTRODUCTION

WE are accustomed to assign to every period in history its own type of beautiful woman, and in determining this type we are largely swayed by the works of great artists of the particular epoch. When, for instance, we think of the Ancient Greeks, our imagination instantly conjures up some Pheidian or Praxitelian type, dignified, perfectly proportioned and athletic, classic in its purity of feature and attitude; or in the same way for the seventeenth century a divergent type comes to mind, that perpetuated in the art of Rubens and his school, healthy and full-blooded, firm of flesh, generous of limb, and indolent of movement. To speak of a "Botticelli" or a "Titian" face has become a commonplace. All of these types live for us in our mind's eye, and reviewing them we can assign to each its characteristic attitudes, gestures, expression, carriage, and so on.

So, in the same way, does the mode of attire synchronize in each case, and just as the favoured type alters, so does Fashion change and vary. We can contrast the exquisite beauty and suitability of the Greek tunic with the stately flowing lines of Mediæval robes. These in turn give way to the conceits of hooped skirts, laced-in waists, farthingales, crinolines, and bustles, till we find in the twentieth century a marked tendency towards a reversion to simpler forms and more fundamental principles in feminine fashions. It is to be hoped that some future generation will evolve an attire as graceful, hygienic, and perfectly fitted for usage as that of the Golden Age in Greece.

Fashion is notoriously fickle and liable to sudden change. Nature knows no change but the slow steady march of evolution, in which a thousand years are accounted as so many seconds. Infinite as are the variations of the human body—one tall of stature where another is short, one fair of skin when another is dark, one so much more perfectly formed and proportioned than another—yet all are built on the same logical plan, all are wrought by Nature to fulfil her scheme to the highest degree. The human form is in every case endowed with a rhythm and harmony and constructed with a masterly logic which the artist must seek perfectly to understand before he presumes to set his hand to interpret its beauty.

Man may be satisfied in possessing a more rectangular and somewhat compact frame. A woman's outline sways wave-like along her body in a rhythmic arrangement of curves affecting every shape from head to foot, sinking and rising in logical sequence, enhancing the beauty and harmony of the whole. How innumerably subtle are the variations which it registers in the grace of its natural attitudes, in movement or repose, bending, stretching, kneeling, reclining, or engaged in innumerable occupations or recreations! How fascinating is the balance and muscular tension of the dance, the ripple of muscles as the body bends or stretches, the statuesque dignity of the final position!

Now, at last, woman has attained her long-desired freedom and is on an equal footing with man. She has dared to become natural, to show herself as beautiful as Nature made her. The woman of to-day is a healthy, blithe being who wants to share man's joys in a healthy, blithe life. The ideal type of the present is slim and muscularly perfect; she loves exercise and is physically, as well as mentally, energetic. But at the same time she retains her essentially feminine characteristics of grace and elegance, and her attire, while remaining loose and free for exercise, still retains all the charm of femininity. The dress she favours is a fit covering for a beautiful body, one that preserves its outline and rhythm, and gives at the same time a full, comfortable play to the limbs.

Just as the Historical section of this book portrays through the work of old Masters the essential types of beauty and attire at each period of the past, so in our section of " Standard Poses " we have attempted, with the collaboration of our models, to build up a series that will depict by camera the woman of to-day in all her infinite charm and variety, draped or undraped, in action or repose, at work and at play. We have sought by these means to produce a series which shall be of real use and significance to all who seek to represent the female form—illustrators, commercial or fashion artists, designers, and the like, as a source of ideas and inspiration. In the matter of dress we have sought first to determine, then to demonstrate the fundamental forms and folds which are to be found underlying the modes of dress of every period, and to show their application in as large a range of positions as possible to the most graceful types of female figures. With these fundamental dress-forms we believe it to be quite essential that all who concern themselves with the representation or adornment of the female form should familiarize themselves. Obviously, an adequate knowledge of the anatomical, physiological, and mechanical conditions relating to the human body must be the starting-point, and give us the right foundation.

It is evident that clothes must be made for people who are built on a certain plan, who move about and use their limbs in various ways, and are dependent on external influences such as cold, heat, light, rain, wind, dust, etc. But apart from these considerations, and disregarding entirely ethnographic, historic and fashionable problems which enter into the question of dress, the moral and æsthetic demands are important. Intelligent cutting and assembling and putting together of suitable materials respect all the conditions which have been mentioned.

A perfect garment should fit the body without clinging too closely to it, without impeding any of its natural functions, such as circulation of the blood, breathing, digestion, the swelling of muscles during work, the free and easy movement at the joints, the dilation of the skin during heat ; and yet garment and body should give the impression of an intrinsic unity.

FIGURES AND FOLDS

The cross-section of the human trunk is an ellipsoid the diameters of which diminish towards the centre. The transverse diameter is longer than the saggital dorsoventral one, but in the middle of the trunk the horizontal section approaches the circle. At the back there is a shallow groove corresponding to the furrow within which the vertical column lies embedded between the ribs and dorsal muscles, so that the actual compass of the section is rather kidney-shaped. There is another shallow trench at the front of the breast, caused by the sternum which retreats between the ribs, and the fleshy pectorals.

The waist in women is a natural phenomenon, and the nobler the human form the more elegant and nicely curved is the waist line. Often a slim waist goes with rounded hips and finely-shaped limbs and other signs of a pure race, such as a high instep and delicate joints. It is partly a matter of anatomical training ; the women of some African tribes have most delicate waists, and features also influenced by training. A fine roundness of the chest, in a soft curve beginning at the throat and shoulder, lowering itself at the ribs and sternum, may be regarded as particularly beautiful.

It is no fault if the breasts are only small in comparison with the finely-curved thorax. Added to straight, well-proportioned, beautifully-rounded limbs, to good symmetry throughout the body, they ensure that complete harmony which is so admirable in a perfect figure.

Varying in detail, especially in the direction of their planes, the configuration of the shoulders is of the greatest importance. The shoulders are the principal key to habiliment. Good shoulders are square or slightly sloping ; they begin at the base of the neck and envelop the clavicles, the head of the humerus, and the upper part of the scapula. Their highest point coincides with the head of the humerus beneath the Deltoid muscle. A good shoulder is wide and also full from back to front.

Next in importance to the shoulders are the hips, the roundness of which, just below the waist, enables men, and especially women, to use them as supports to a waistband of varying width (the corset may be designed as such), from which garments may be suspended; and they play no mean part in the evolution of costume.

Fortunately for modern mankind, at the present day dress designers respect the delicacy of the abdomen, and trust the shoulders with the work of supporting the garments, for which their strong, bony, and muscular structure certainly fits them admirably. Athletics and hygiene have taught us to reduce the number of garments worn together at any one time to a minimum, and this fact has considerably lightened the burden which the shoulders need carry.

In reality, a form of dress based on the principle of suspension from the shoulders or hips was adopted very early in the most various countries, and developed by the more civilized peoples throughout the ages. Whereas the close-fitting garment which enfolds the shape has the advantage of greater protection of the underlying form, the suspended garment gives freedom to the body, and, thanks to its amplitude, lends itself to a more varied æsthetic treatment. In the combination of close-fitting and suspended garments, we can hope to attain that perfection of clothing for which mankind, through the medium of fashion, has ever striven, and which it has actually accomplished at various times.

In running rapidly through the history of costume, we will see these two complementary principles in use, sometimes one predominating over the other, but hardly ever used independently from each other. But even before starting our investigations we will award the Greeks the palm of good taste and also pay them our tribute of admiration for their thorough understanding of the art of dressing (as of so many other accomplishments). They alone understood how to blend the rhythm of their own beautiful bodies with the rhythmic lines derived from a well-thought-out drapery. By utilizing the wide transverse planes of bust and abdomen for the production of horizontal folds, by opposing to the wave-like rising and falling of their relief vertical pleats and cascades of undulating meanders, they achieved effects of dignity and plastic beauty of which their statues give us a vivid idea.

The intersection of the horizontal and vertical system of draping in semi-transparent materials over the well-shaped form produced that wonderful unison of vestment and figure, such as only the highest artistic genius and the noblest taste were able to evolve. The Caryatides of the Erecthion and the Niobe of the Acropolis demonstrate the beauty of vertical and horizontal folds; in the Caryatides the long tunic is pulled up and arched over the abdomen and hips, thus producing an effective break and a display of beautiful proportions.

In the section entitled the "Anatomy of Dress," we have dwelt at length on the design of Greek vestment, and given numerous illustrations. The object was twofold—firstly, to show by a number of examples of fundamental simplicity, the numerous applications of which the square or oblong piece of material was capable; secondly, being struck with the similarity between the Greek and modern outlook on life, to show why dress designers should pay particular attention to Greek costume.

Modern dress is nothing more than the Greek tunic adapted to the mode of the day. Drapery is being studied again, and Paris, where Professor Ruppert has a large following among dress designers, makes use of its particular understanding of this long lost art, in applying it to its creation.

The couturier invents little that is new; he knows his model, his material, and his history of costume, and it is by having these three notions well fixed in his mind that he evolves tomorrow's *chef-d'œuvre*.

It would seem to us of first-hand importance that the artist of every kind, besides making a detailed study of the anatomy of the human body, should at the same time turn his attention to the anatomy of costume which we have briefly touched upon above. For the designer or producer of clothes such a study is absolutely essential, and it would seem equally indispensable for any artist who is to attempt the depiction of the clothed figure. The aspects which draperies and folds present according to the pose of the body are innumerable, and are shown to as full an extent as is possible in the plates of this book. How such folds synchronize with the lines and contours of the body beneath, pick up and adopt its rhythm and create a unity out of the whole is not one of the least fascinating studies in the field of art.

This book deals with the living woman, the woman at work or at recreation, in all the diversity of her moods and attitudes. The greatest pains have been taken throughout to register those poses into which the graceful body falls naturally in the course of its everyday activities, and we believe that, if we have succeeded in our purpose, the book should prove a fount of suggestion for the art-worker. Finally, we do not pretend that this or any other book could in any way replace the use of an actual living model. It is intended rather as a supplement, a guide, and a work of reference, in which the female countenance and clothing as depicted by great artists for all time are shown in association with representative womanly forms of the present day.

DRAWING THE FIGURE AND THE FACE

MANY artists draw the figure regularly in the course of their duties, and also during the whole of their career.

Their object may be one of practice, in the same way as the musician practises his scales; or they may wish to use the figure in their compositions or designs; or their studies may aim at being pictures and studies at the same time.

It is curious that fashion artists and dress designers whose work is founded on the figure should mostly draw from imagination, sometimes using the glass and drawing from their own image to correct details, or else use photographs and design their figures from these.

To this majority the photographs reproduced in this book will be welcome.

But it seems a pity that drawing from life should not be more generally in use, especially among fashion artists. To be able to pose a good figure just as required, for a definite purpose and with the idea fresh in mind and filled with the enthusiasm of creation, is not only fascinating but the simplest way of doing justice to a difficult task.

Artists who always draw from imagination must stagnate. They are like people with a good vocabulary but who are not in touch with life; they can string words together and say a large number of things, but what they say lacks imagination. It is dull and uninteresting. People who live, on the other hand, who partake of the joys and sorrows of existence, who possess the spirit of adventure, and who take their share of human affairs, are usually attractive talkers, and shine by their mode of expression and by their individuality.

In the same way, working from the undraped model imparts the necessary inspiration, enlarges the understanding, and gives vitality to the work.

To draw well from a model is nevertheless a difficult performance. There is so much that passes through the mind of the artist while he draws, so much of interest that can be transferred to his drawing, that a narrowing down of his interest is advisable.

By thinking out the design beforehand a great deal of concentration of thought becomes possible, and better results are attained.

A dress parade, a show, a window, a magazine, any incentive might be the primary source of inspiration, but the fact that a design has been thought out enables the artist to look for definite things while he draws from his model, and perhaps by exaggerating these points ever so slightly, to give more force to his design.

It may be the curve of a shoulder which becomes more marked, or the line of a leg which is made more abrupt, or some shifting of one or several features which the seeing eye of the designer will be able to visualize in a position that would be naturalistically correct.

In fashion as well as in fine art, design has taken the place of naturalistic representation. The renewed interest in design does not seem to be a passing phase of art, but a logical development on lines diametrically opposite to those of science.

In science we cannot be exact enough, and realism is necessary. But the realism of science has killed the realism of art, and too many of the things which we can represent truly are due entirely to the machine. This fact alone should be enough to divorce the artist from absolute realism, and to make him incline to convention.

There are, however, many artists who will not take any notice, and who consider the exact imitation of nature as the most wonderful accomplishment of art. Among these are some very eminent artists and at least one fashion artist, who can claim to be right at the top of the profession.

But these people are so filled with the love of nature that they do not reflect whether there is or is not any scientific competition with their art ; they do that which pleases them, and do not trouble about consequences. Sometimes the consequences are in their favour. The fact of their love of nature expresses itself somehow, and their work abounds with the individuality of their outlook and reflects their feelings.

But only the talented or the pertinacious can afford this fanaticism and independence of action ; the others must fall into line with the leaders of the day.

Whether he aims for realism or convention, the artist should seize every opportunity of working from the living model, and connect his design, this term being taken in its most complete sense, with the figure in front of him.

Accidents of light and shade, colour, the setting, the material with which he works—everything, in fact, which establishes a live contact between the artist and his work—flashes intelligence to his mind and helps him to attain his ultimate goal.

Besides the artistic there is the practical aspect of figure drawing from the dress designer's and fashion artist's point of view.

How is the human body shaped, where are its widest and narrowest measurements, to what extent can the limbs be considered as tubular ? The slope of the shoulders and the width of the hips have a great deal to do with dress. How certain poses lend themselves to a fine display of drapery, what are the proportions of the various parts of the figure in relation to one another, these and many other questions must occur to the practical man who uses the living model, and their solution can only have a beneficial effect on his production.

The finest foundation to a costume drawing is a well thought out and well executed figure.

Many masters have clothed and are still clothing their figures on the solid rock of the undraped form. The conscientious fashion artist and the aspiring dress designer cannot do less than the master, for they also must aim at becoming masters in their own particular line.

The fashion artist, and particularly the dress designer, ought to change their models as often as possible, and each new model should be as different as possible from the old one in build and countenance.

He must study his model with his eyes, and with his imagination alert, draw her as she appears to be, and also make idealized drawings of her—make improvements which his experience or task might suggest.

In a book entitled *The Human Form in Art* I have concluded my reflections on drawing the figure by discussing the time factor. I believe that a drawing, to be live and interesting, should be done rapidly. Otherwise it lacks spirit, looks tame, laboured, and unconvincing.

" The Oriental draughtsman has solved the problem by delaying the drawing until he has given it ample preliminary consideration. The draughtsman as we know him gives little thought to his object beforehand, but tries to rivet his attention while he draws it. But apart from precedence of thought over action, rapidity of execution depends on quick reactions, on concentration, and on a certain feverish excitement. These conditions induce an exalted state of mind which helps creation, enlivens our work with the spark of emotion and with flashes of inventiveness. By practising three-minute poses we train ourselves to unhesitating action, to immediate decision. We learn to waste no time on trifles, while we strain every nerve to express all we perceive.

" To counteract any undue haste to which we might become accustomed, we ought to alternate these short-time exercises with others lasting for hours.

" During these long sittings, we should pay the greatest attention to measurement, the foundation of all good draughtsmanship ; to composition, as being essential in a work of art ; to light and shade, as revealing tri-dimensional form ; to linear and aerial perspective, as stressing the illusion of reality ; to the underlying structure, for helping our understanding of flesh and bone.

" The notions which these mature exercises will have bred in us will gradually become part and parcel of our artistic equipment and, sinking into our subconscious mind, acquire the power to express themselves automatically.

" We shall then be ready to impart to our rapid work the energies accumulated in the pursuit of truth and excellence, and to shine by our knowledge and spirited execution."

Assuming that they draw only from models, very few artists, except with constant practice, are able to concentrate their minds so completely that they can make everything they know about the figure enter into their work, and at the same time pay attention to such important points as essential action, beauty, grace, which are not always perfectly expressed by the model holding the pose.

The artist's personal feeling and imagination coming into play, his art will fill the gap between reality and ideal.

Where there is action—and without it a work of art is dull—the action which the artist is to reproduce should re-echo in him. Every nerve within himself must vibrate in unison with those of the model, and while he draws he must be mentally espousing the same attitude as that he wishes to depict. If he can do this he will have achieved something much more vital than a mere display of knowledge, for he will have put his own individuality into his work. When his understanding transcends that of mere learning, his drawing, instead of being a cold record of facts, acquires the warmth and animation of real intelligence and life.

Beauty and grace are ubiquitous, but do not necessarily lie on the surface of every human form. It is the nobility of the artist's mind which makes them rise to the surface and appear in his work.

The craftsman who can see the goddess in the human figure that stands before him betrays his admiration ; his thoughts and feelings are reflected in his craft.

Does this mean that the artist should neglect the study of anatomy, light and shade, perspective, and let feeling and imagination take the reins ? Not at all, because his competence depends on his knowledge and technical skill more than anything else. But he must draw with all his heart and soul as well as with his head if he wants to shine.

To make their drawings look smart and attractive, especially to a public whose interest in Art does not go beyond outward appearances, artists need devote a great deal of attention to the faces they depict. Then, again, it is advisable that they should be thorough and not content with some banal, insipid, doll-like head.

It may be going too far to wish that every fashion head should be a striking and smart portrait, full of the character and charm of real personality ; but a near approach to it would be an achievement within the powers of the gifted.

The artist who has a bent for psychology will need no encouragement, and knows the world of difference which exists between one face and another.

And yet how much there is that all faces have in common ! Their structure is the same; one skull resembles another. A standard skull should be sought out and learnt by heart. It is of the greatest importance that the artist should know every detail concerning the skull, how the frontal bone curves towards the eye-sockets and upwards and backwards, how the eye-sockets are shaped, how the jaw-bone is connected with the temporal bone, the exact position of the nose in relation to the eyes, and everything else concerning the skull.

It is not sufficient to draw from the skull to know all about it. One must measure the component parts with a pair of compasses and note the various distances. The planes of the skull and their position in relation to one another should be well understood.

After the skull come the various features. A standard face of a man, woman, and child could be selected among the numerous casts which can be purchased from the museums or shops. In the same way as with the skull the faces adopted should be learnt by heart, each feature being attentively examined and drawn with the utmost care and understanding. Simplicity of interpretation should go hand in hand with close observation of form.

Drawings of the standard heads shown in the illustrations and every one of their features should be made from many different positions, always paying attention to the altered perspective.

The heads should be arranged to stand successively level, slanting, high, low, far and near, and always drawn to life size. It is wasting precious time to make studies of faces and features on a small scale.

A little exaggeration and sharpness of treatment in making the various planes diverge from each other is desirable. On the other hand, the planes that merge into each other or that are wedged together should be clearly constructed.

Your standard skull and standard faces well fixed in your mind, you are now ready to draw from the model, and able to represent all the similarities and all the differences between the standard face and that of the model.

The thorough knowledge which you have gained from your standard skull enables you to detect and to connect salient parts and depressions in the model's face with the skull you have in mind, and thus to *construct* your face with a good deal of power.

The features will differ more or less, in most cases very considerably from those of your standard face, but if you have learnt to draw those of your standard face with desirable precision and profoundness, you will find it comparatively easy to represent those of your model with the same verisimilitude.

To get your likeness, remember that your first object should be to reproduce the proportions and the character of the face.

Measurement of the various planes and distances and due regard to perspective will give you the right proportions, and you will arrive at a satisfactory likeness. So that the likeness be complete, you must also catch the character of your model. This is more subtle and complex.

Character may lie in the whole of the face or be dominantly expressed by one particular or various features.

It is the discovery and correct rendering of the one or several features which results in a striking likeness. The successful caricaturist has the faculty of finding out the dominating character of a person, only his medium is exaggeration.

In the same way the expert portraitist can seize upon the character of a face and give emphasis to it in his work, only in his case without the comic or aggressive touch. Sometimes by elongating an eye, bending a nose, curving a lip a little forcibly, but not violently or jerkily, the character of the person depicted is revealed or emphasized.

Apart from character, expression enters into the composition of the face, but the truthful reproduction of expression it is not given to every artist to perform. Fully exhibited emotions, such as laughter, terror, hatred, surprise, are not within the compass of this dissertation; they do not interest the commercial or fashion artist, and the portraitist himself fights shy of them.

But subtle emotions which animate the expression almost imperceptibly impart just that degree of vitality which one looks for in a work of art.

Even now, with the innumerable records which the camera is providing, the enigmatic smile of Da Vinci's " Mona Lisa " impresses us by its elusiveness and mystery.

The commercial artist need not, of course, emulate the achievements of the old masters, but many fine shades of sentiment are within his range, and the pleased, polite, dignified, attentive, happy, vain look are part of his stock-in-trade. He should be able to provoke and detect and render these expressions very adequately.

To draw faces well requires a specialized apprenticeship, and the trouble the artist takes in studying the subject should be commensurate with the responsibility of moulding the mentality and taste of the people.

Individual features are not really so different as may appear at first sight, and in drawing them their proportion should be paramount. It is by a nice balancing of one feature against another that he evolves types that win approval. But whatever he does he must not neglect reality, and his faces must remain true to life.

The best method by which to impart beauty, character, and individuality to the drawing of a face is to draw from one which nature has endowed with similar perfection. Lucky the artist who possesses such a face, and to whom a mirror or two are all the help required. In the majority of cases the artist has to invent the beauty which he shows in his work or to improve that of his models.

FACES

AS REPRESENTED BY GREAT ARTISTS AND SCULPTORS OF THE PAST, GRADED ACCORDING TO THE ANGLE OF DEPICTION

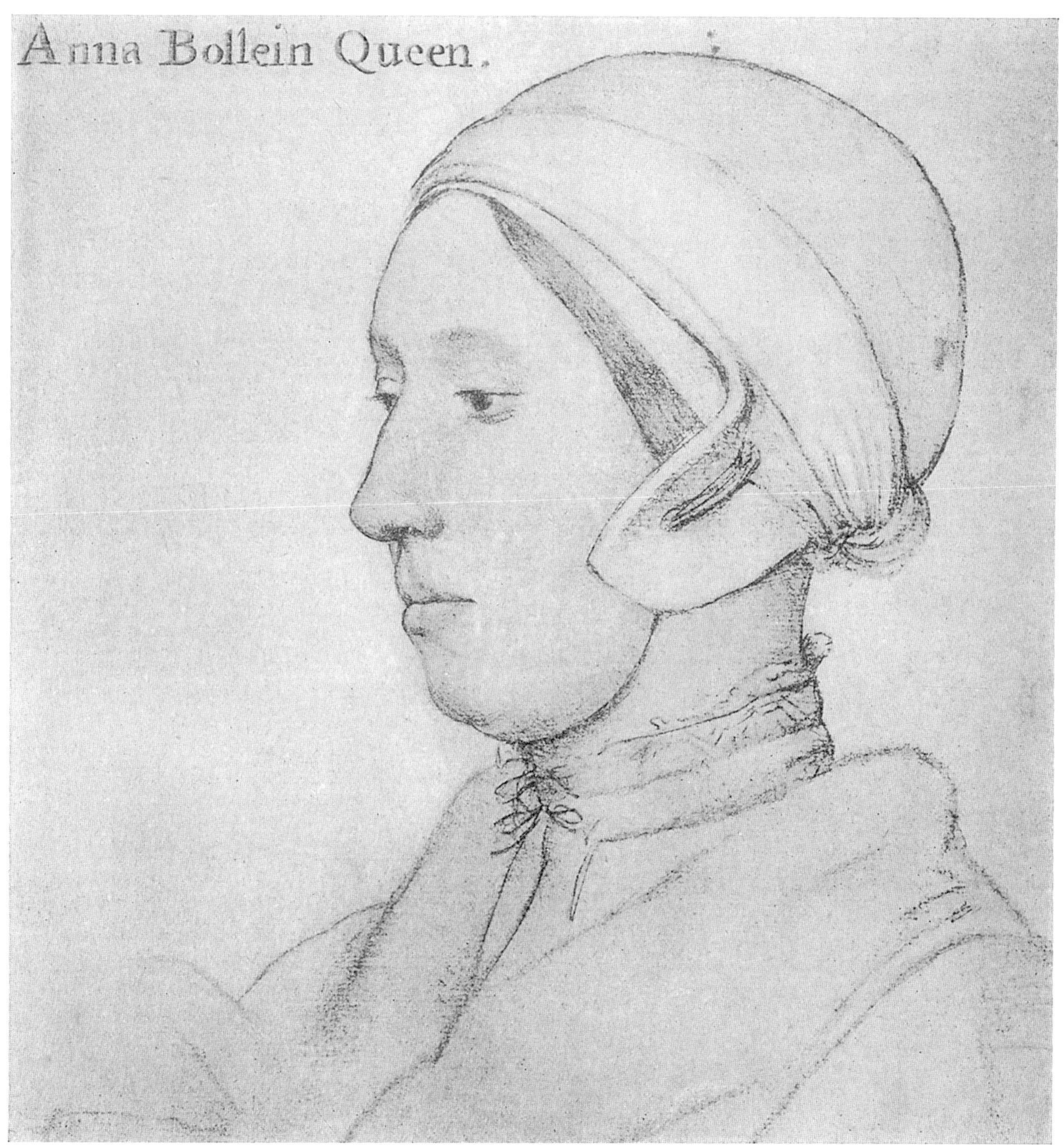

Ann Boleyn, by HOLBEIN.

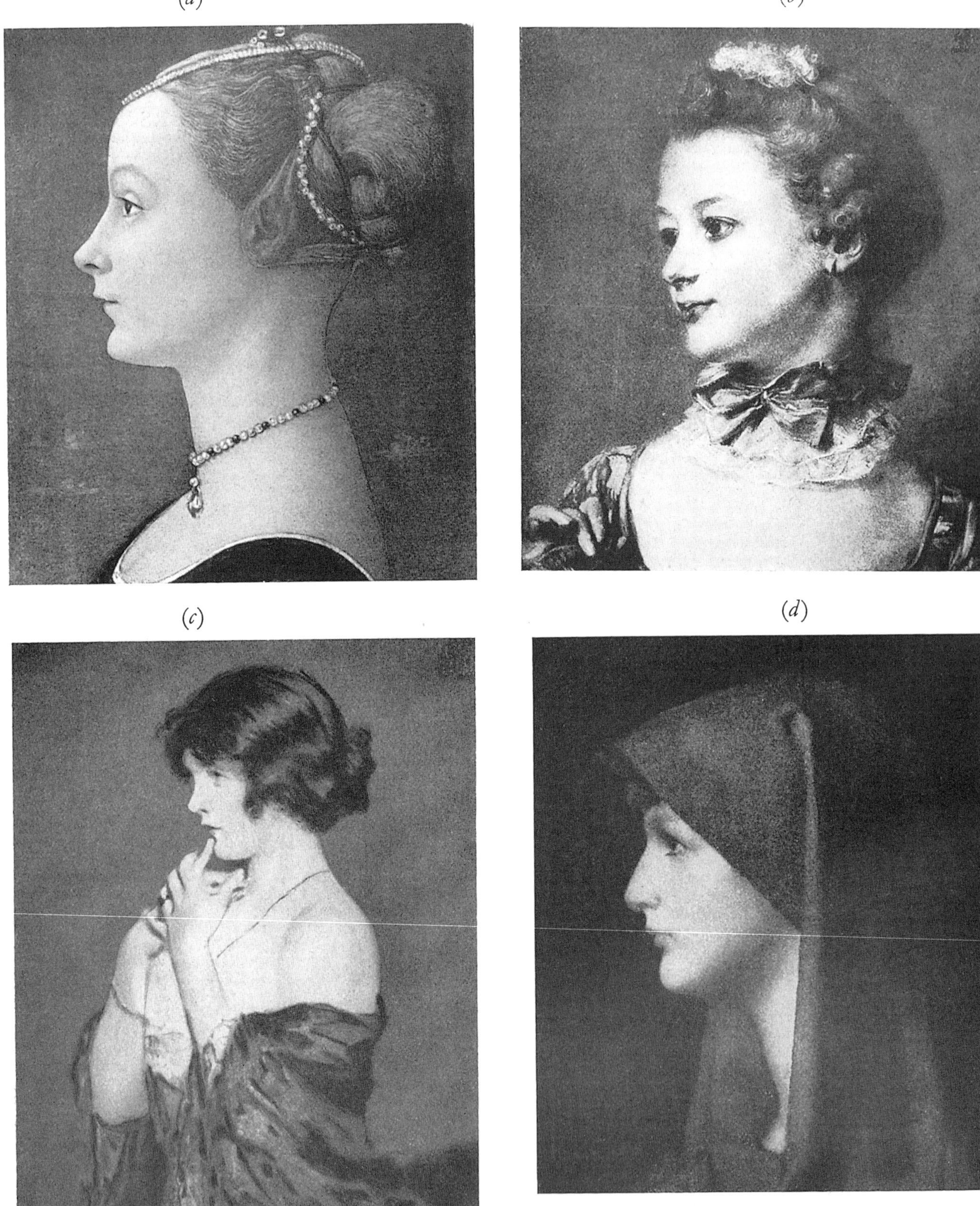

(*a*) By Piero della Francesca. (*b*) By Perroneau. (*c*) By Gabriel Nicolet. (*d*) By J. J. Werner.

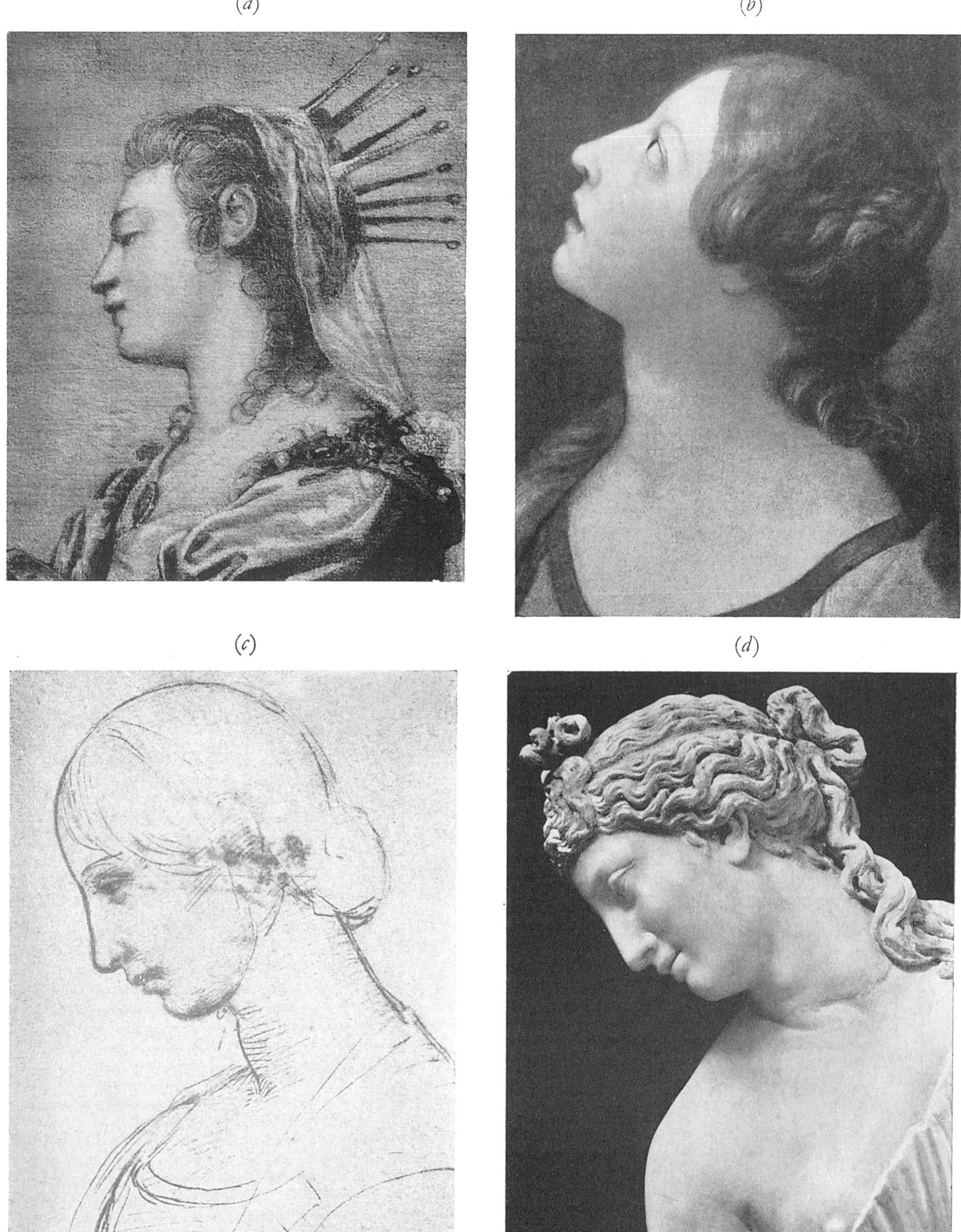

(*a*) By Tintoretto. (*b*) By Guido Reni. (*c*) By Raphael.
(*d*) Detail of the Venus Callipige shown on page 40.

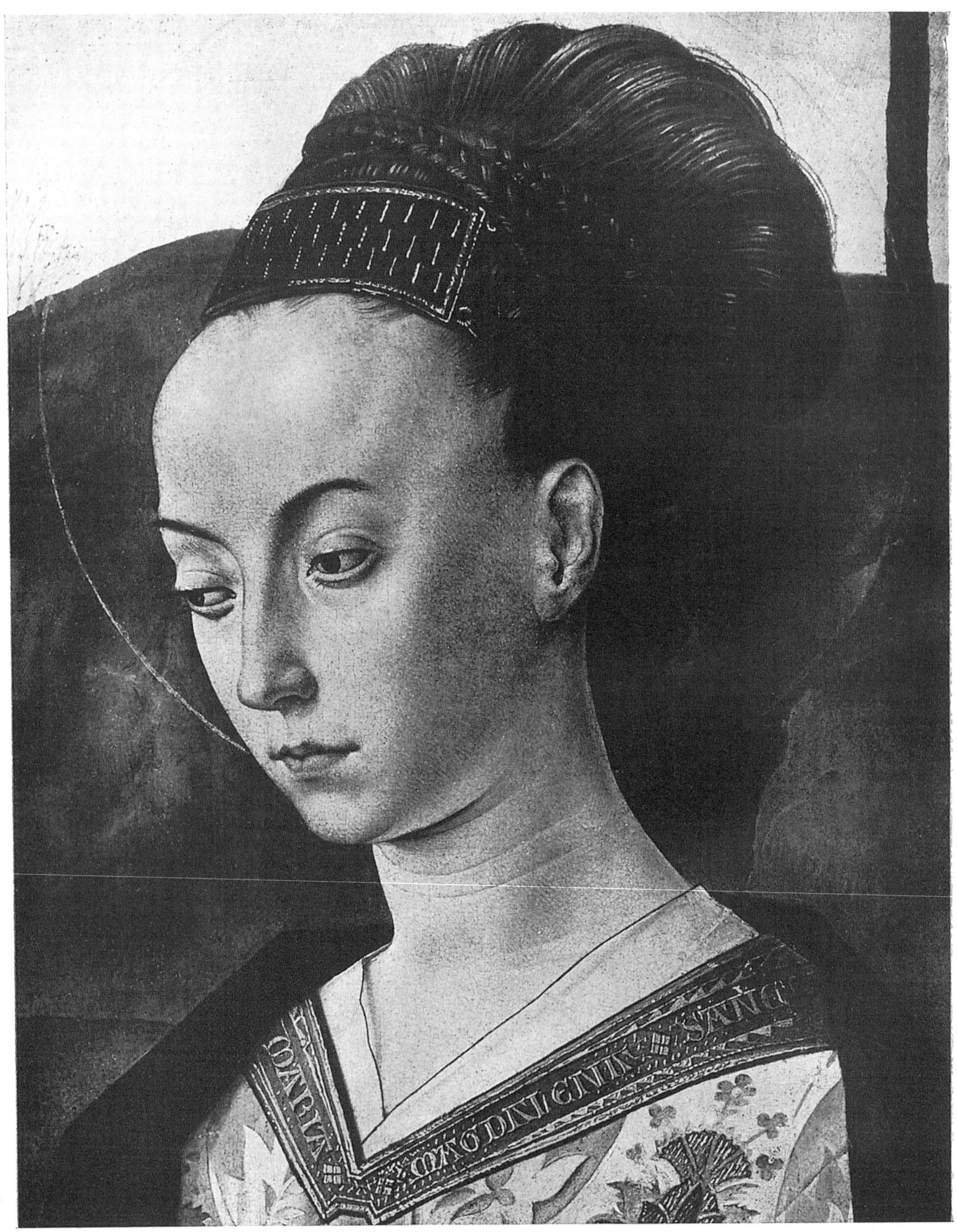

Head of the Magdalen by VAN DER GOES.

(*a*)

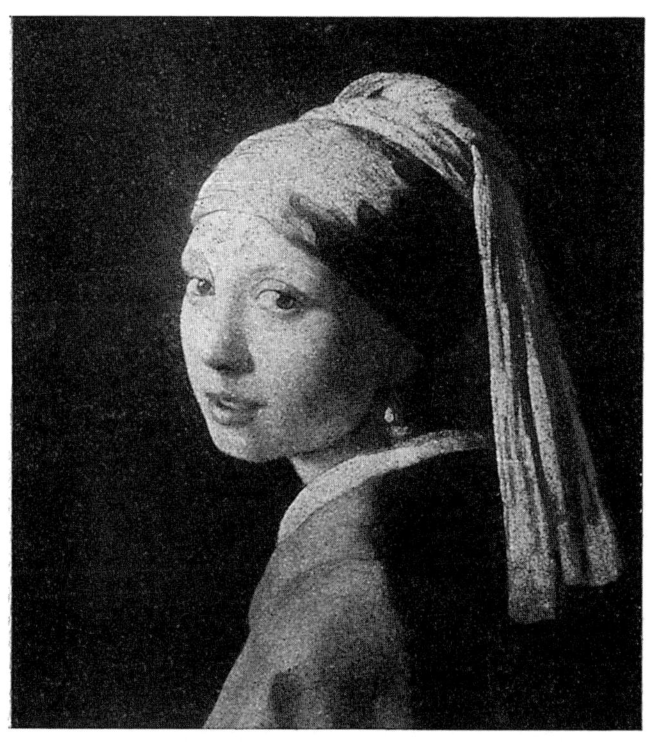

(*b*)

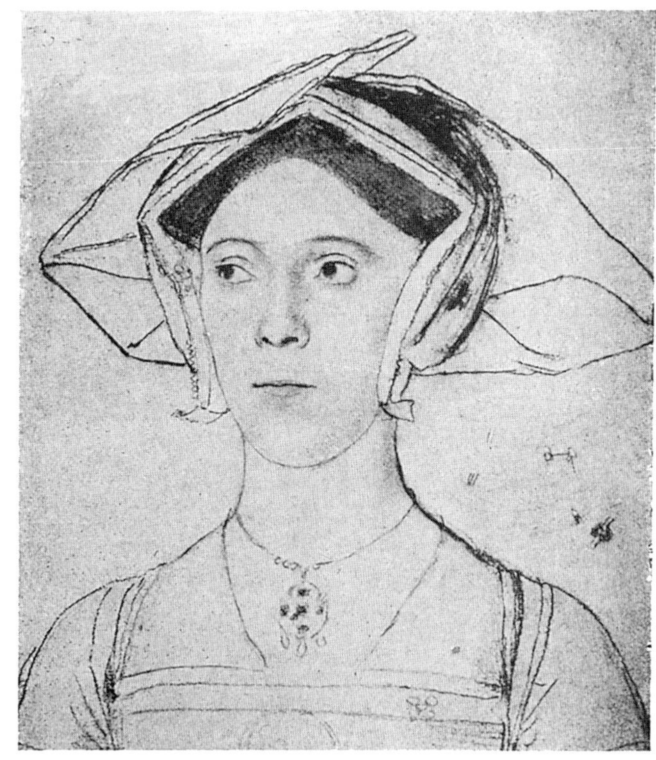

(*c*)

(*d*)

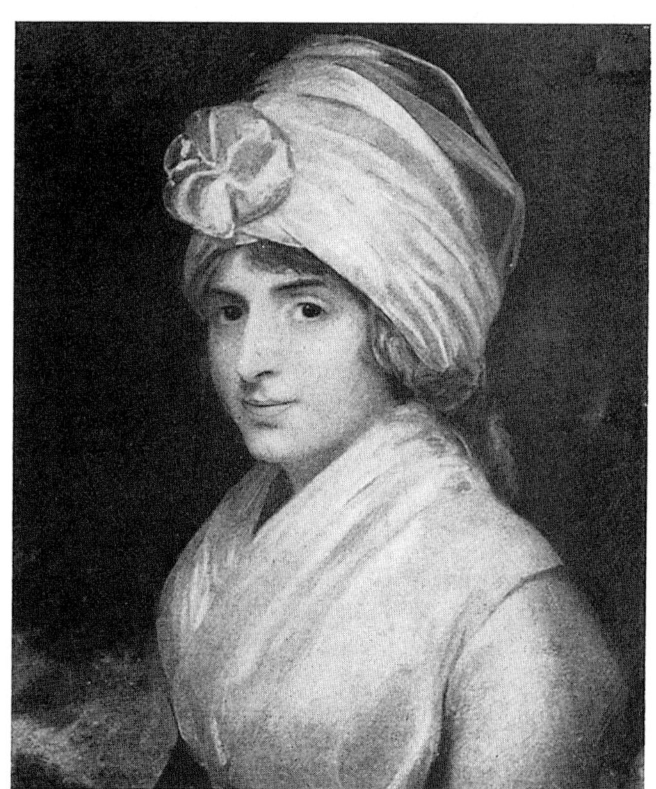

(*a*) By Vermeer. (*b*) By Holbein. (*c*) By Memling. (*d*) By Sir William Beechey.

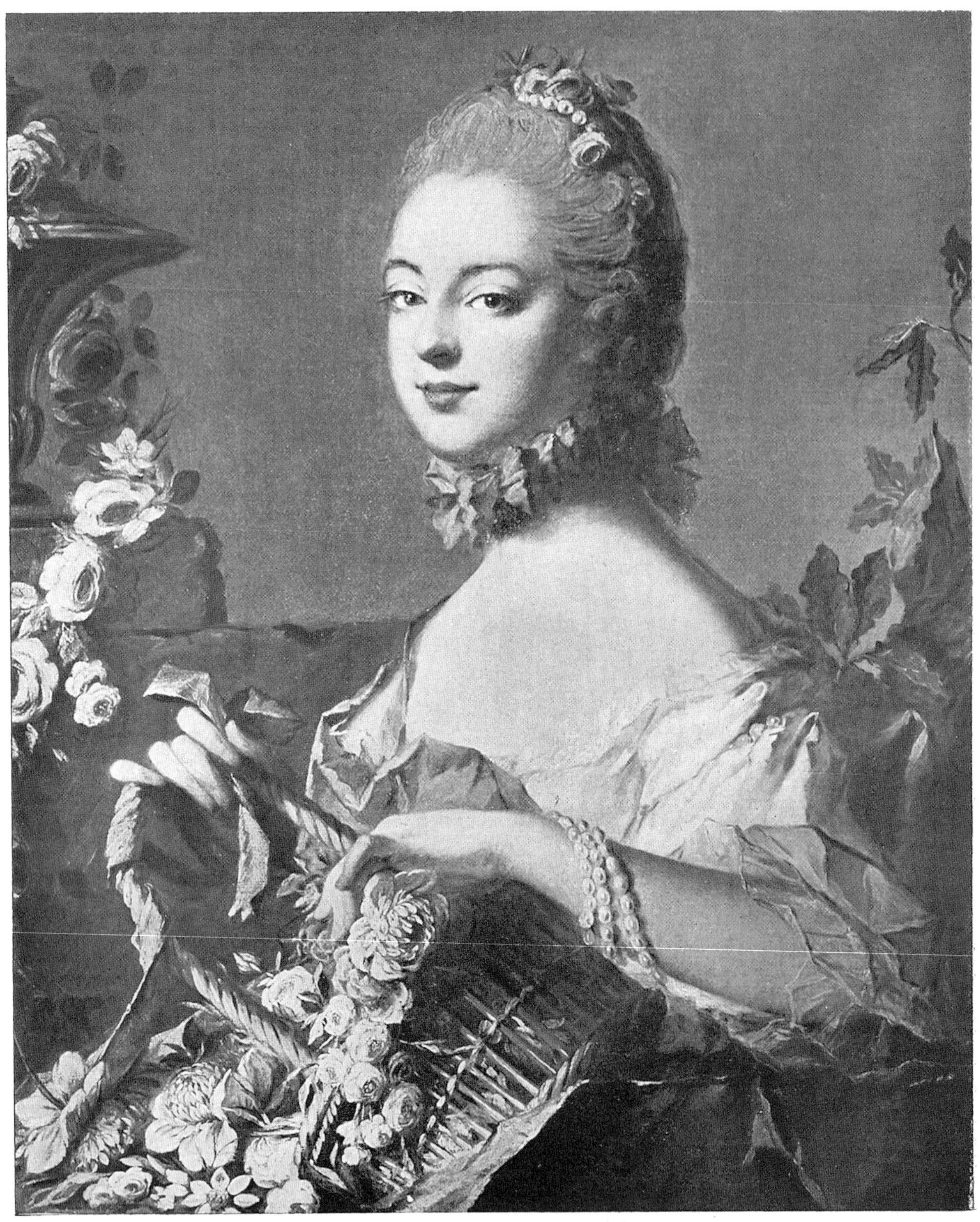

Detail of a French Eighteenth Century Portrait.
Artist unknown.

(*a*)

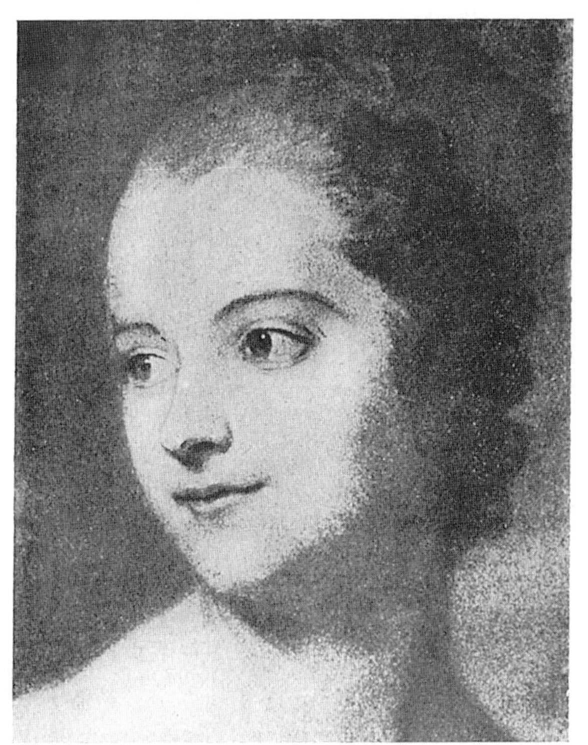

(*b*)

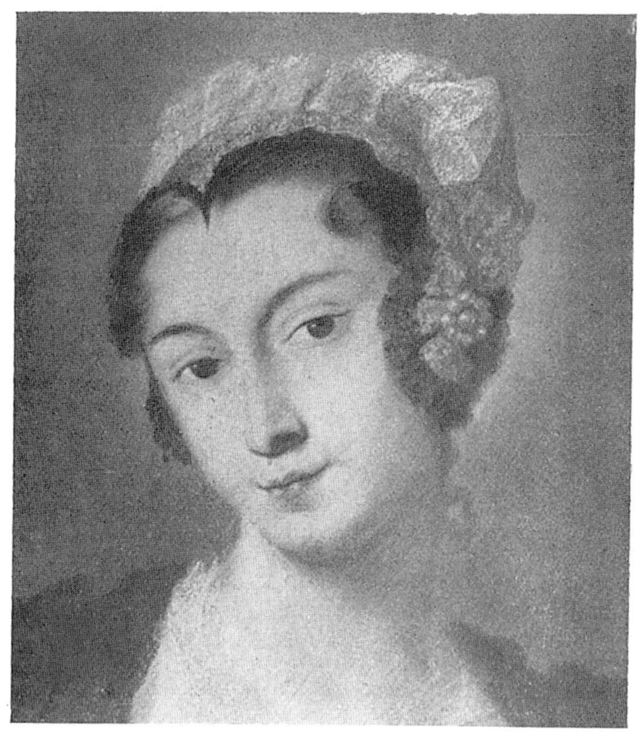

(*c*)

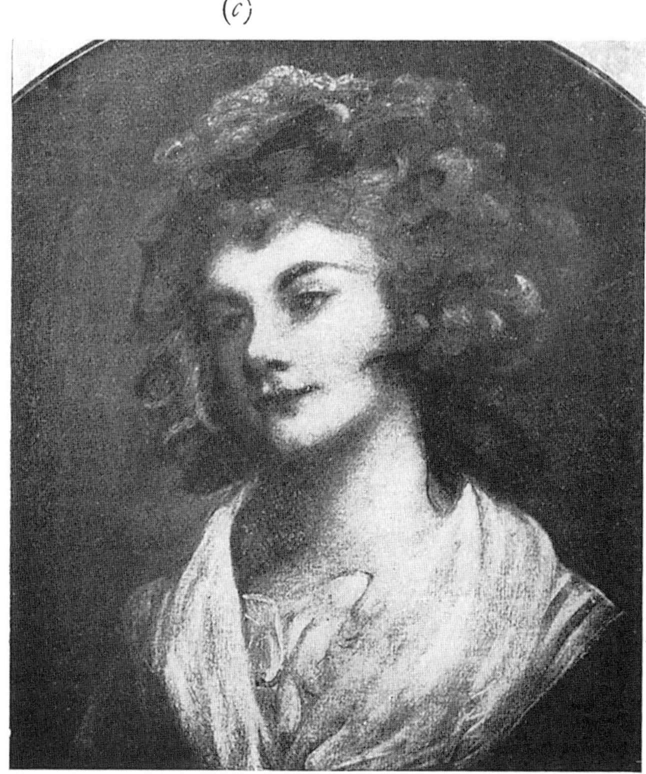

(*d*)

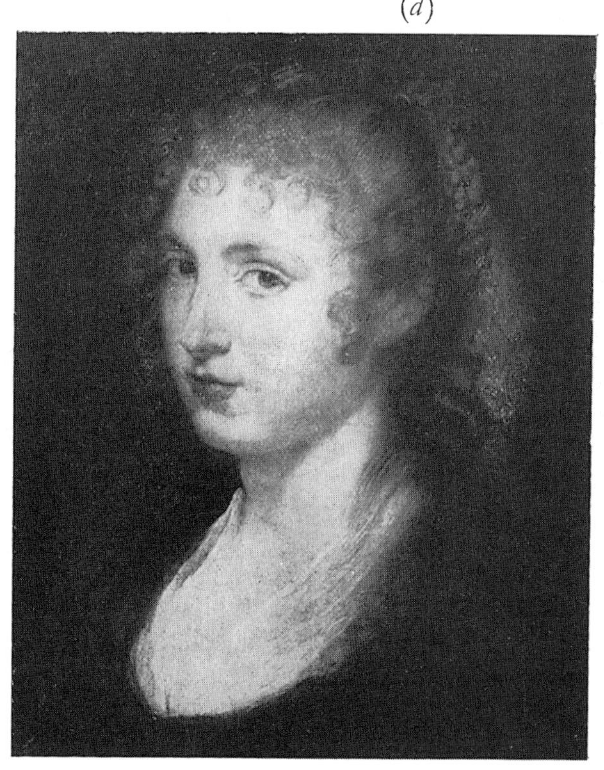

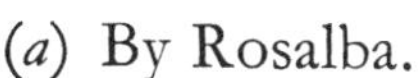

(*a*) By Rosalba. (*b*) By De la Tour. (*c*) By Romney. (*d*) By Rubens.

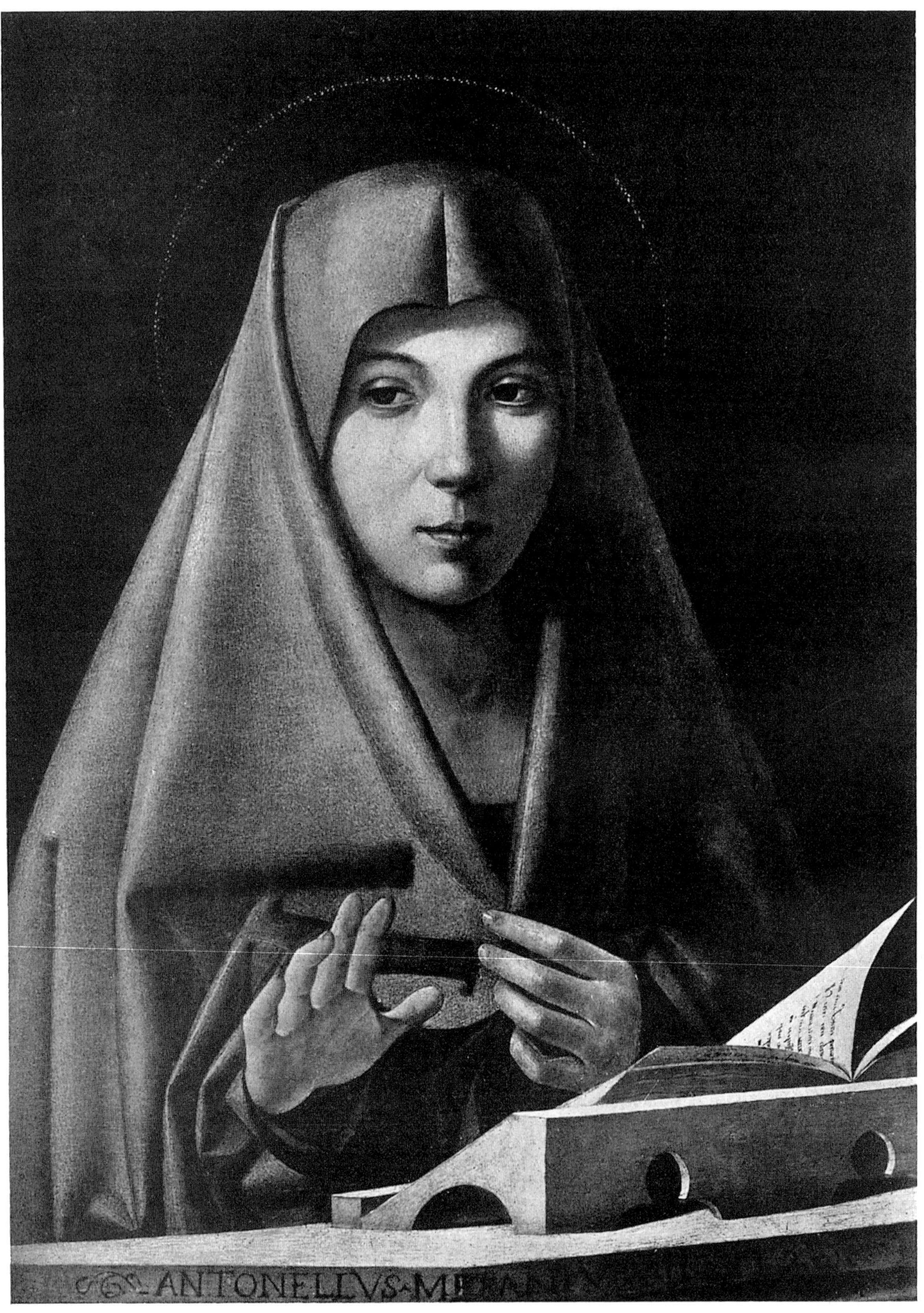

Detail from an "Annunciation" by Antonio da Messina.

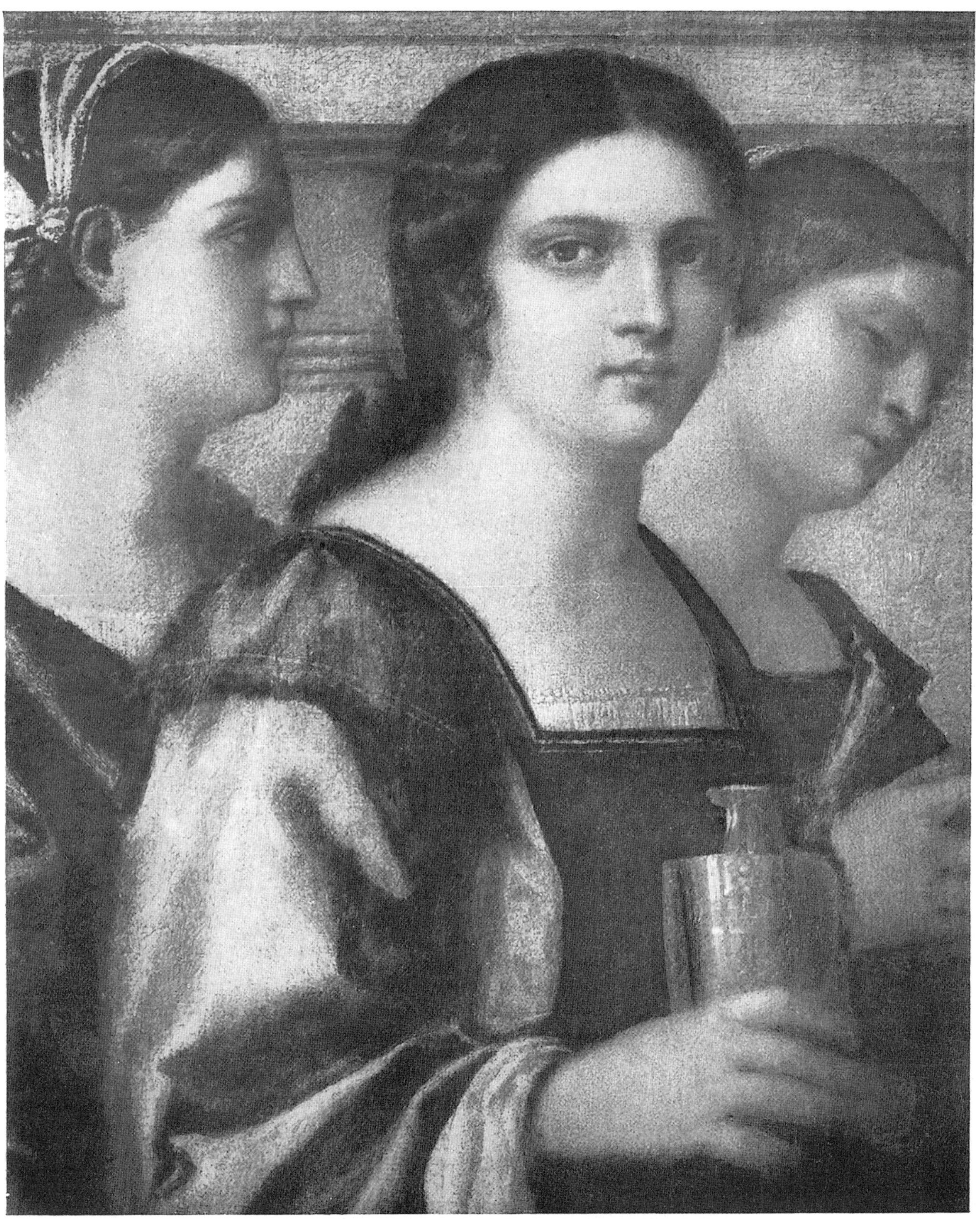

Detail of Heads from a Painting by SEBASTIANO DAL PIOMBO.
Three interesting positions of the same head.

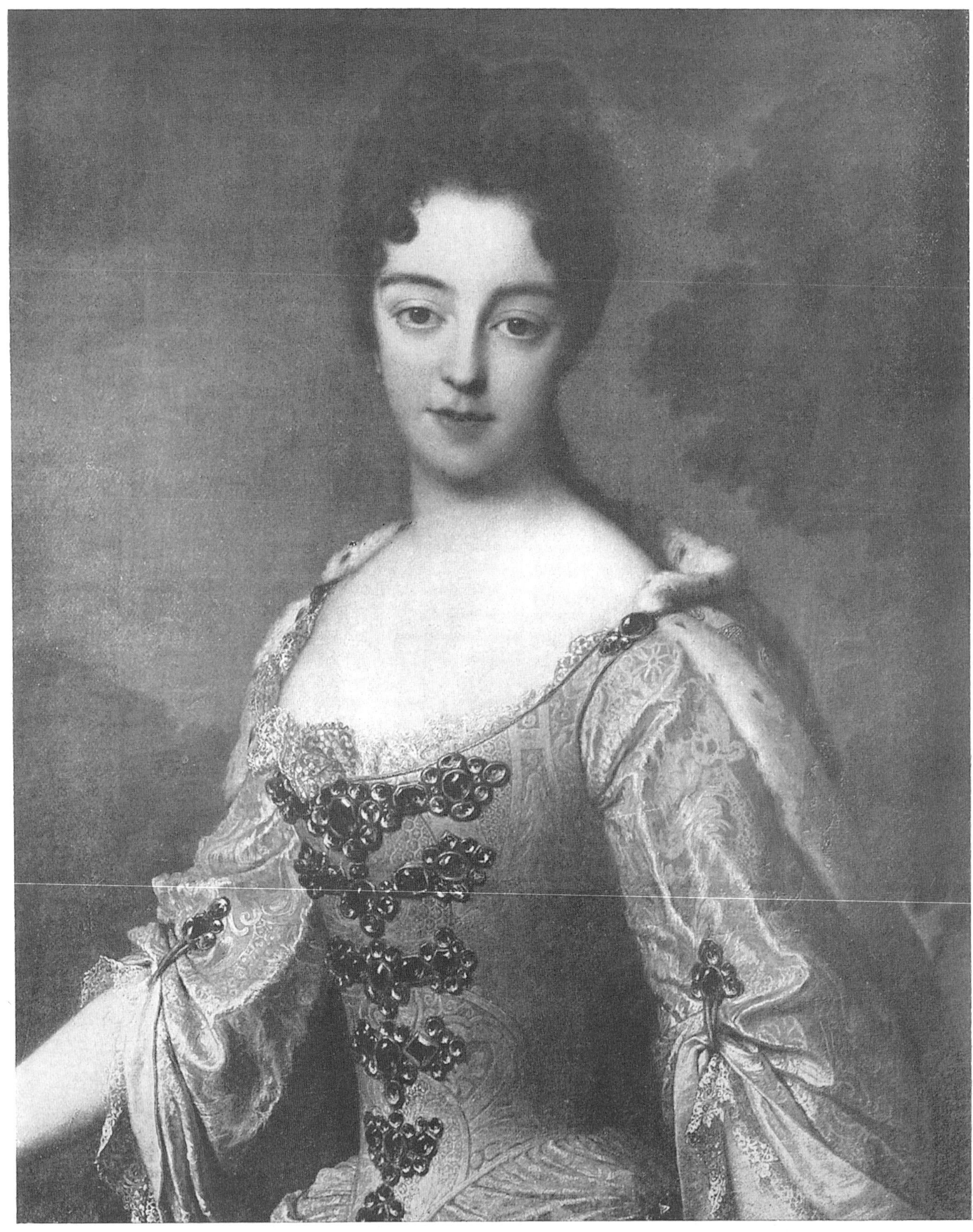

Detail of a Painting of the Duchesse de Bourgogne, by SANTERRE.

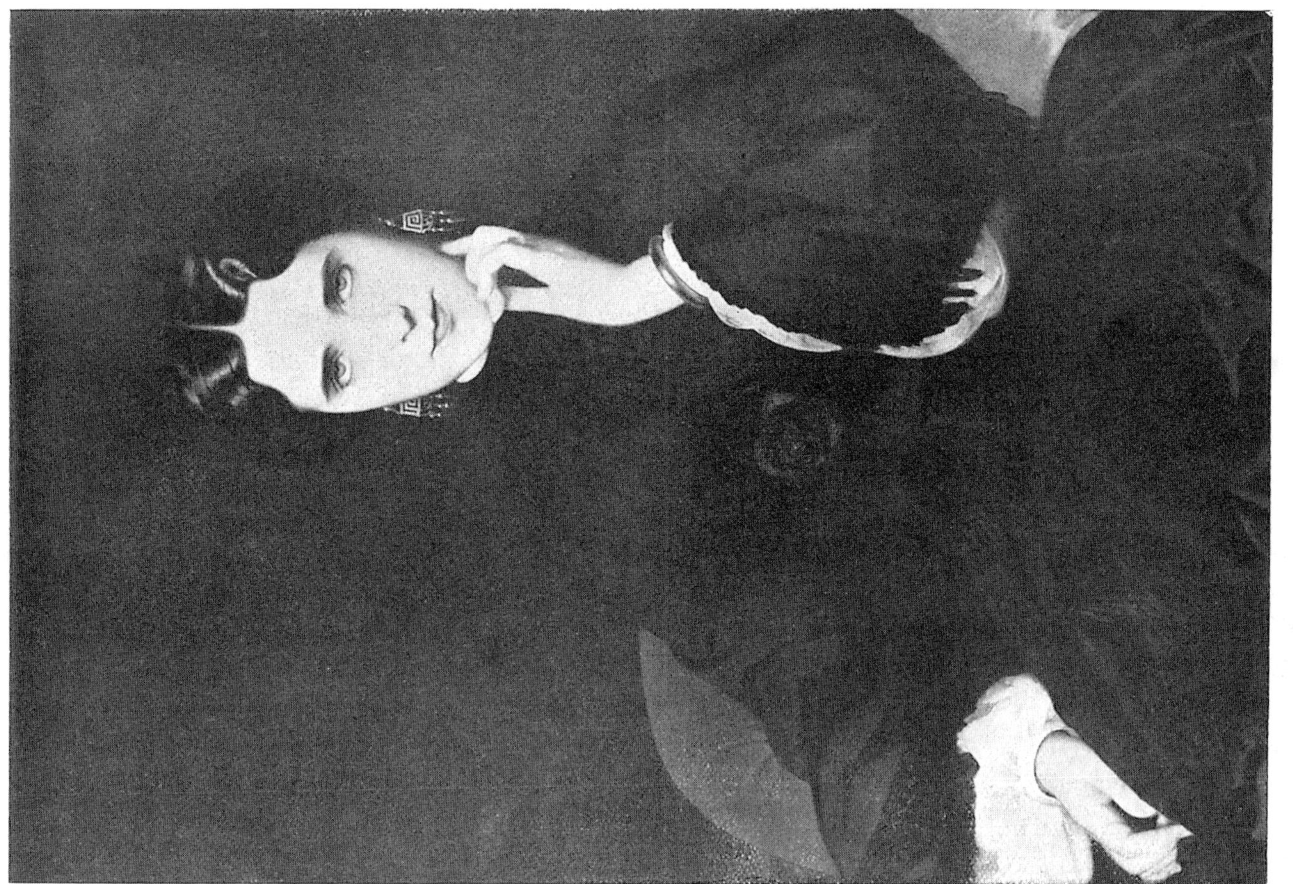

(*b*) By Amoury Duval.

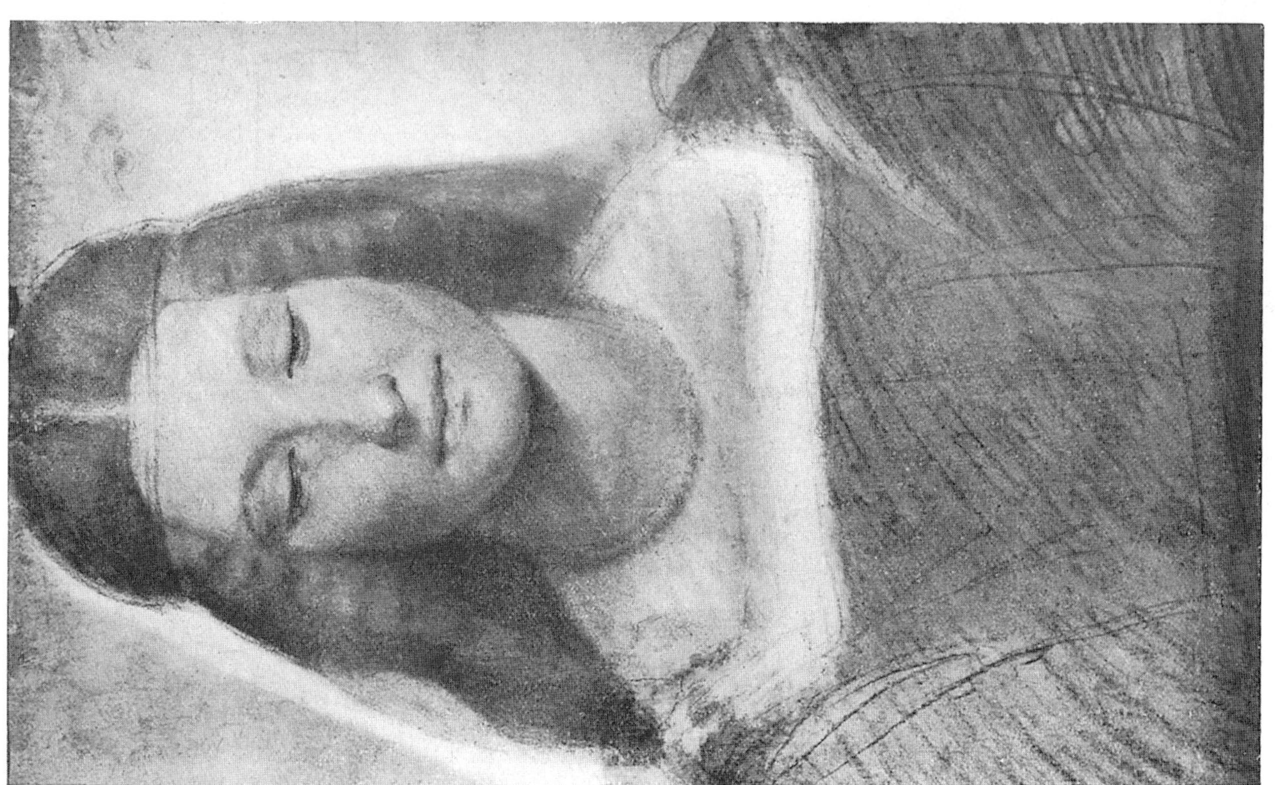

(*a*) By Beltraffio.

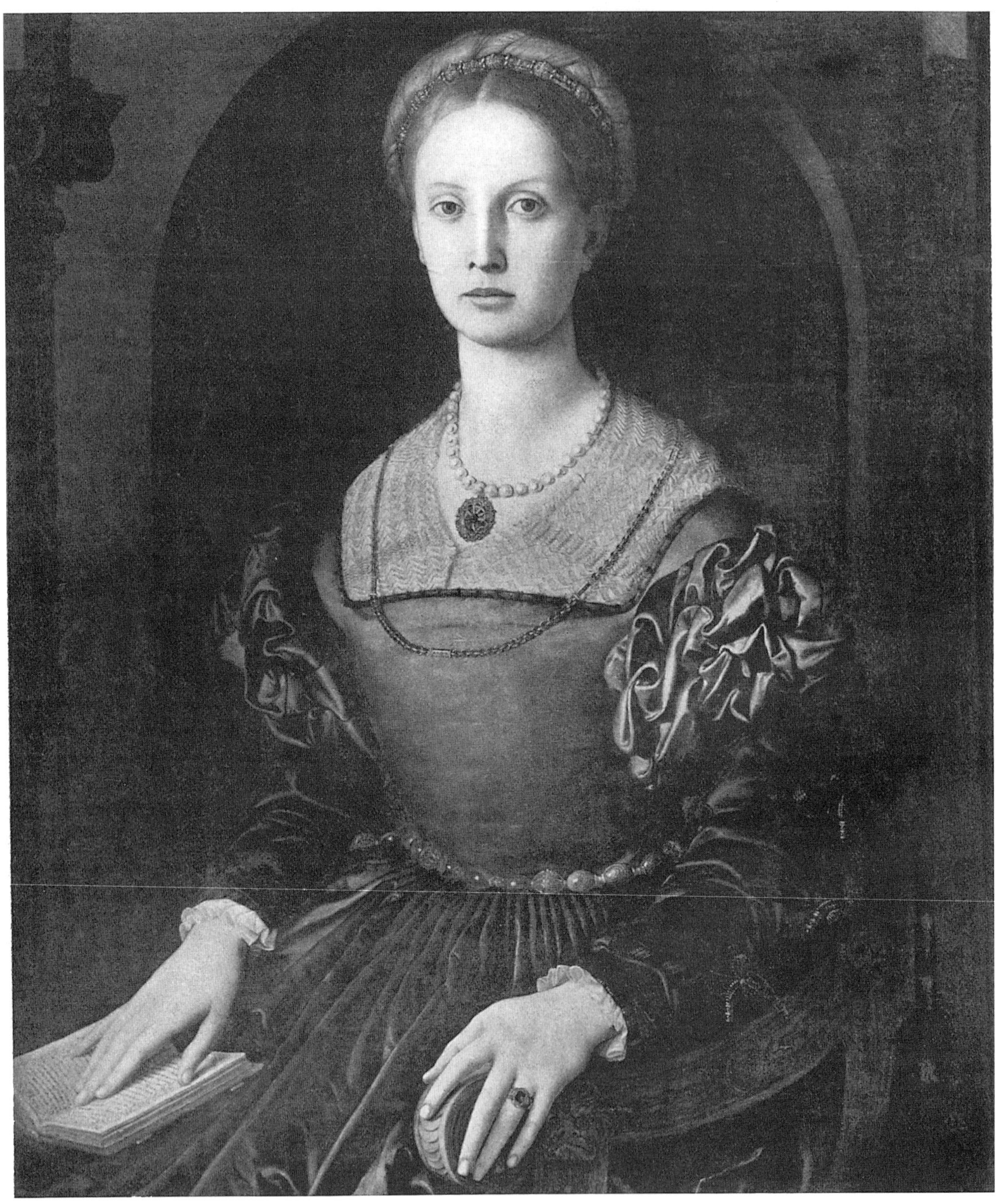

Detail of Portrait of Lucretia Panicalichi, by BRONZINO.

(a)

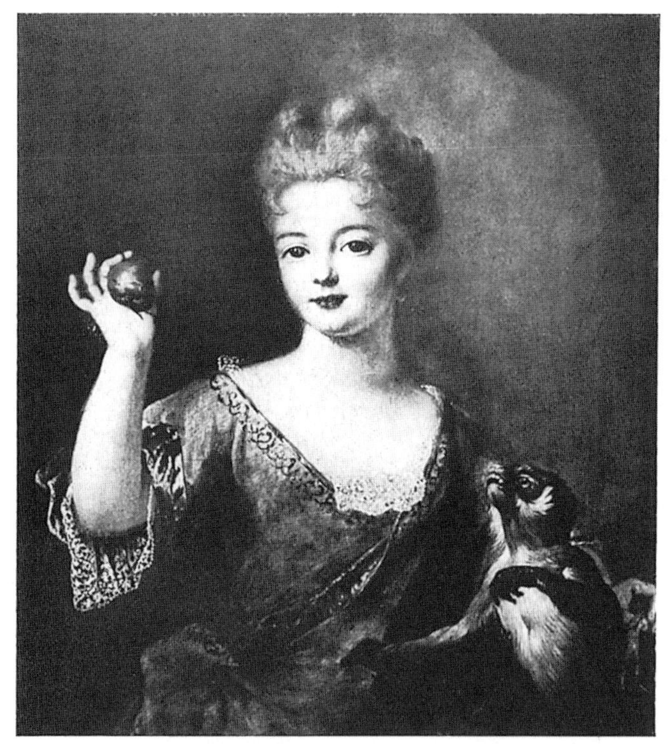

(b)

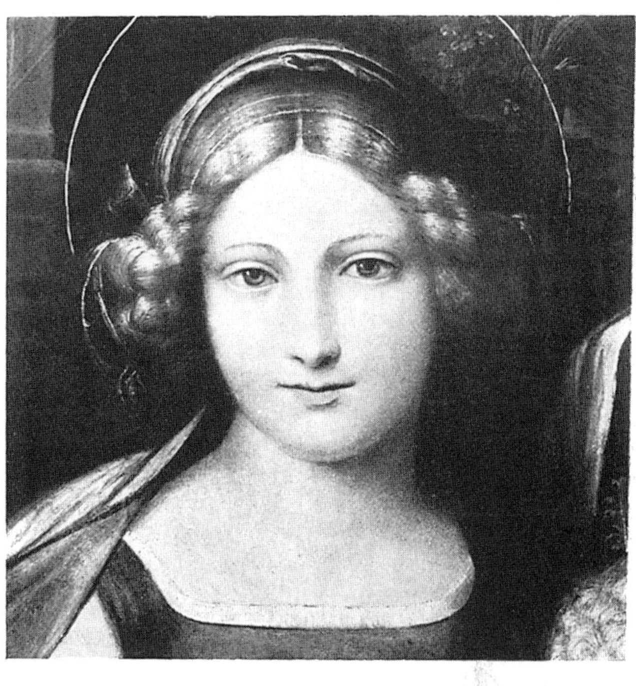

(c)

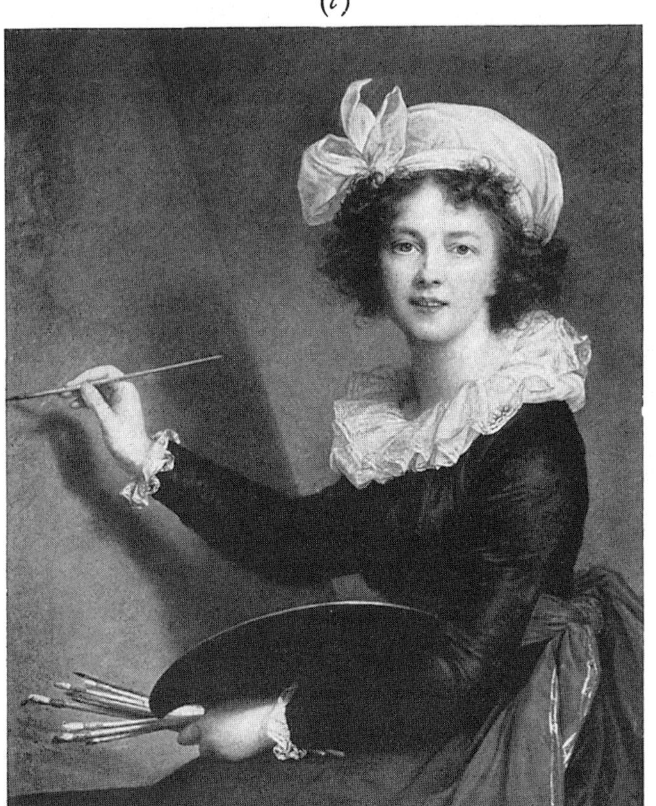

(d)

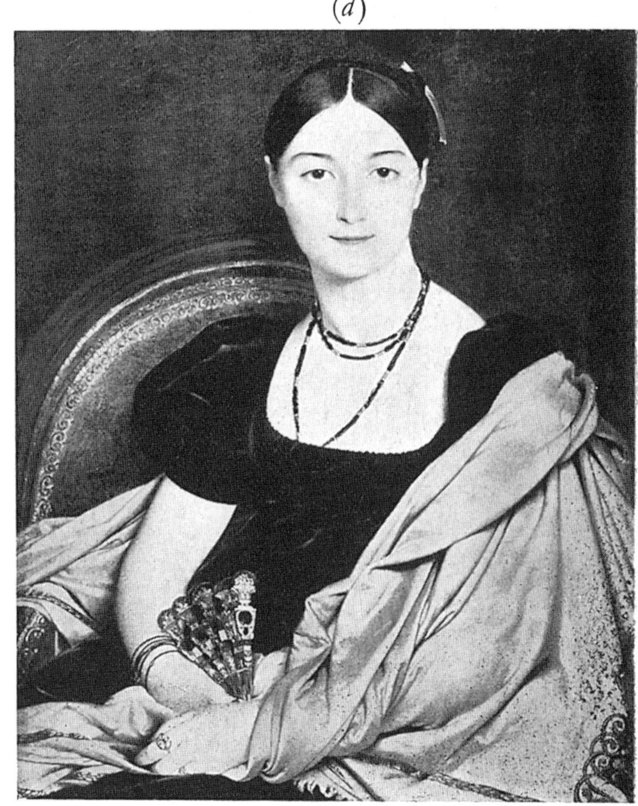

(*a*) By Nattier. (*b*) By Garafalo. (*c*) By Vigée-Lebrun. (*d*) By Ingres.

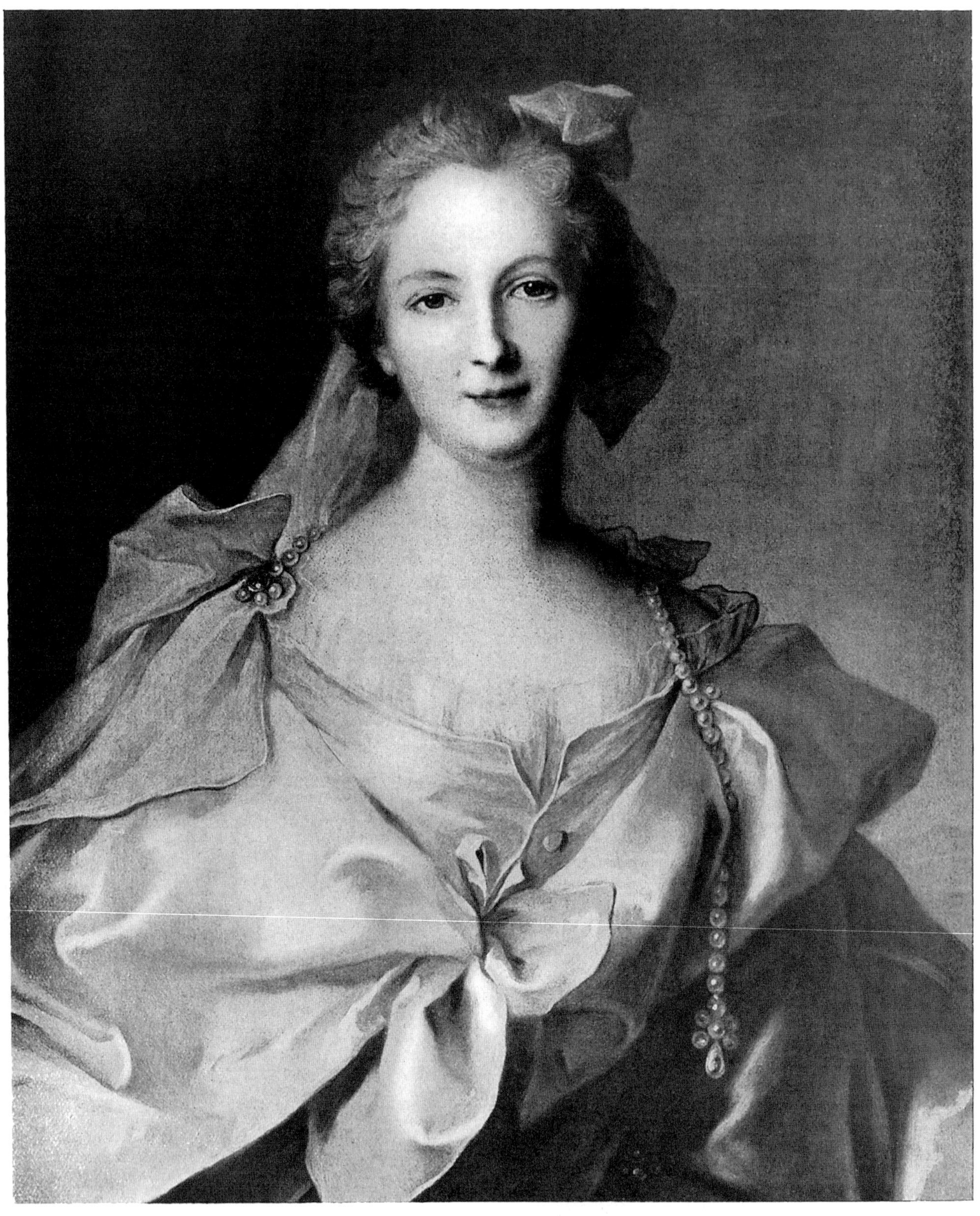

Detail of a French Eighteenth Century Portrait.
Artist unknown.

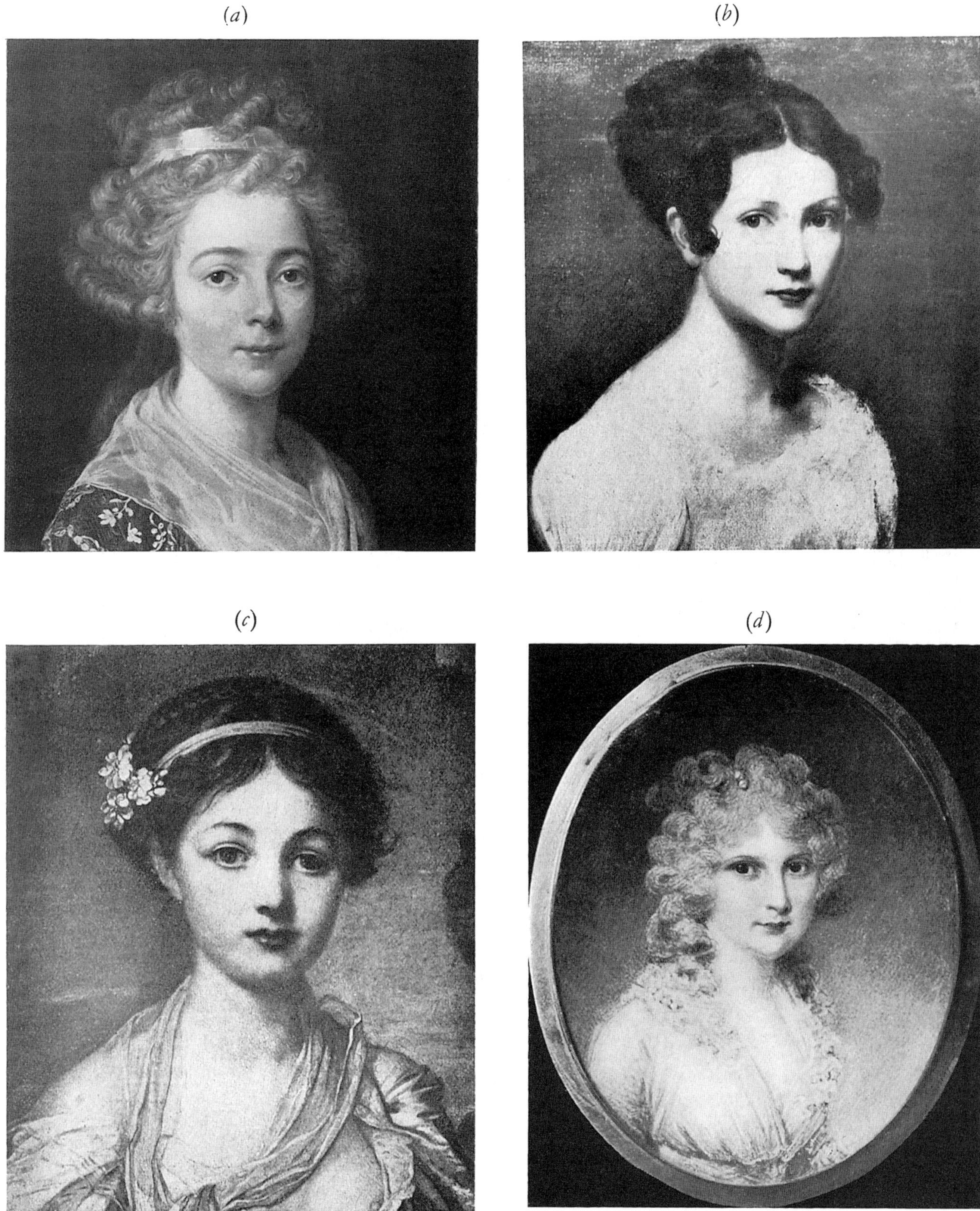

(*a*) By Antoine Vertier. (*b*) By Larivière. (*c*) By Greuze. (*d*) Miniature by Samuel Shelley.

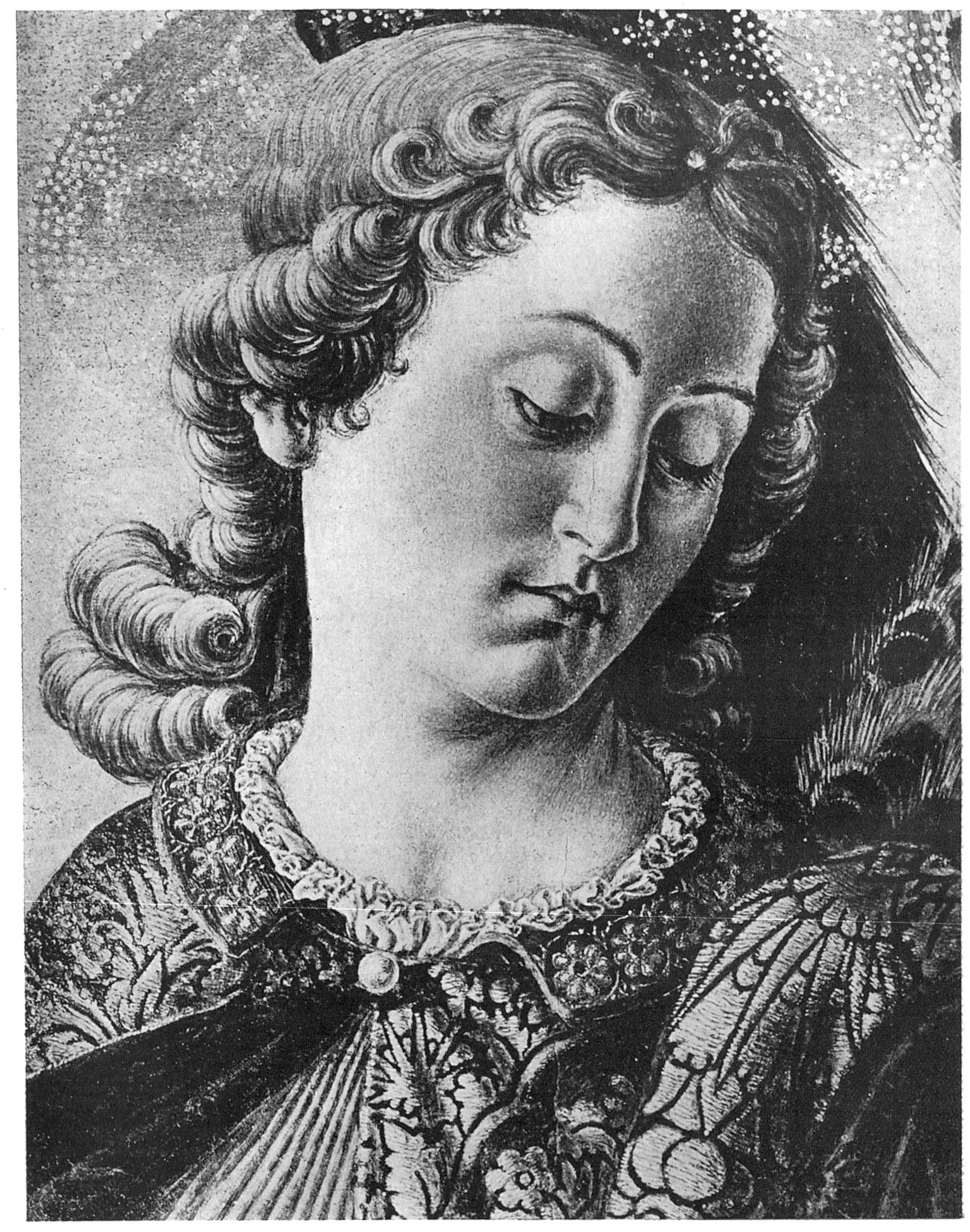

Detail of a Head from "The Three Archangels" by BOTTICELLI.

(*a*)

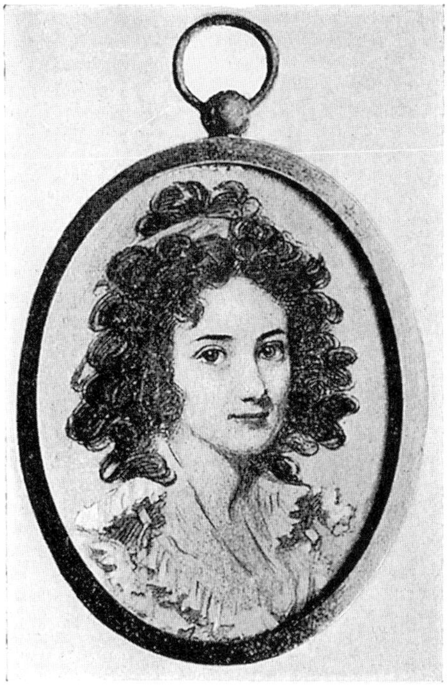

(*b*)

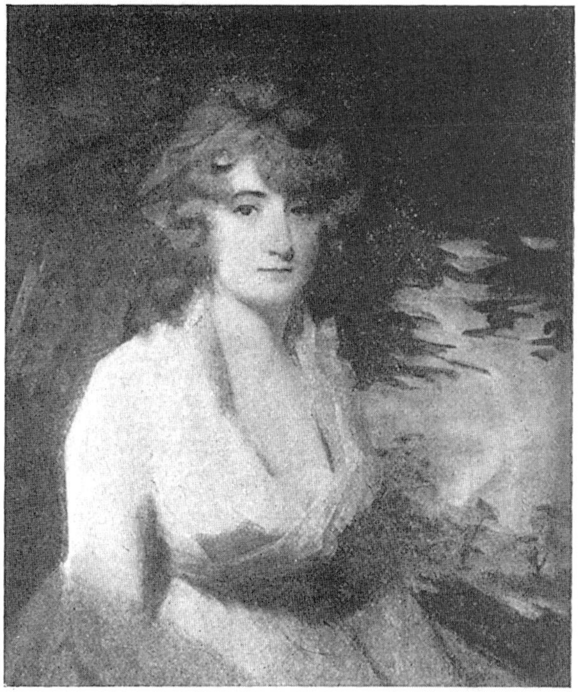

(*c*)

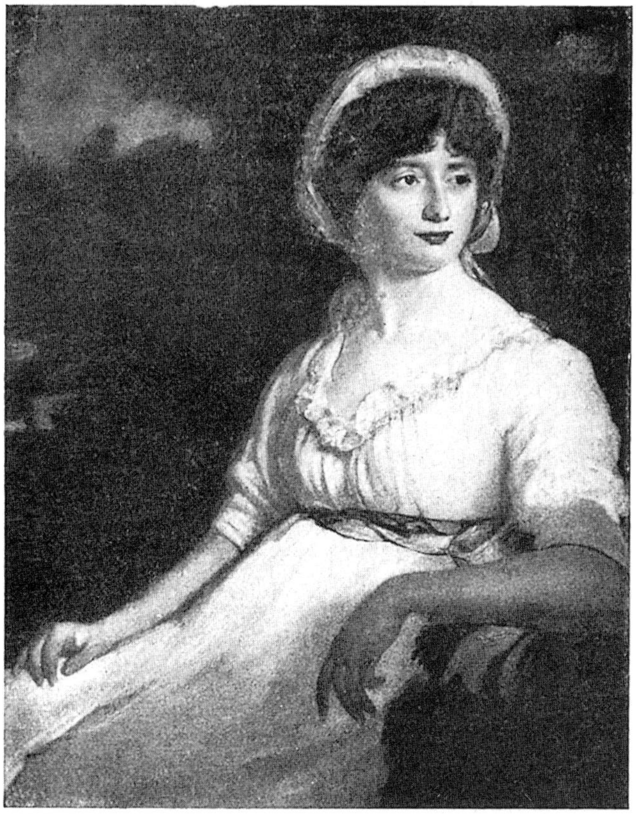

(*d*)

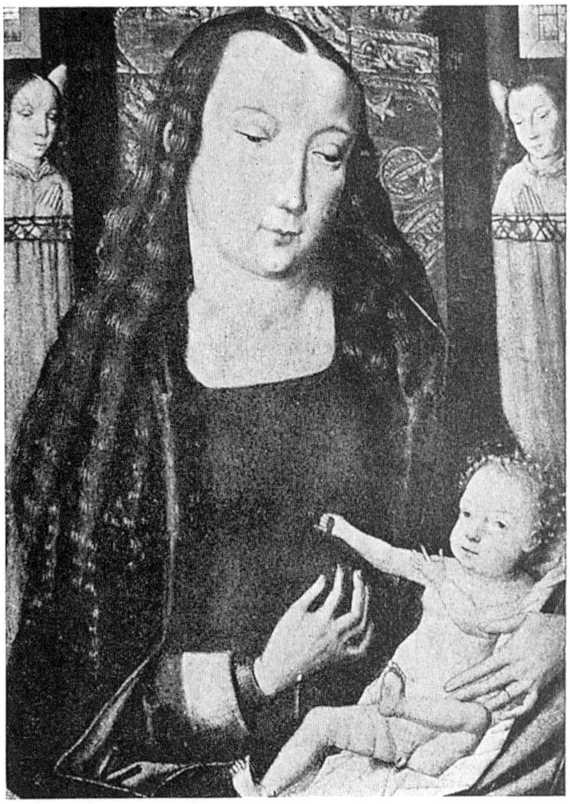

(*a*) Miniature portrait by George Engleheart. (*b*) By Raeburn. (*c*) By John Opie. (*d*) By Daret.

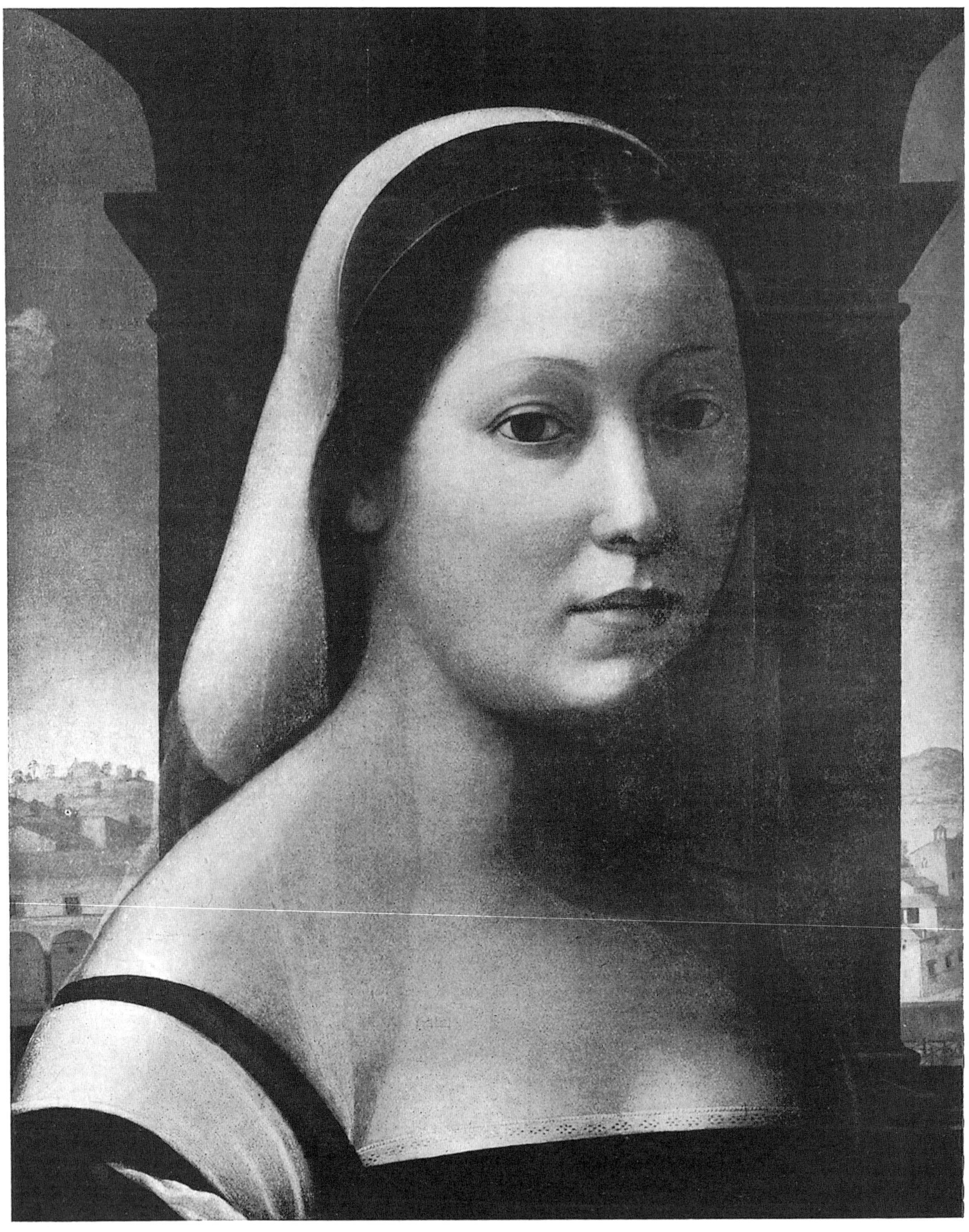

Unknown Portrait by LEONARDO DA VINCI.

(*a*)

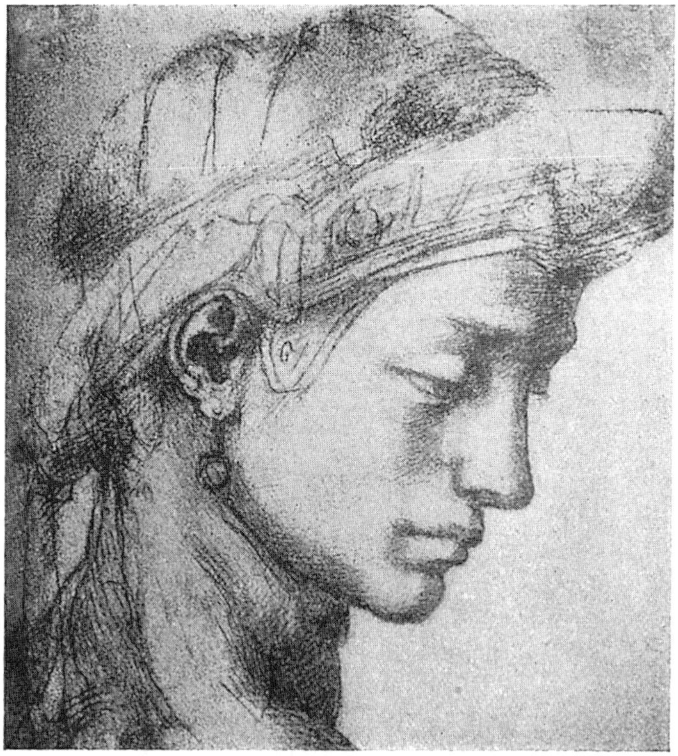

(*b*)

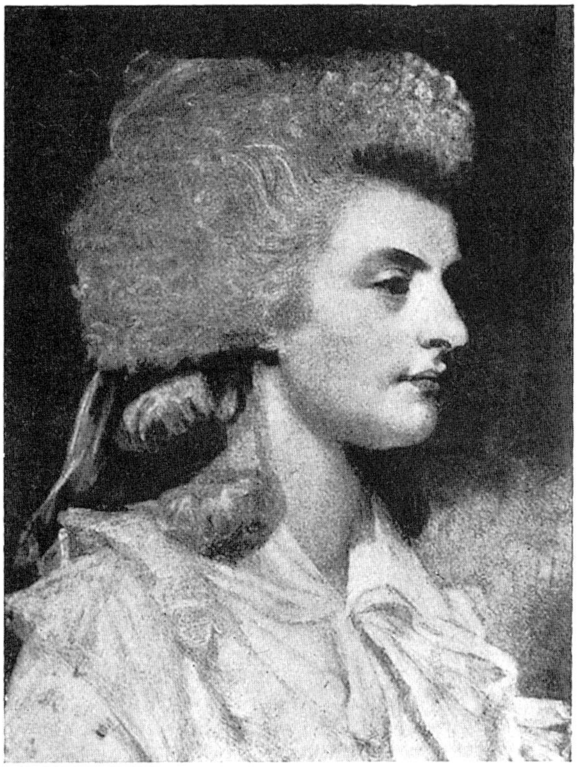

(*c*)

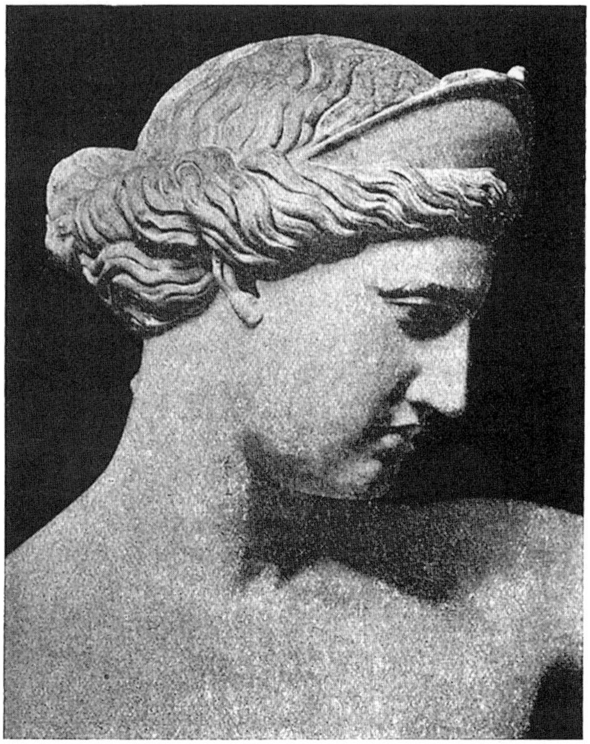

(*d*)

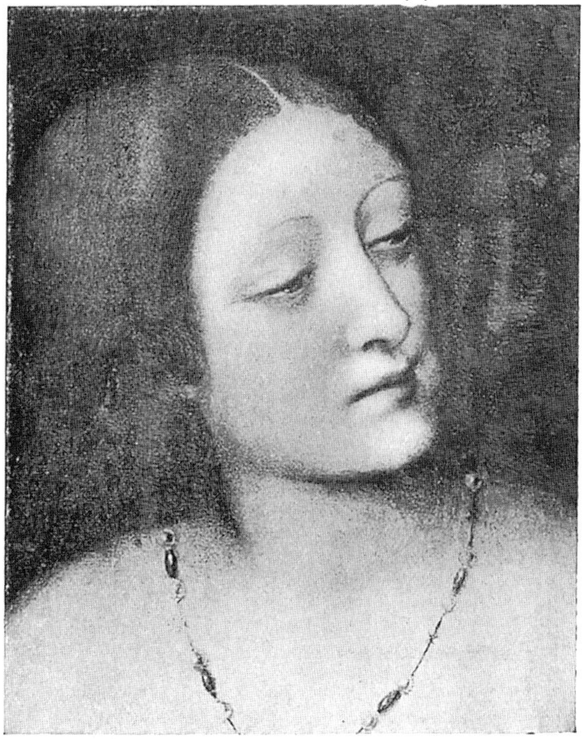

(*a*) By Michel Angelo. (*b*) By Reynolds. (*c*) Detail of antique Statue of Venus. (*d*) By Luini.

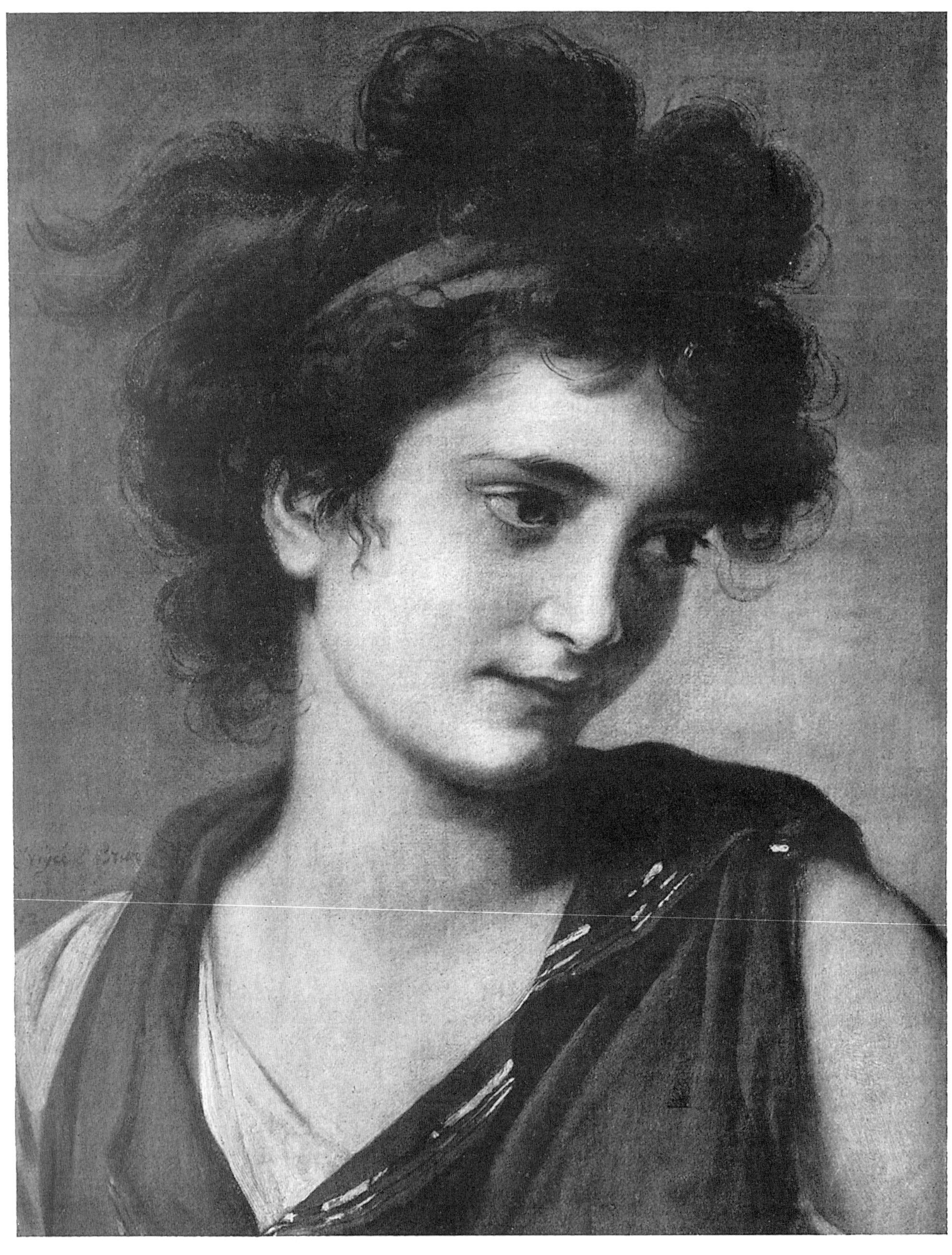

Detail of a Portrait by VIGÉE-LEBRUN.

(*a*)

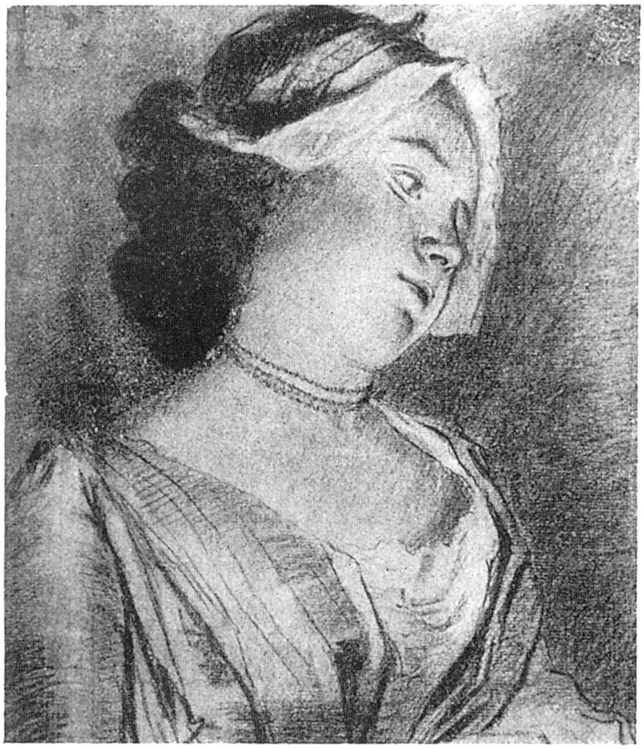

(*b*)

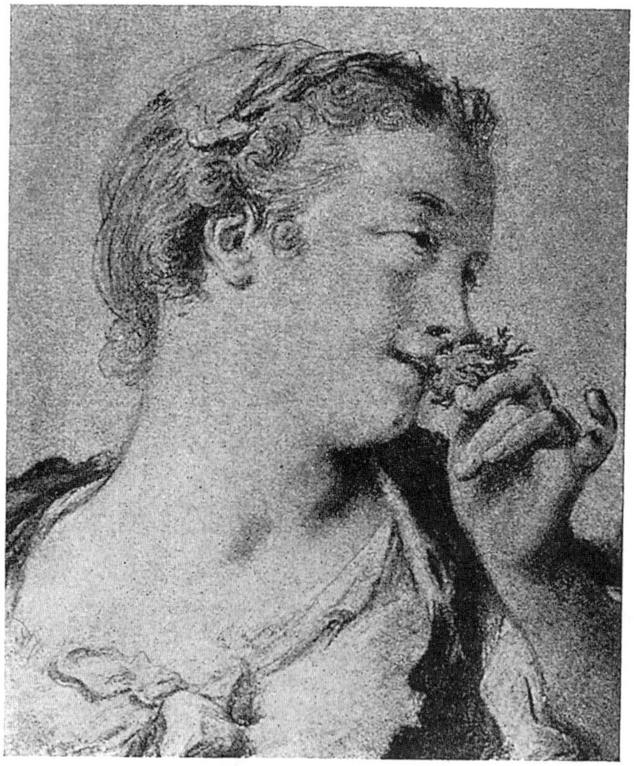

(*c*)

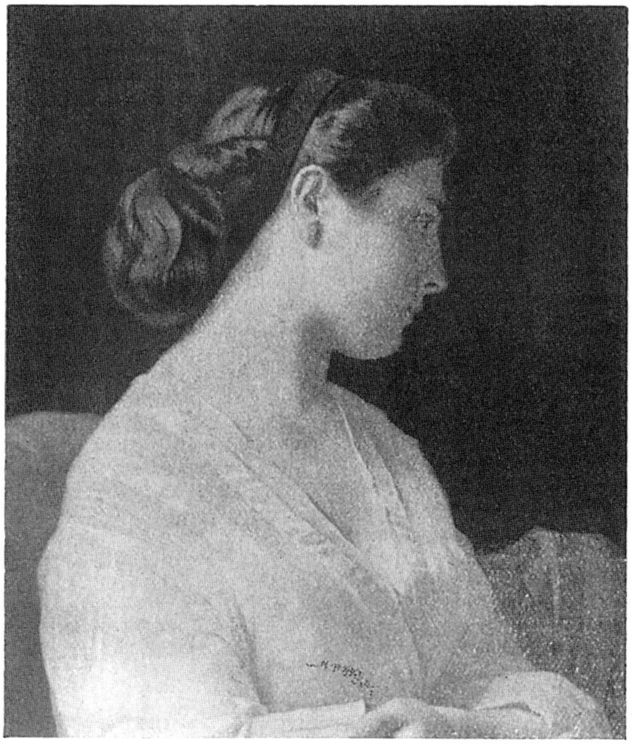

(*d*)

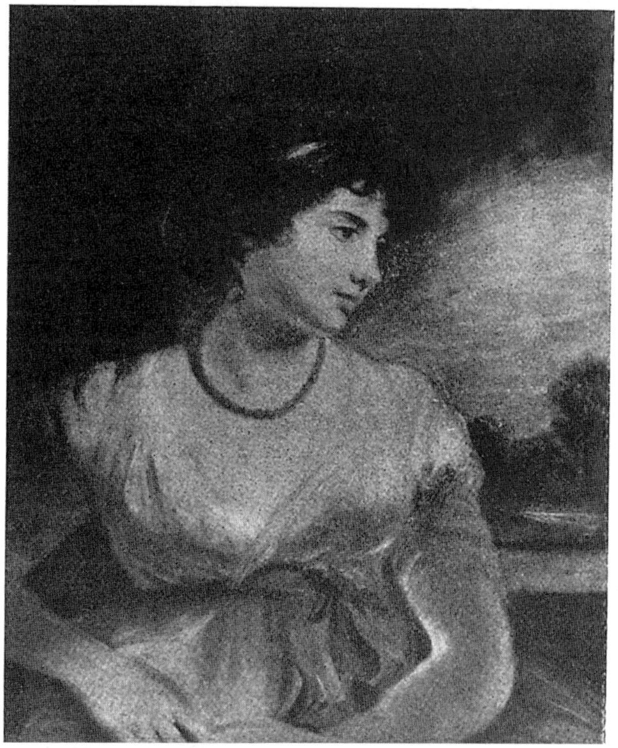

(*a*) By Portail (*b*) By Boucher (*c*) By J. H. Flandrin (*d*) By Hoppner

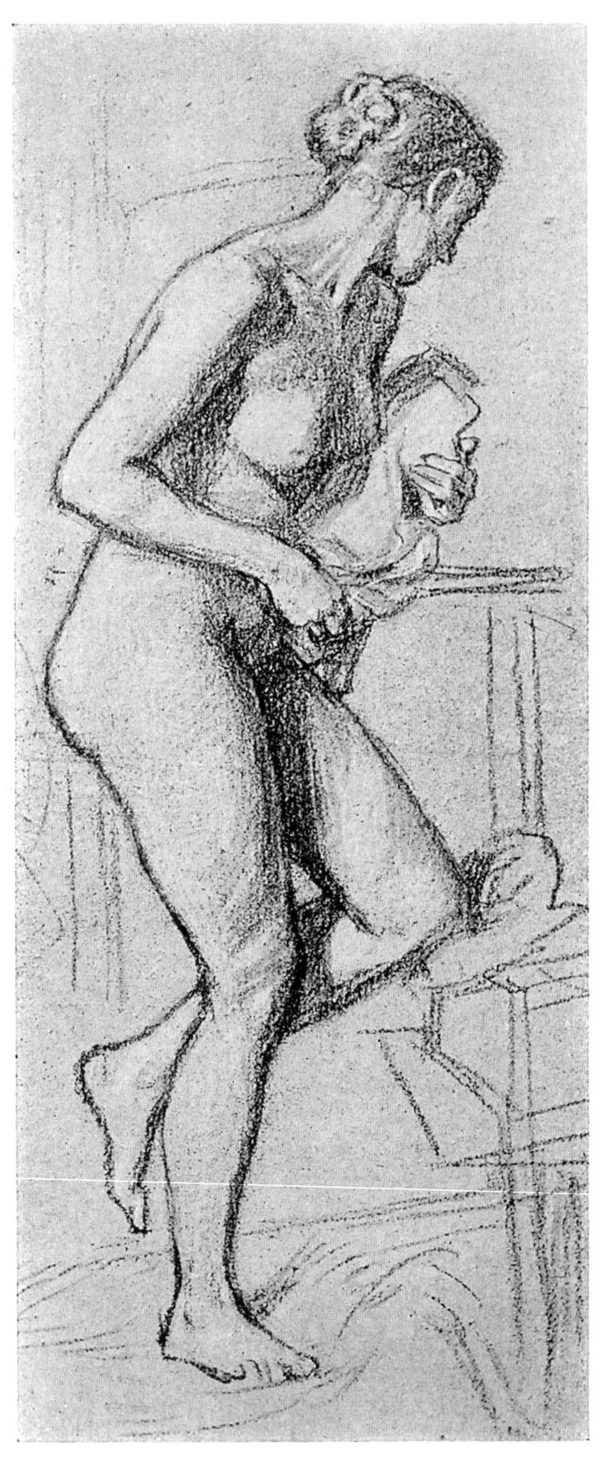

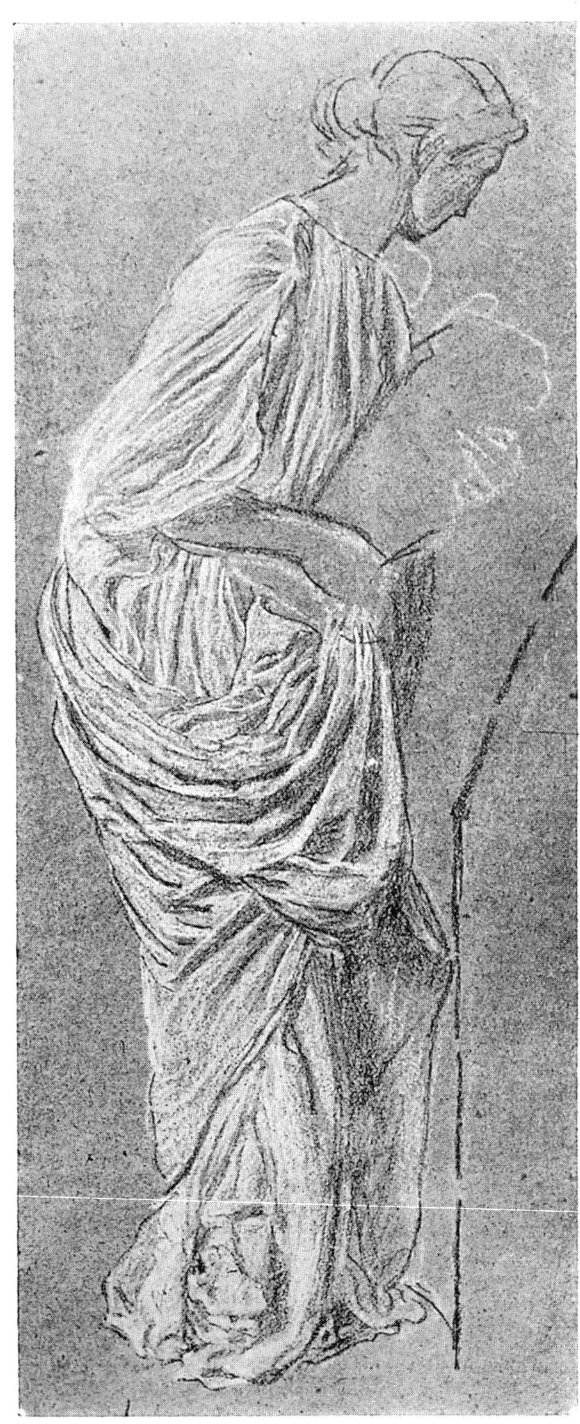

Draped and Undraped Studies of the same Figure, by ALBERT MOORE.

DRAPERY

THE origins of Drapery are a matter for the ethnographical student; the student of fashion must place this fact first—that it conforms to the use and comfort of mankind.

In its advanced stages it aims at a decorative system of lines, which serve as a foil to the figure, setting it off, explaining it, underlining its beauty, giving it amplitude, emphasizing or improving its natural proportions.

To represent a figure in action, drapery will be of the utmost utility, not only because movement alters the direction of the folds, but also because conversely a system of folds may be arranged to suggest movement.

Thus, snapshots or cinematographic stills of moving drapery do not necessarily convey with the same intensity the action with which they are connected—such as running, dancing, flying—as an artificial and reasoned arrangement of folds may do, and the general impression may not be so satisfactory.

As in other domains of art, simplicity of treatment of folds is to be preferred to elaboration, and all creases, depressions, and reliefs of the drapery, and their relationship to one another and the general pattern, should explain themselves without difficulty.

All good dressmaking has its foundation in skilful draping. The principal on which folds are produced is simplicity itself. Gravity makes and shapes the folds.

Drapery is either attached to, or supported by, some fixed smaller or larger surface, from which it falls downwards in obedience to the law of gravity.

The number, size, and length of the folds depend on the weight and resilience of the material and the size and location of the points or surface of support. If suspended from a point the folds radiate from that point.

Their formation is closer or wider according to the texture and weight of the material used.

The thin, transparent materials which the Greeks used produced narrow, pipy folds, whereas the heavier cloths of the Middle Ages produced the stiffer, squarer folds with which mediæval statues and paintings have made us familiar.

During the Renaissance, light and heavy cloths, made of silk, linen, or wool, were in use, and it is interesting to contrast the elaborate and finely felt arrangements of folds of a Botticelli with the simple rugged drapings of a Michael Angelo.

When the same piece of drapery has two or more points of support or attachment the folds radiate from those different points, and the closer these are together the oftener it happens that the different systems of folds meet and either dissolve themselves in a common curve, or intersect and form an angle or a break.

Points of support which are situated on the same level, such as the shoulders, breasts, hips, bring forth symmetrical arrangements of folds which, owing to their combined crispness and softness, to their varied lighting, must be considered as elements of plastic beauty.

Sometimes these folds look like tiers of festoons, lightly fastened to their supports; sometimes they hang elegantly, in sweeping curves, from one attachment to the other.

Rippling and swaying, they add their own grace to that of the supporting figure.

Cascades of waving curves, binding the radiating folds to each other, originate from single points of support, whereas double supports produce the broader cascades of rich and ample garments, which look so well on the rich and ample forms of Greek goddesses.

Belts tied over loose garments are points of attachment from which numerous folds radiate upwards and downwards, or the garments may be pulled over them and arrange themselves in bunches of gracefully curved folds.

Buttons, fibulas, brooches, may be points of attachment and the centres of radiating lines. Sometimes a tight attachment of ample material to a limb produces a wavy zig-zag line of folds, as in the bunched-up sleeves, the fashion of which has had periodical revivals.

Beautiful and stately are the long folds of upright figures draped in ample robes.

When the drapery is attached—that is, fixed rather than supported—the points of attachment are also points of resistance, and they will pull the drapery towards them, wherever they may be situated. Thus a tight belt will tend to monopolize and straighten out the folds which would otherwise have appeared in oblique and partly in horizontal lines across the breast.

When figures are seated the points of support of the lower part of the drapery or of the undergarment are the knees. Quite impressive cascades of folds may descend from the thighs down to the ground.

Sleeves are sometimes beautifully draped. In ancient costume they really do come under the heading of drapery, owing to the ample material which, in the tunic, for instance, hangs from the shoulder along the side and arm.

In the sleeves of close-fitting garments a series of folds occur at the bend of the arm and along the upper arm, especially when the arm is raised or bent.

THE STUDY OF DRAPERY

For the student, the study of drapery falls most naturally between the actual copying of simple objects, still life, and their translation to life and movement.

Still life (that expressive word for all the latent interest in things) is memory work, for only that slight space of thought intervened between looking at the object and looking at the drawing. It is an assimilation of facts and a translation of facts, but does not require that definite collecting and correlating of knowledge used in drawing from the moving life figure.

When drawing from the life, even the almost statuesque life of a long standing model in the life room, there is much more drawing from knowledge. In drawings of movement the student has nothing to copy from except his own knowledge.

To explain: study some instantaneous photographs. The most active movements—a dog leaping a fence, or a man running, fail to give any appearance of speed.

The fact that the dog is leaping a fence, and the man is running, will tell your mind that these actions are going on; but there is nothing to tell your eye of the fun and the movement. The dog is pinned against the sky with his legs a foot above the fence; the man, in a curiously strained attitude, stands on one leg in the middle of the road. Those are the facts of the case. It shows all that was taking place at the instant those photographs were taken.

Study now what it is the artist does in his drawing to give not only the facts, but also the impression of speed. You will find that the artist has taken the movement that *has been* and the movement which is *going to be*, and bottled them both up into one complete movement, the movement which *IS*. He has drawn from knowledge. The movement that had happened is gone; the movement that was going to happen has not come; but he knew all about both, and drew them *from knowledge*. It is a thing most difficult to explain. A sculptor once expressed it as the single stationary point in the very centre of the spinning wheel of movement. The actual pose seems to pause, for just one fraction of time, between the intensity of two movements. You do not draw the movements; you draw that pose.

Drapery seems to explain this almost more easily than anything else. Therefore let us see what drapery is.

Just as a scientist could tell you, speaking scientifically, of the material of which plants are made, so one can speak, equally materially, of the substance of which drapery is made. On pages 66 to 68 is a section upon "Materials." The student of fashion has, we hope, got plenty of pieces by him. Drapery, as thought of by the costumier, is material, fabric, stuff. For the artist, there must be more subtle understanding. Woven material may be his medium, but not the stock-in-trade of his knowledge.

The clinging and folding of growing things, the very colour and substance of light itself, have a quality of drapery. No matter what tremendous amount of difference there is in the materials, the medium through which he thinks out his designs, he will never find too many, and the more analogies he can feel between the things he sees and the material he has got to work with, the more spontaneously will his ideas come, and the fresher they will be.

FORM

Drapery has no form of itself—a simple statement which seems to cover the entire subject. Take a piece of material (it is not yet drapery) and lay it flat out on the floor; it will lie there, quite flat, quite smooth, quite quiet, quite dead. Pull it by one corner, and instantly the whole of it is alive. It is one complete system of radiating lines, every single one of them directly depending upon the life and strength you have given it through that one tug. There is not a fold nor a crease in that drapery (it is drapery now, not material) but points directly to the corner you pulled.

One simple, but tremendously important lesson! You must always find out and account for and understand the pull and force that has brought your material to life and made it into drapery.

It will not always be easy. Pull the second corner now. The two opposing forces will make interesting lines. Pull the third and the fourth corners, and go on pulling and studying what happens for yourselves.

We have said that drapery had no form of its own, but was dependent always upon other things. Now study this.

Your drapery on the floor had the form of your pull. If you lift it up into the air it hangs, every line of it, entirely dependent upon your support. If you take your hand away it falls quite limply.

A banner floating in the sun is the beautiful movement of the air made visible. A strip of cloth in running water will show you the moving and the waving of the ripples. The less substance in the cloth itself, the less personality that it has of its own, the more easily will it take its life from other things.

Realize, therefore, that you must never hope to draw the form of drapery itself. *You must draw the thing which makes the drapery*. The underlying cause of its existence.

Now we will study the material, the medium in which you are going to work. For the want of a better name, we will call it the anatomy of drapery. This anatomy will vary as much as the substance it is made of. You must have on hand crisp, papery silks, soft smooth materials, limp and tractable, stiff reluctant pieces of felt, light woollen blankets, and heavy, thunderous plush. Study them as material, that you may know what to expect when they come to life as drapery. For example, take a piece of medium-weight calico, or sheeting, and hang it up by one corner. The radiating folds are tubular. Now what happens when you bend a tube? It will break like macaroni, or curve like a bit of lead piping, or it will crack with a curious definite angle, like a piece of drapery. Take a sheet of newspaper and roll it up into a tube and bend this tube until it cracks. You will find a similar form and section. The tube will flatten at the bend so that the diameter is actually greater at the angle, which makes it "stick out" farther than the rounded tube piece. The outer side of the angle is drawn tight, the inner side has material to spare, and cockles up. The whole makes a little knot or "eye," which is a very important piece of anatomy. Study it in various materials. In thin stiff ones, it is crisp and definite; in thick heavy ones, it is almost diagrammatic. Some thin silken materials have so little life of their own it is almost impossible to get an eye at all: the tubes of folding flatten down too easily.

When you have made, studied, and drawn these things in as many materials as possible, you will have understood a great deal about the anatomy of drapery.

Remember this tubular form in drawing any fold and see the shade on the fold itself, the reflected light, and the cast shadow. It is the varying quantity and quality of these three things that will help you in the study of material description.

As a practical point to understand and help with the actual representation, we recommend a large and heavy blanket, a soft piece of crêpe de chine, and a piece of crisp cotton material, all three thrown over similar chairs and observed simultaneously; the differences will be obvious, and from the list of materials on pages 66 to 68 you will readily understand their various characteristics and personalities.

The wear of material is important.

In some pliant materials the beauty is actually increased through wear; the fibres give, and the movements of the figure induce their own subtle folds; in others a crisp freshness is the essential charm. Tulle, glacé silk, taffetas, and some stiff muslins must be appreciated for their own folds rather than the folds induced by wear. This is a vital matter for the designer considering the usefulness of the designs.

In drawing drapery the quality of the material and its subsequent anatomy is the first consideration, as all materials in drapery are dependant on the underlying form, but equally all express this underlying form through their own personality.

For example, some one sitting with legs crossed in a skirt of soft clinging material will show outlines of both legs with close modelling over the knees. A crisp, papery glacé silk will show a very definite angular cracking at the knee-level, and the folds will be definitely formed by the crossed legs, though they may stand out at some distance from them. In both cases it would be necessary to draw the legs first.

Another quality is the wet and dry effect; though not applicable directly to a fashion artist, their indirect bearing as a quality of weave is very important. Take an average woollen material and arrange it upon the model; having noted the folds, try the same effect with the same drapery put on wringing wet.

The difference is one of weight and tension, and serves to demonstrate the effect of heavily loaded materials as contrasted with the lighter and more pliant ones. This is specially important in these days when so many curiously dressed materials are on the market; the weight of these is often disproportionate to their thickness. Heavy brocade and metal fabrics should also have special consideration on these lines.

N.B.—Very heavy materials should be left hanging up for some time or specially arranged in short folds in consideration of their weight.

SURFACE DESCRIPTION

Having understood the anatomy of the various fabrics, their surface description is a natural corollary to the artist. The materials bending in wide, heavy, tubular folds will catch and hold the light differently from the angular materials whose narrow creases and facets must necessarily condense it more. A soft material tends to diffuse light, a crisp material makes for definite planes of light and shade.

ARRANGEMENT OF DRAPERY FOR STUDY

The much maligned lay-figure can be very useful as a rule. It depends whether you are merely studying effects of drapery or using the lay-figure to help you formulate your ideas of the same drapery upon a living person.

Always arrange your lay-figure as model, that is, arrange the drapery upon it first, and afterwards make it take the required position through movements approximately as closely as possible to the natural movements of the figure.

That is to say, see that the drapery folds are the result of the assumed movements of the lay-figure within. Do not tamper with the folds or attempt to rearrange them from the outside, or you will have, not a figure making drapery, but material draped over a lay-figure—an important distinction.

When any movement is to be shown, you must twist the lay-figure so that it actually does that movement, to avoid an artificial effect.

In this way the lay-figure can be of real use, especially for long poses and intricate drapery designs; but again care should be taken not to lose freshness.

The mobile nature of drapery (even quite stiff drapery) is very easily lost, and any drapery left in position too long sinks and becomes stiff and lifeless.

Many and varied attempts have been made to set drapery: a good example is the billowing canvas on the small sailing ship models. In these the material is soaked with some mixture of plaster or glue and dried while blown out in a strong draught. They certainly set stiff in a good impression of wind, and the same method has been tried by artists who were studying drapery in motion.

They are all interesting, experimentally, but in the end you will draw from the knowledge obtained through your observation rather than the result in your plaster.

DRAPERY IN MOTION

We have spoken of the instantaneous photograph and the value of combined actions in expressing movement and of the value of drapery in demonstrating this.

Imagine a weight swinging freely, like a pendulum, backwards and forwards on a cord. A certain definite rhythm is understood and expected. Break that rhythm so that the weight swings unevenly and the cord is not straight but curved, and a quick jerking movement is understood and realized.

Thus, in a moving figure, the swinging drapery will show direct swinging movement, and as the movement flows outwards from its cause in the moving body, you will often find two or three movements following each other down a single length of cloth. Thus, in a figure descending, all the lines of the drapery will float upwards. When the figure alights some of the drapery lines will become horizontal, while others are still descending, and the arrested movement will be clearly demonstrated.

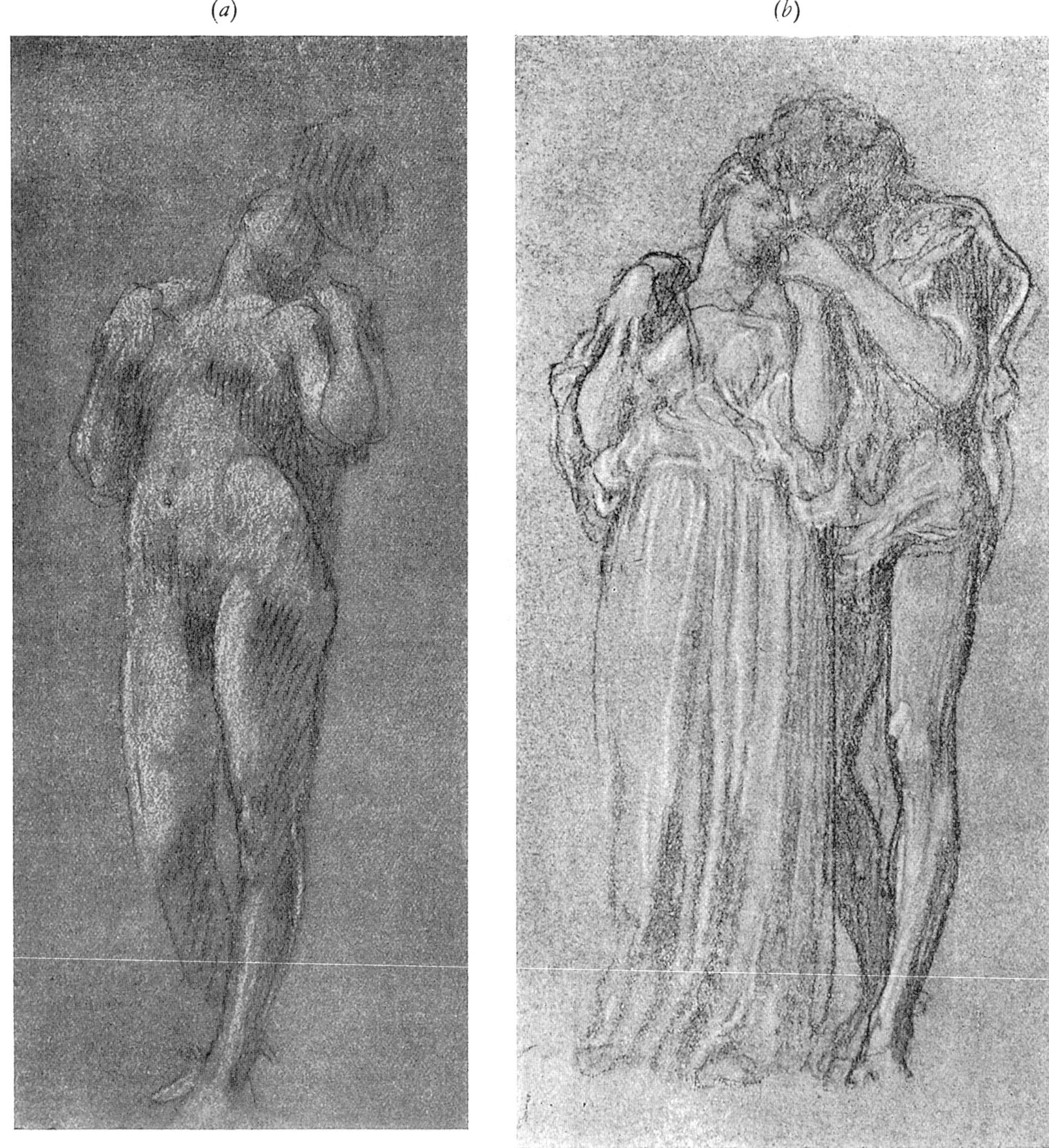

Studies by Lord Leighton.
The undraped figure (*a*) is drawn as a preparatory study for the draped figure in (*b*).

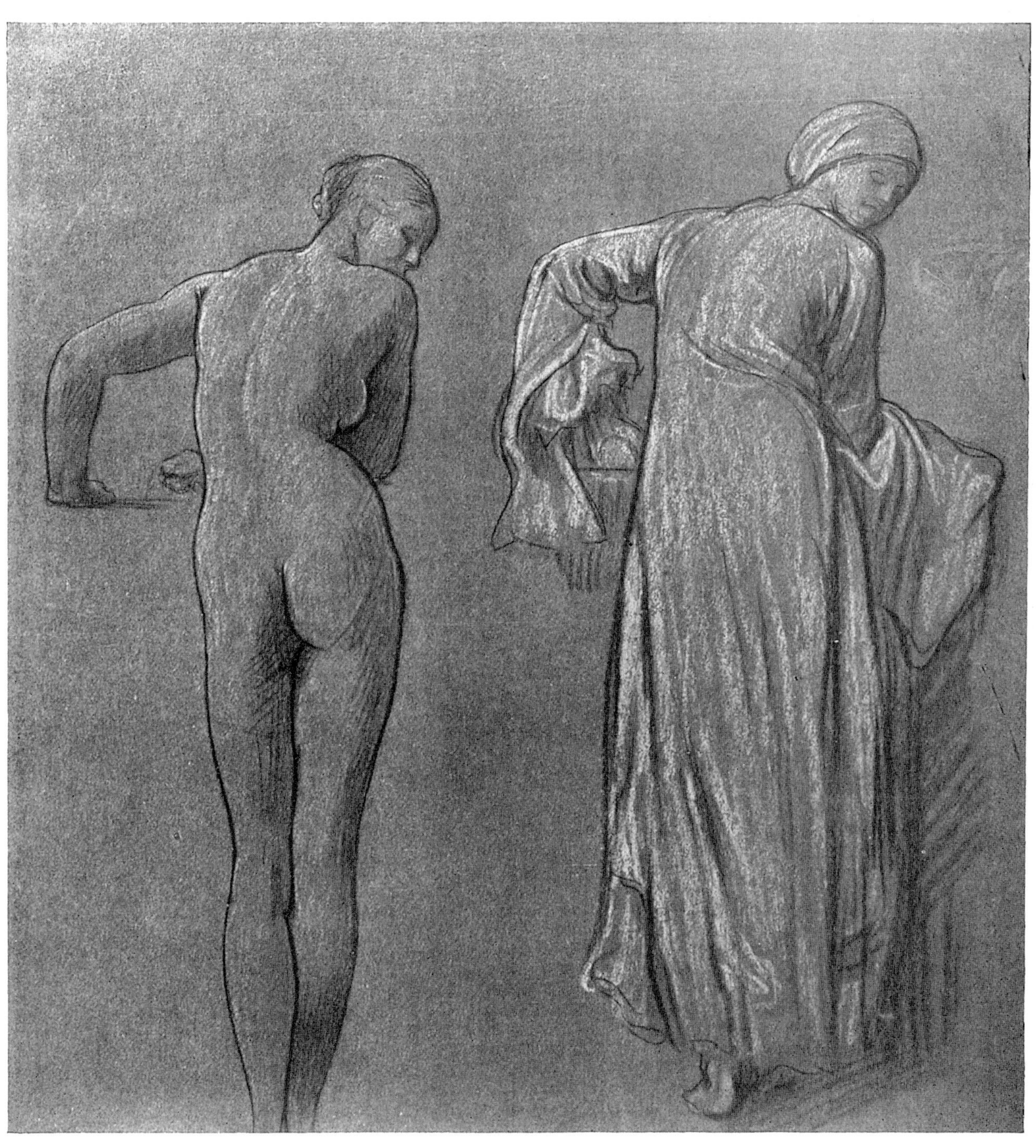

Studies by Lord Leighton.
The same figure, draped and undraped.

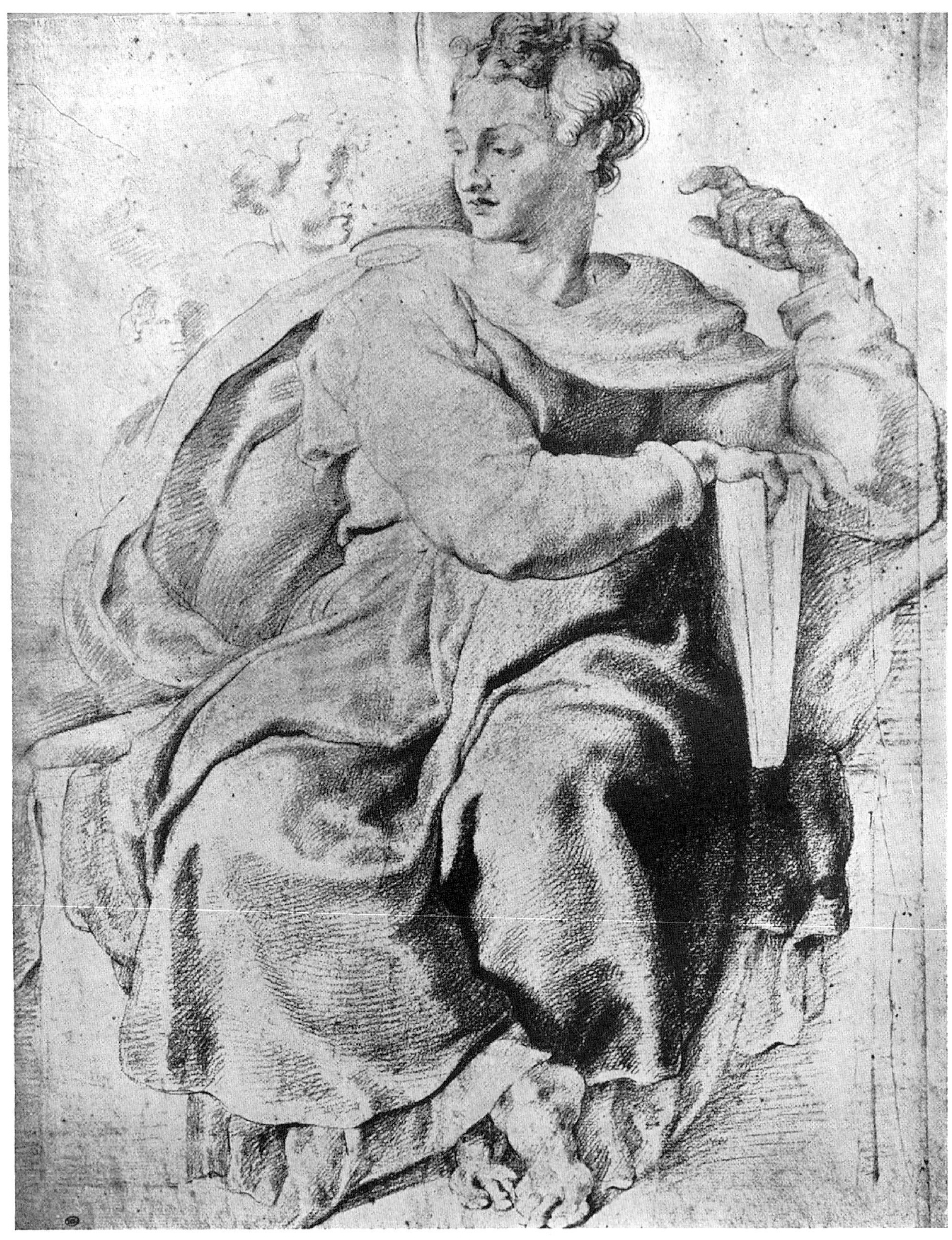

The Prophet Isaias, by RUBENS (after Michel Angelo).

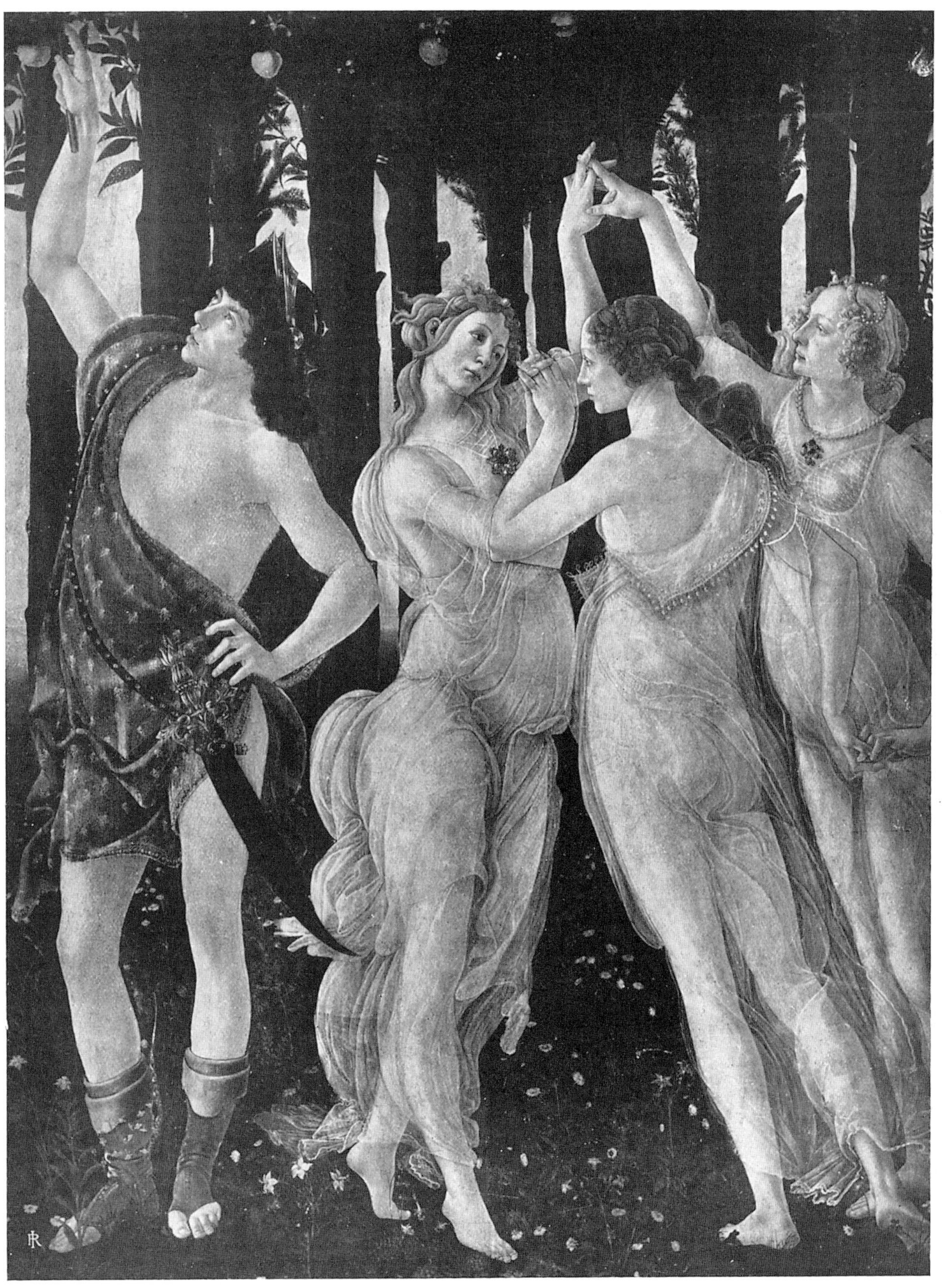

Detail from the "Primavera" by Botticelli.

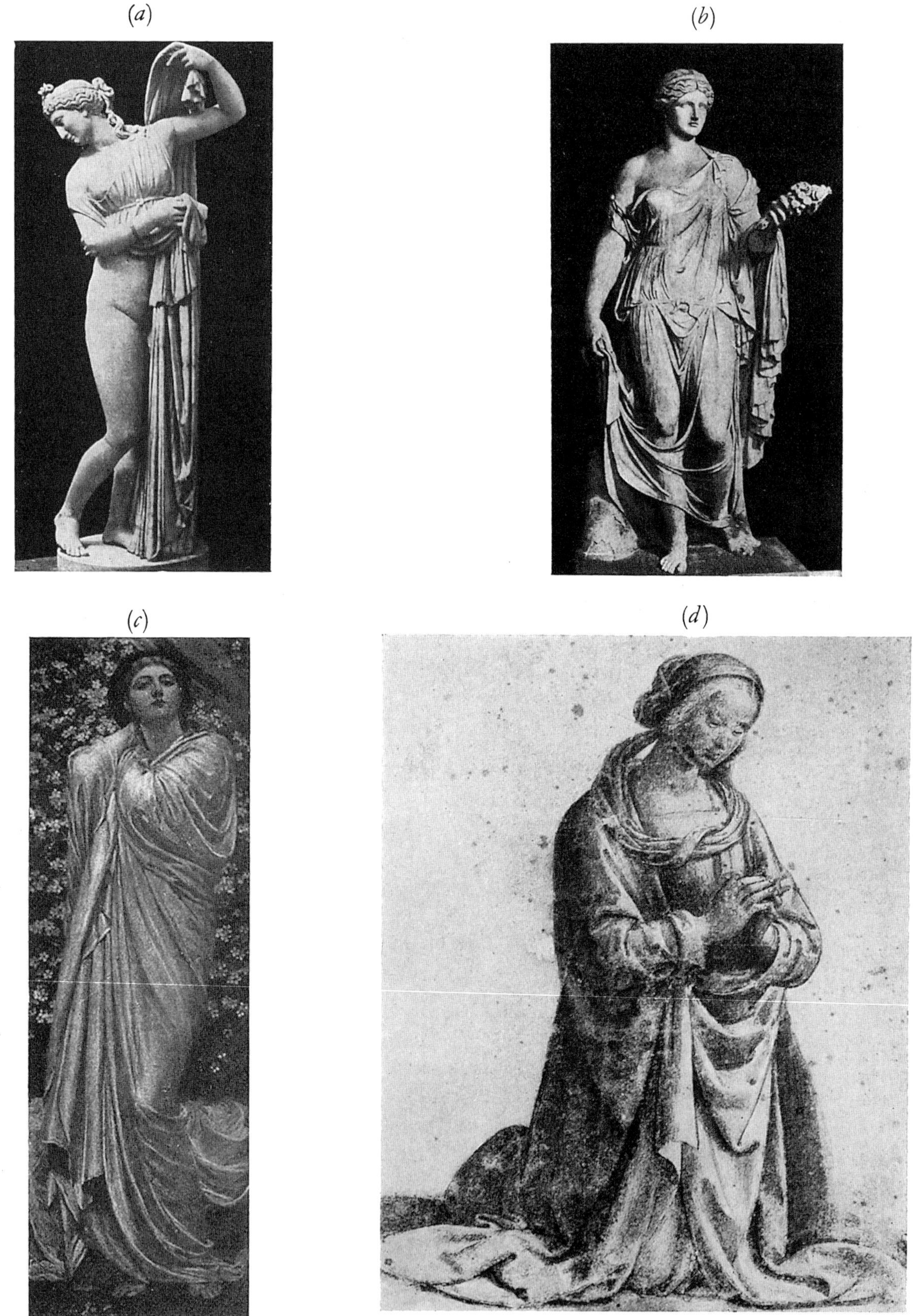

(*a*) Ancient Greek statue of "Venus Callipige." (*b*) Ancient Greek statue of "Flora." (*c*) By Albert Moore. (*d*) By Perugino.

(*a*)

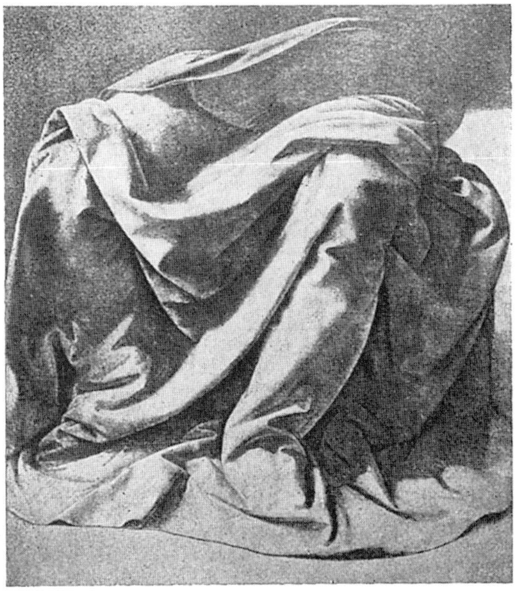

(*b*)

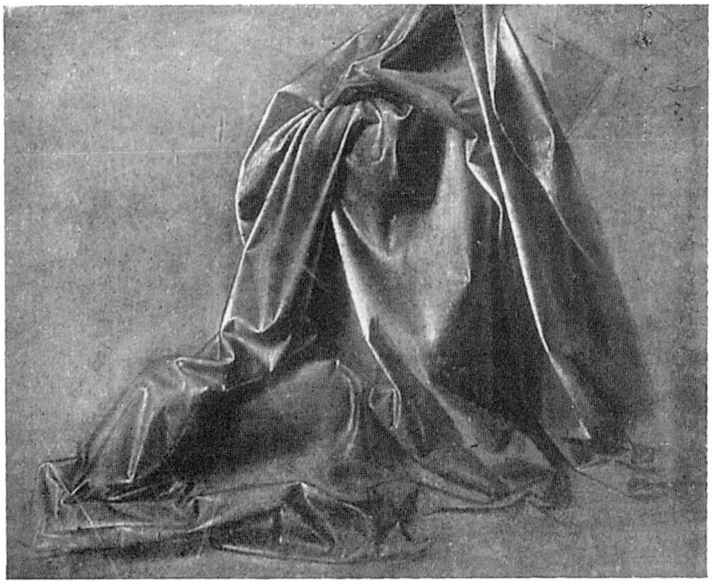

(*c*)

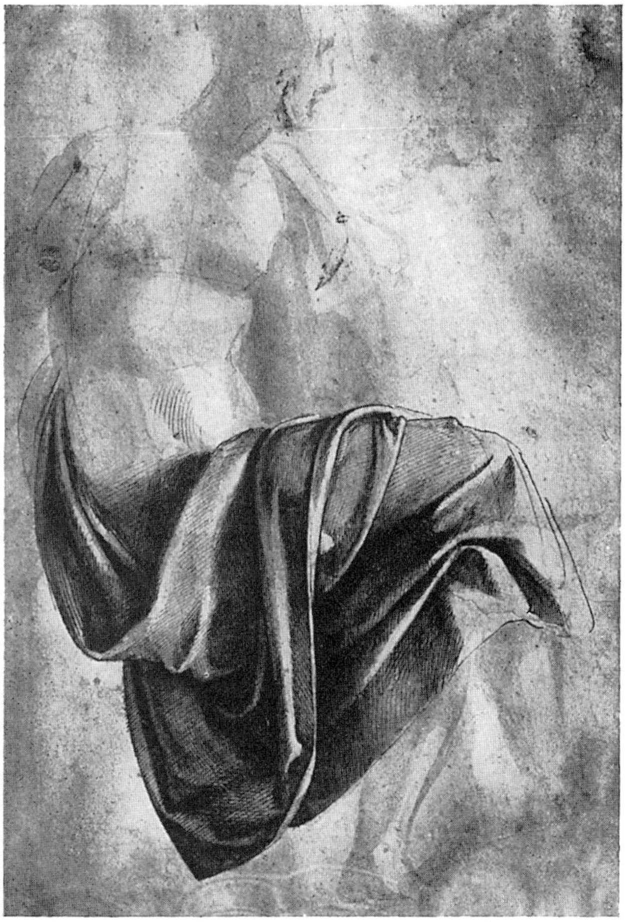

(*d*)

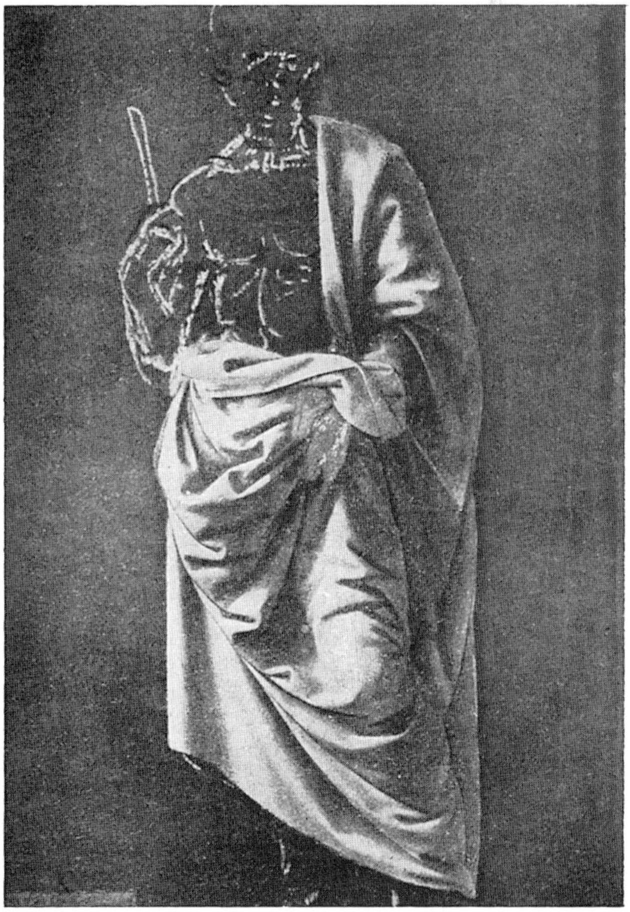

(*a*) and (*b*) By Leonardo da Vinci. (*c*) By Michel Angelo. (*d*) By Lorenzo di Credi.

(*a*)

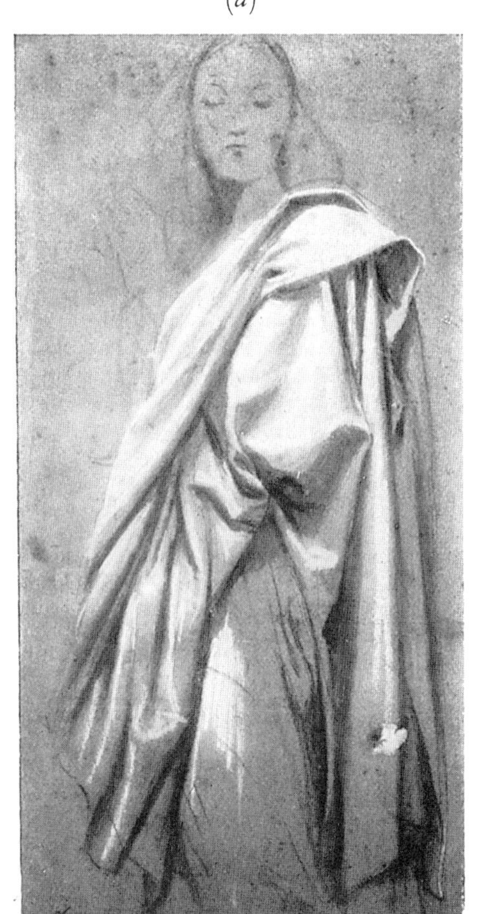

(*b*)

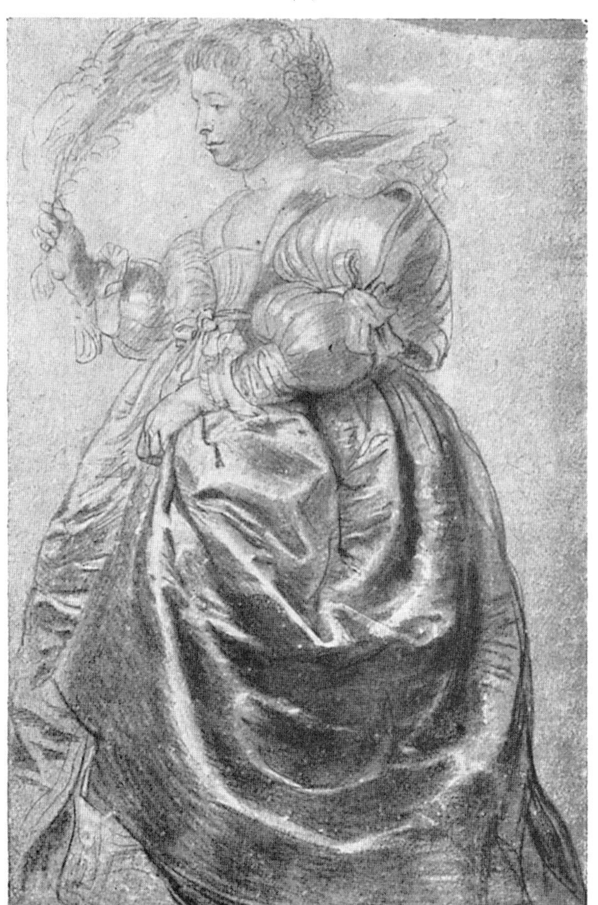

(*c*)

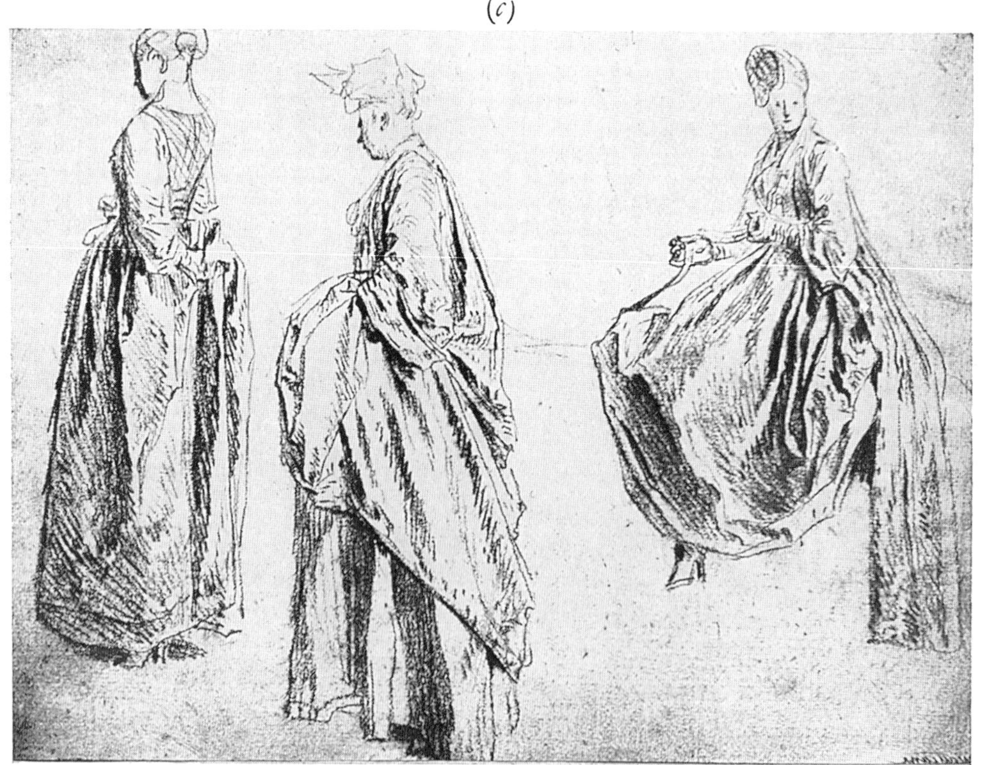

(*a*) By Ingres. (*b*) By Rubens. (*c*) By Fragonard.

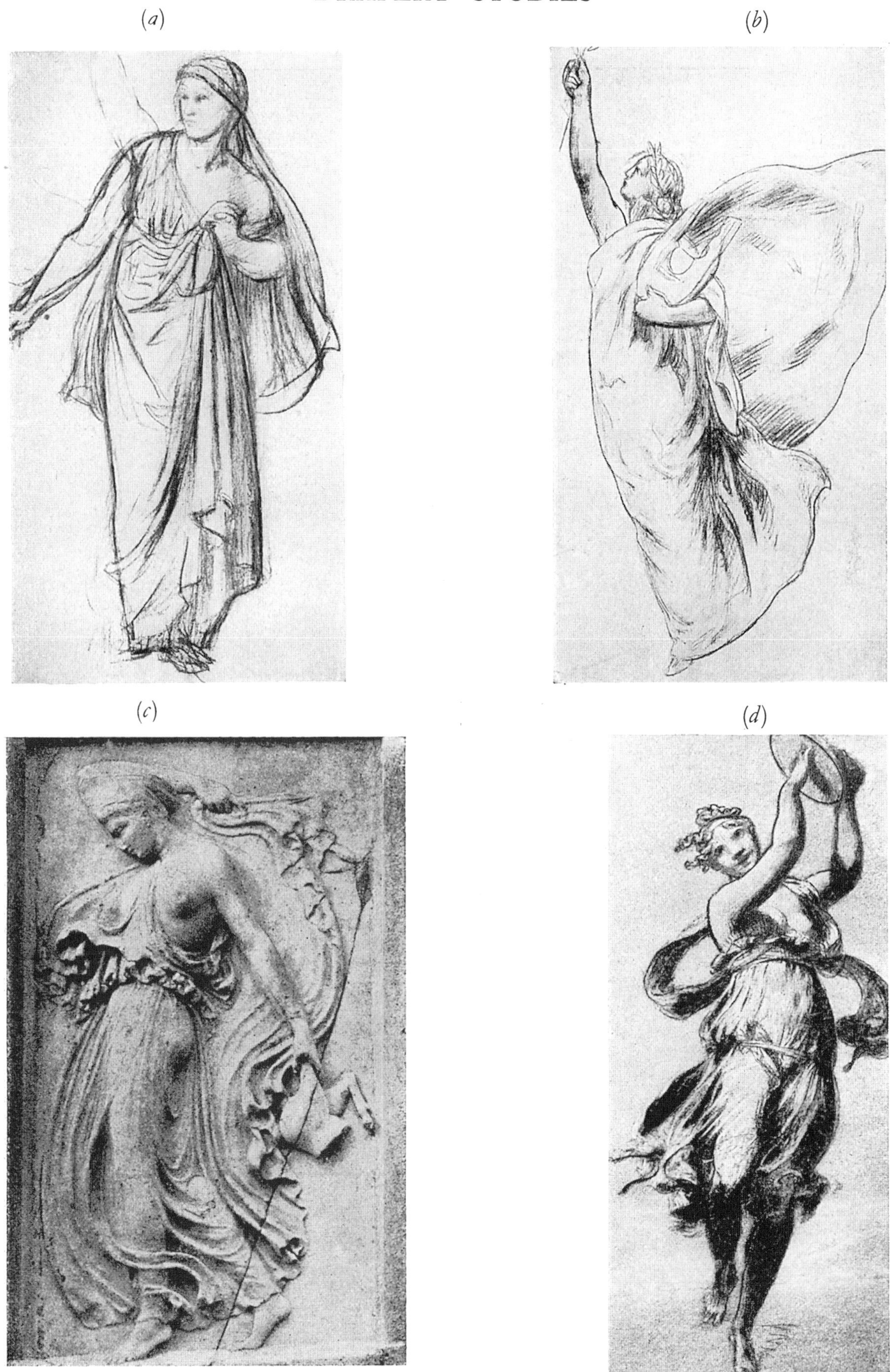

(*a*), (*b*) Puris de Chavannes. (*c*) Maenad in Frenzy (Greek relief). (*d*) By P. Prudhon.

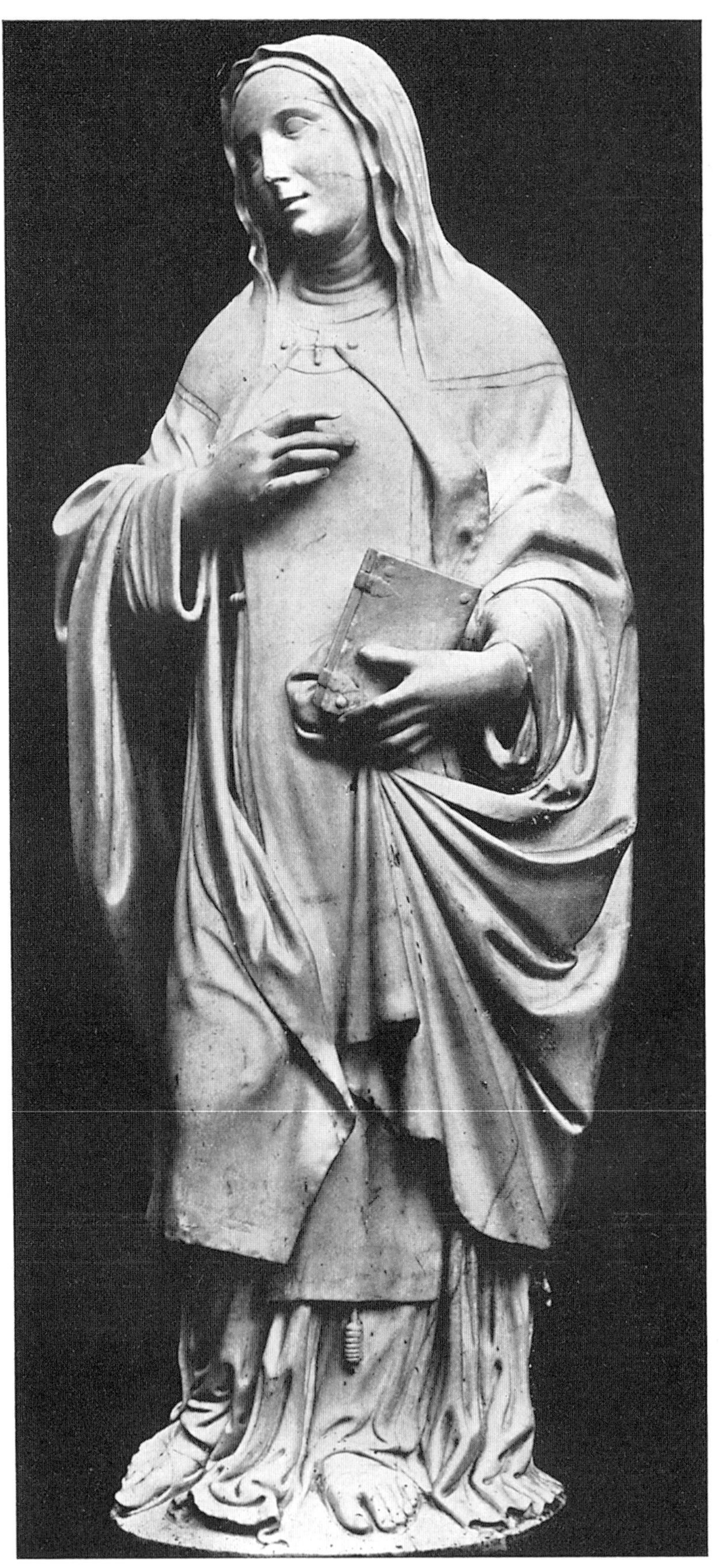

Statuette of a Nun in white marble. Italian, Sixteenth Century.

(*a*)

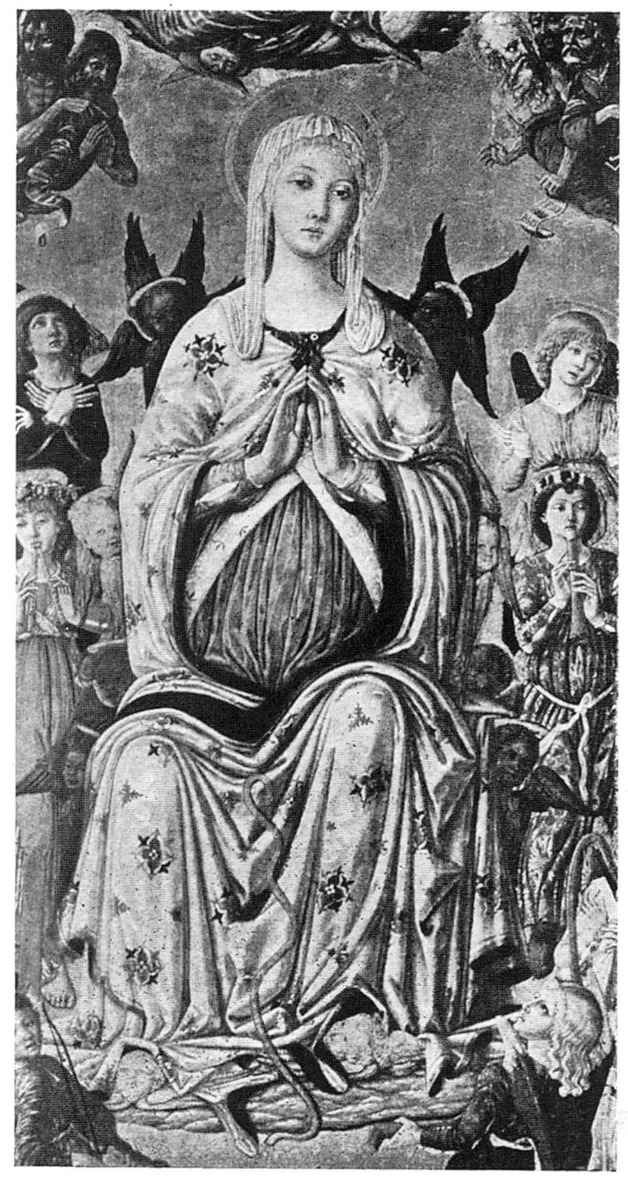

(*b*)

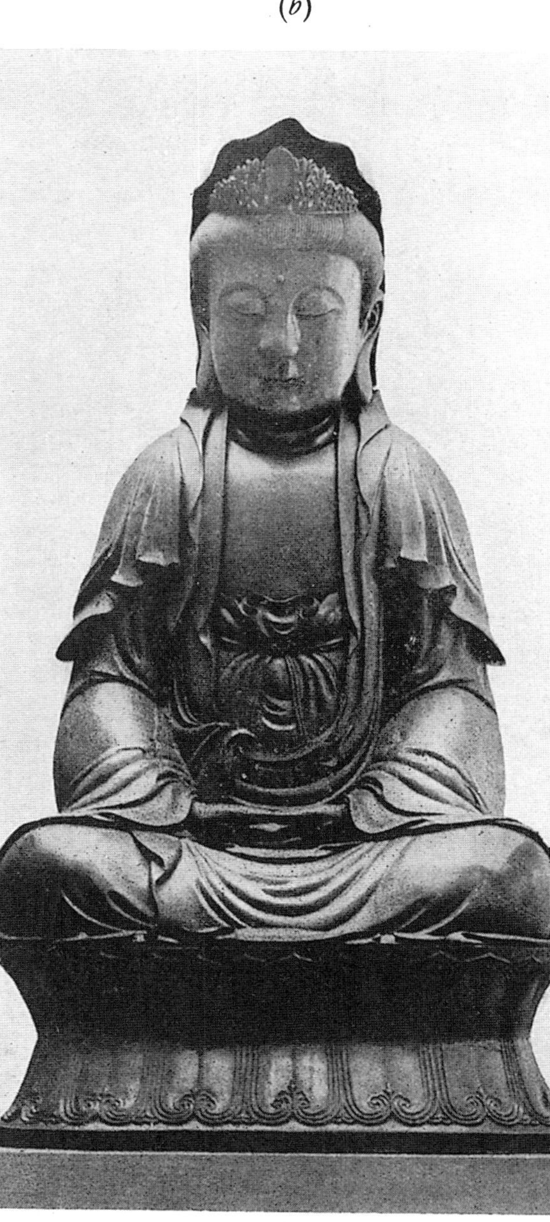

(*c*)

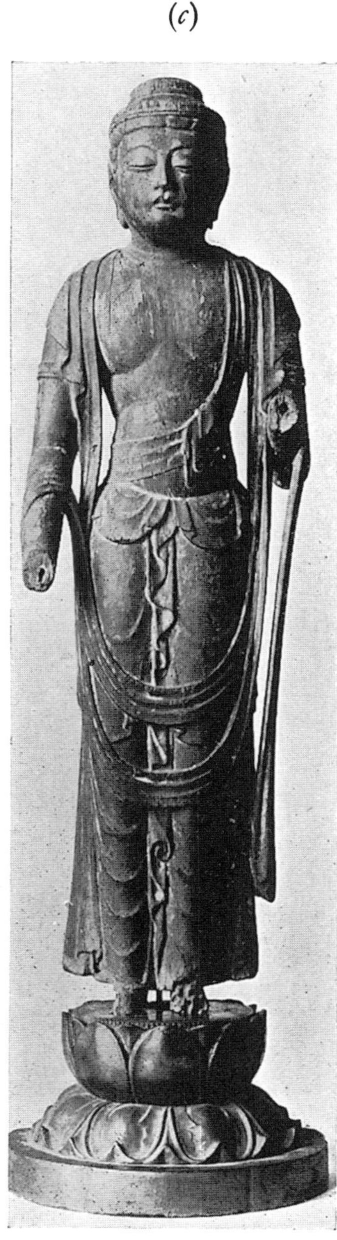

(*a*) Detail of "The Assumption," by Matteo di Govianni. (*b*) Large bronze figure of a Buddha.
(*c*) "Kwannon," ancient Japanese statuette in wood.

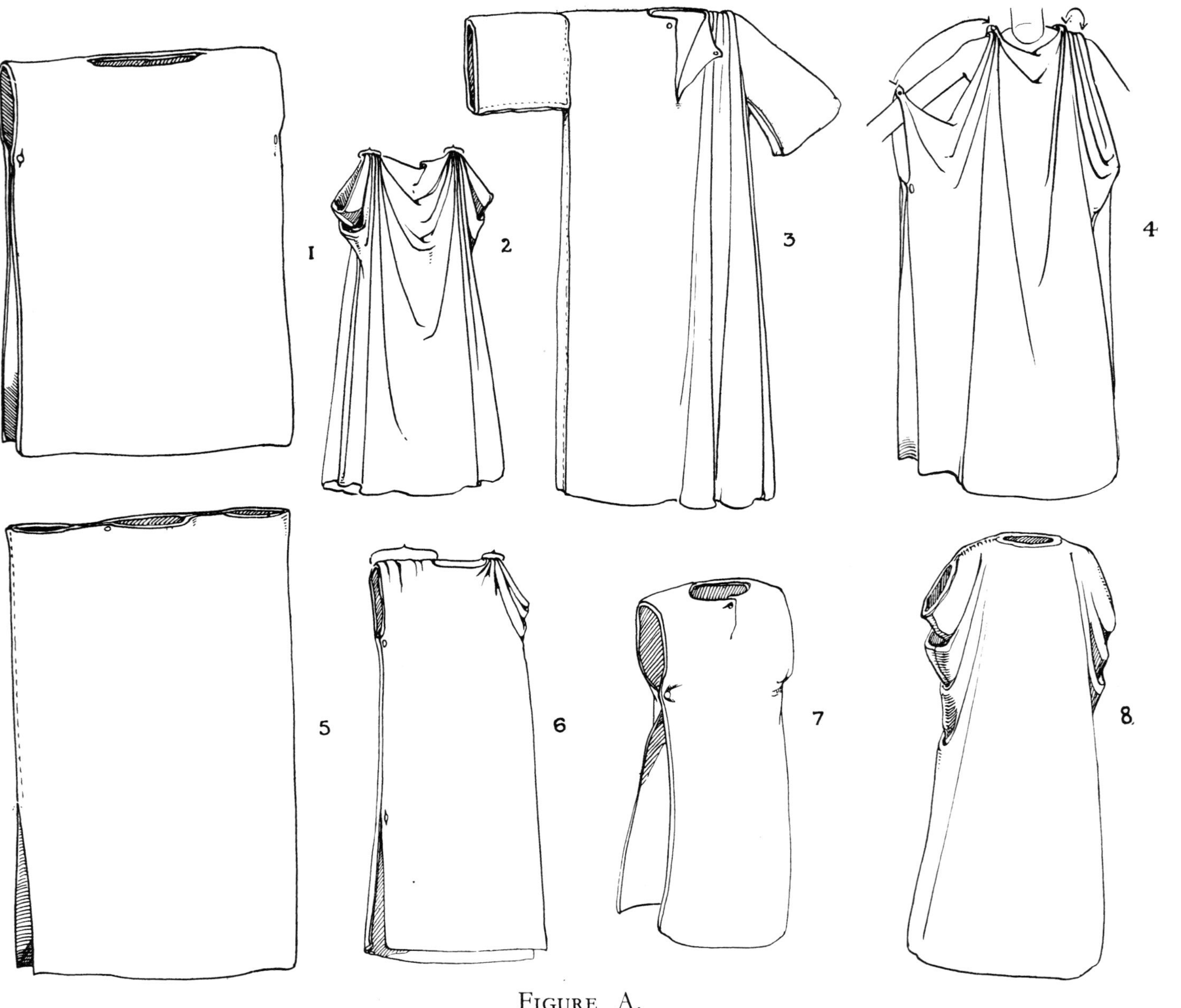

FIGURE A.

1. Basic Tunic No. 1. 2. The same with shoulders gathered. 3. The same with inset sleeves. 4. Lightly constructed form of Tunic No. 1. 5. Basic Tunic No. 2. 6. Tunic No. 1 with shoulders gathered. 7. Tunic No. 1 closely cut and fitted to the figure. 8. Basic Tunic No. 2 in wear.

THE ANATOMY OF DRESS

A FLAT piece of cloth has no form, its life is of the figure that supports it, its soul the movement it remembers in its folds asleep.

The drawing of drapery is a study from life, but not still-life. It must be studied with understanding; it cannot be copied. Every student of drapery should make and study the simple basic forms described below.

Avoid at first cutting or tying up the simple straight forms of the cloth and choose a plain, rather heavy material that will drape well. Realize the significance of the yard measure, the ordinary widths of the material, 36 in. or 52 in. It is based on the human form. The little dressmaker measuring a yard, fingertip to turned chin, is using the old principle of the arrow or yard-shaft of the archer, whose three yards (*i.e.* three times his own arrow-stretch) of Lincoln green constituted his cloth allowance.

It is the single loom measure of one worker's shuttle throw—the double width used two workers, one at each side of the cloth.

THE LONG TUNIC

(*See Figs. A, B, C, and illustrations on pages* 51, 52, *and* 54)

This basis robe is carefully anatomized on Fig. A. Nos. 1 and 5 are diagrams of the two main types of tunic.

Get three and a half or four yards of plain, rather heavy material, and make one tunic of each type. Study them on the moving model, watching their individual character. It will be seen at once that the subsequent folds entirely depend upon the position of neck and arm openings.

In No. 1 they come at the side, below and at right angles to the neck. In No. 5 they are level with the central neck openings.

The first tunic, when gathered on the shoulders as in No. 6, is usually best for light-moving drapery. Very sombre and statuesque effects may be obtained by developments of No. 5, especially if worked out in thick, slowly folding material (see Nos. 2 and 8). The superficial likeness and fundamental difference between these two tunic types can only be appreciated in action upon the model. They demonstrate the first principles of drapery in relation to the figure.

In action No. 1 narrows, any upward movement of the arms tending to force the drapery inward upon the neck, narrowing the sum total of width across the figure by increasing the number of folds. In action No. 5 spreads wide the folds, restricting arm movements, but giving an impressive stolidity of outline.

No. 1 swings clear from the arm opening; No. 5 webs or muffles it, tending to evolve a sleeve effect. The very loose, light freedom of No. 4 further develops No. 1 tunic, and No. 3 is its logical conclusion as a tunic with inset sleeves. No. 7 is the same basic tunic No. 1 with side arm-holes, cut in a narrow, heavy cloth.

Figures B and C are other developments of the tunic.

Fig. C, Nos. 1, 2, 3 show the effect obtained by simply making one half of the tunic longer than the other (this form of tunic billowing in the wind moves delightfully upon a dancing figure). On Fig. B, No. 9, is another simple development of tunic No. 1 in Fig. A.

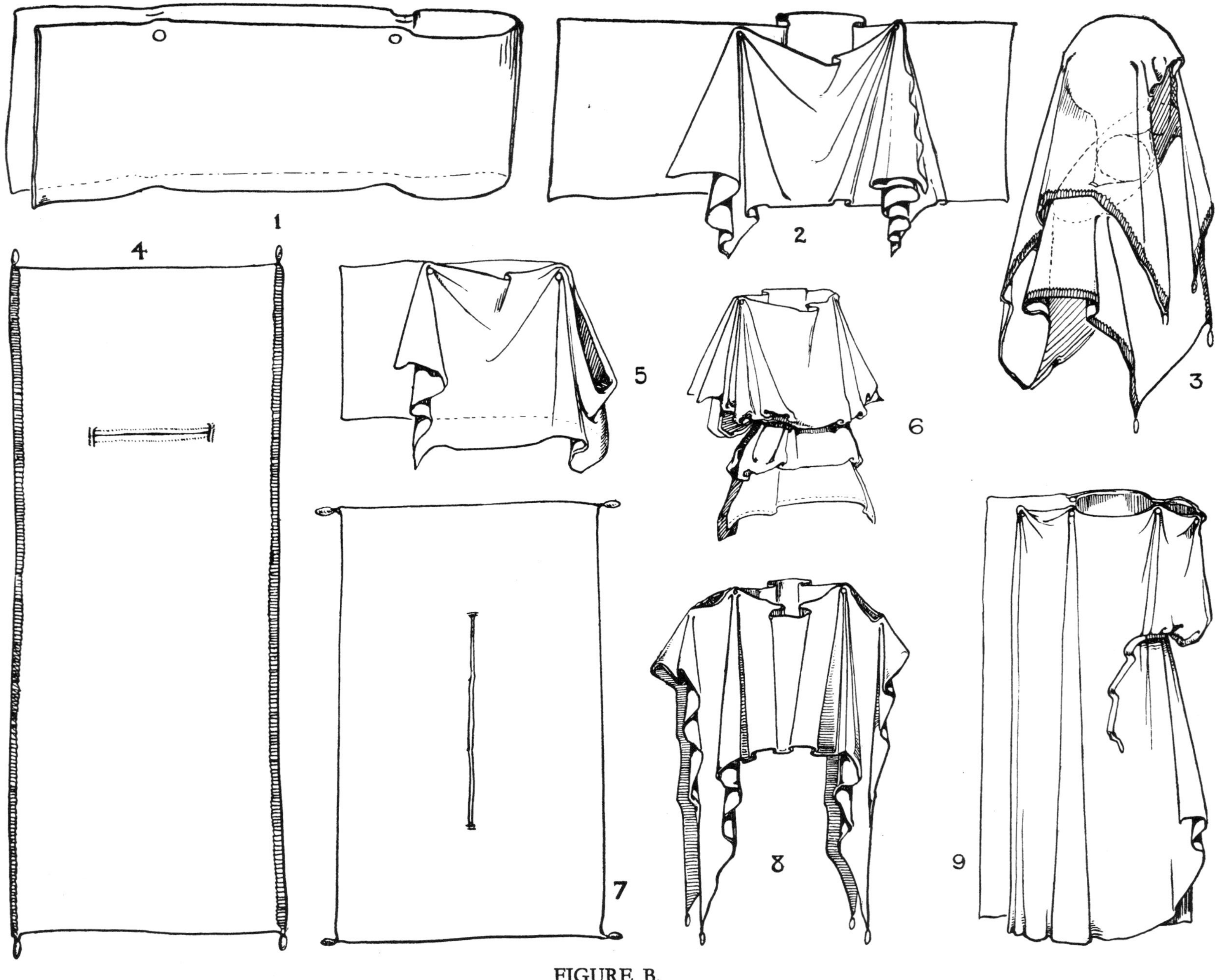

FIGURE B.

1. The single strip of material folded into a short tunic—one arm free, one covered, and the folded end used as a sleeve hole. 2. Two strips of material forming a short tunic, both arms free. 3, 4. An elaborately folded tunic and head wrap and its simple, cut-out pattern. 5. The tunic in No. 1 fastened together for wear. 6. The tunic shown in No. 2, with varied girdle bands. 7, 8. A simple cut-out pattern for an elaborate short tunic. 9. A long, girdled tunic.

THE SHORT TUNIC

(See Figures B and C, and illustrations on pages 51, 52, and 54)

This expresses the same anatomical principles, being a straight length of material, the folds of which depend on the length, width and position of neck and arm openings and bridges, the difference between the tunic proper and the cloak being in the position of its fastenings.

Cut the short tunics, Nos. 1 and 2 in Fig. B first, and study them in action. In No. 1 and No. 5 the free opening and the half-shut, folded arm-hole on the same garment demonstrate well the restricting effect of any form of sleeve, since the folded sleeve is always on the left arm.

Nos. 2 and 6 on Fig. B, cut in two strips, is open under both arms, and its extraordinarily varied folding depends entirely upon its length horizontally and the position of its neck fastenings. When these are set in close to the neck, the chest and back are comparatively smooth, with only a few V-shaped folds, but the two-winged " sleeve " pieces cascade freely downwards in close folds on either side of the figure. (See illustration (*b*) on page 51 and (*a*) on page 52.

In Fig. C, Nos. 4, 7, and 8 all translate and anatomize types of tunics to be found in the illustrations from antique sculpture (pages 51 to 54).

In Fig. B, Nos. 7 and 8 show the apparently elaborate tunic evolved from the simple square with a slit in it. The slit goes over the head and is caught at either side of the neck.

The still more complicated shoulder and head wrap, Fig. B, Nos. 3 and 4, is also a single strip of cloth (No. 4), with a similar neck slit, the longest end of cloth flowing down behind as a train or lifted and folded forwards over the head as in No. 3. The four small weights shown at the corners of these cut-outs will be found helpful as they emphasize the natural hang of the cloth.

Fig. C, No. 5, translates the Nymph's tunic shown in illustration (*d*) on page 51.

Nearly all the complicated foldings of antique drapery can be traced and anatomized by a knowledge of these basically simple patterns.

THE CLOAK

(See Figure D, and illustrations on pages 53 and 54)

The student should again take a straight length of material and study the principles of the cloak in its simplest form.

Fig. D, Nos. 1 and 2, are two cloaks in both of which the material is wrapped round the figure and the folds radiate from a single fastening; but in No. 1 that fastening is set in from the edge of the material, and in No. 2 it is at the extreme corner. The change this makes in the neck-line and whole aspect of the cloak should be carefully studied. As there is only one fastening to tether the cloak to the figure, the lines will radiate from this. The neck opening predominates, and the resulting folds widen in ordered sequence away from the central circle. Of course this principle remains unchanged whether the cloak is clasped from the shoulder as shown, or under the chin or round the chest.

In No. 3 there are two fastenings, one on either shoulder, tending to make the lines steadier and more level, while the rounded piece shown upheld by the left arm soon evolves into a sleeve.

The cut and folded cloak, Nos. 4 to 12, has an interesting simplicity, as will be seen by a glance at No. 6. It is a plain square of material, and must be studied in the material to appreciate the result. The variations that can be obtained in altering the comparative length and width of hood piece and shoulder width will be seen at once. To gather the shoulders, thus bunching the hood, will evolve an entirely different type of cloak, whilst to place the centre of the cloak deliberately out of the centre of the material (leaving one side of both cloak and hood-piece very much longer than the other) will enable the long side of the cloak to be wrapped round and thrown over the shoulder in an impressive sweep, the elongated hood-piece becoming a scarf that may be wound round the neck and allowed to hang down freely.

The hooded cloak shown in Nos. 8 to 12 explains itself. Its making is that of the mediæval hood or the adjusted sack turned inwards, corner into corner, as worn by the modern coal-heaver.

Plate D and the illustrations on pages 53 and 54 show these basic cloaks and hoods very clearly.

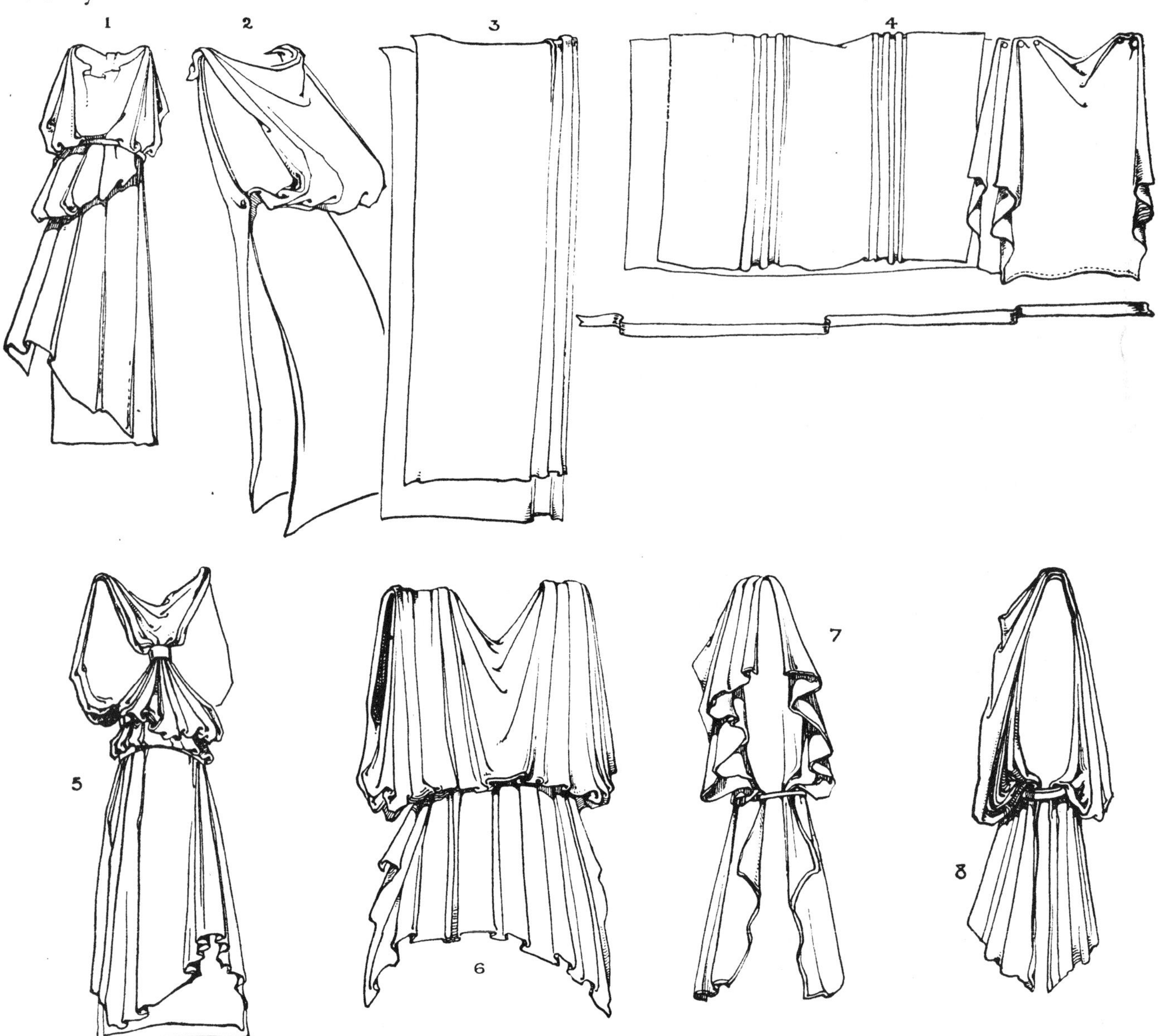

FIG. C.—1, 2, 3. Two straight lengths of material arranged variously, giving a good light type of drapery for study upon a dancing form. 4. The same straight lengths arranged horizontally to form a short tunic. 5. A tunic arranged with a scarf-like collar. 6. The tunic below the breastplate in illustration (*a*) on page 51. 7. The sleeve opening when the fastening comes towards the neck. See also the cloak fastening on Fig. D, Nos. 1 and 2. 8. When the fastening comes at the edge of the material.

GREEK COSTUME

The photographs in this book serve as an introduction to an intelligent study of Greek costume. No designer would transplant the flowing Greek robes directly into modern London,

[*Continued on page* 56.

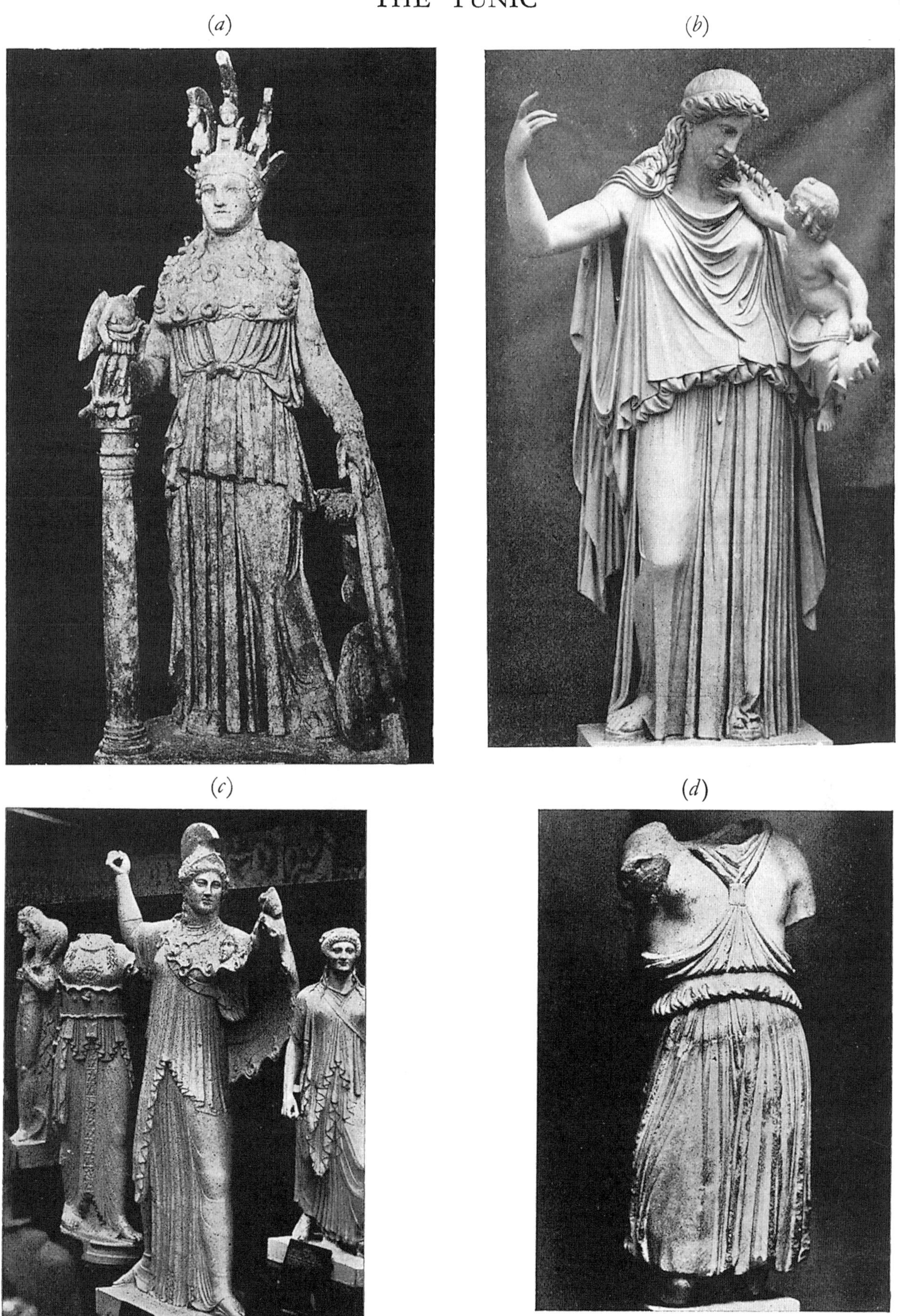

(*a*) See Fig. B, No. 6. (*b*) A short Tunic of simple type worn over a long, girdled Tunic. (*c*) Pressed and fluted folds elaborating a simple Tunic. (*d*) See Fig. C, No. 5.

(*a*)

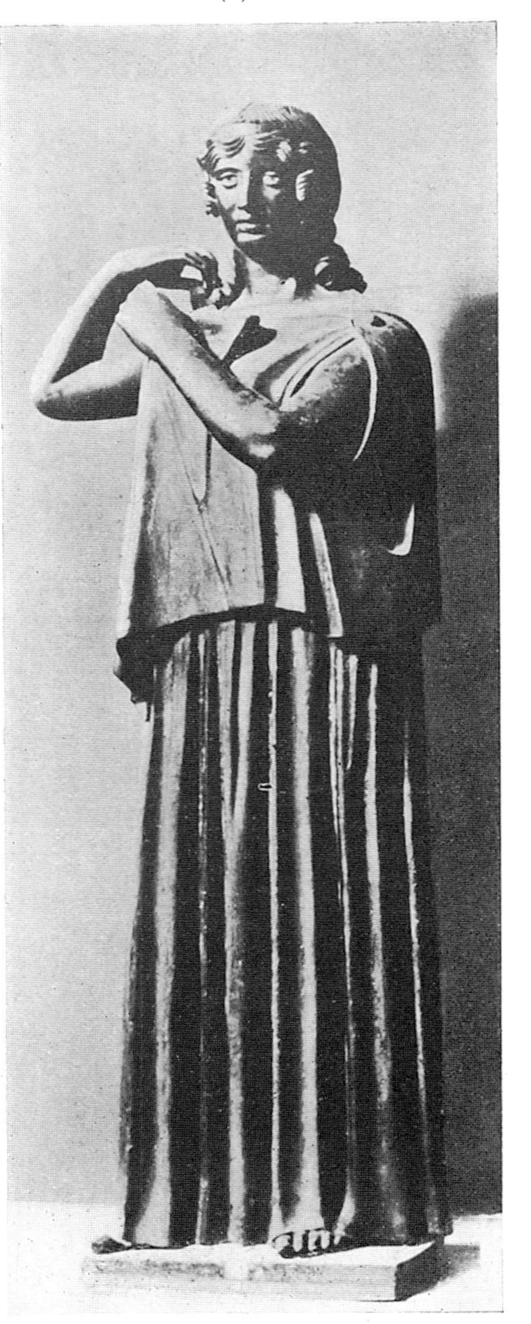

(*b*)

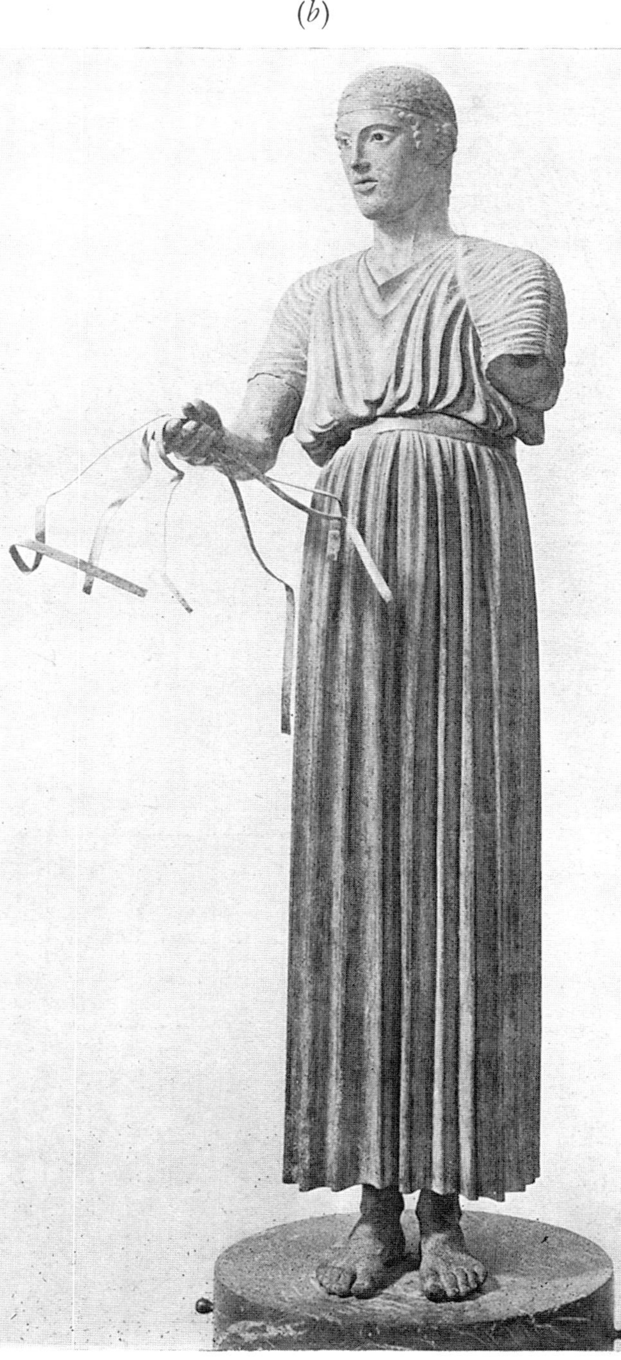

(*c*)

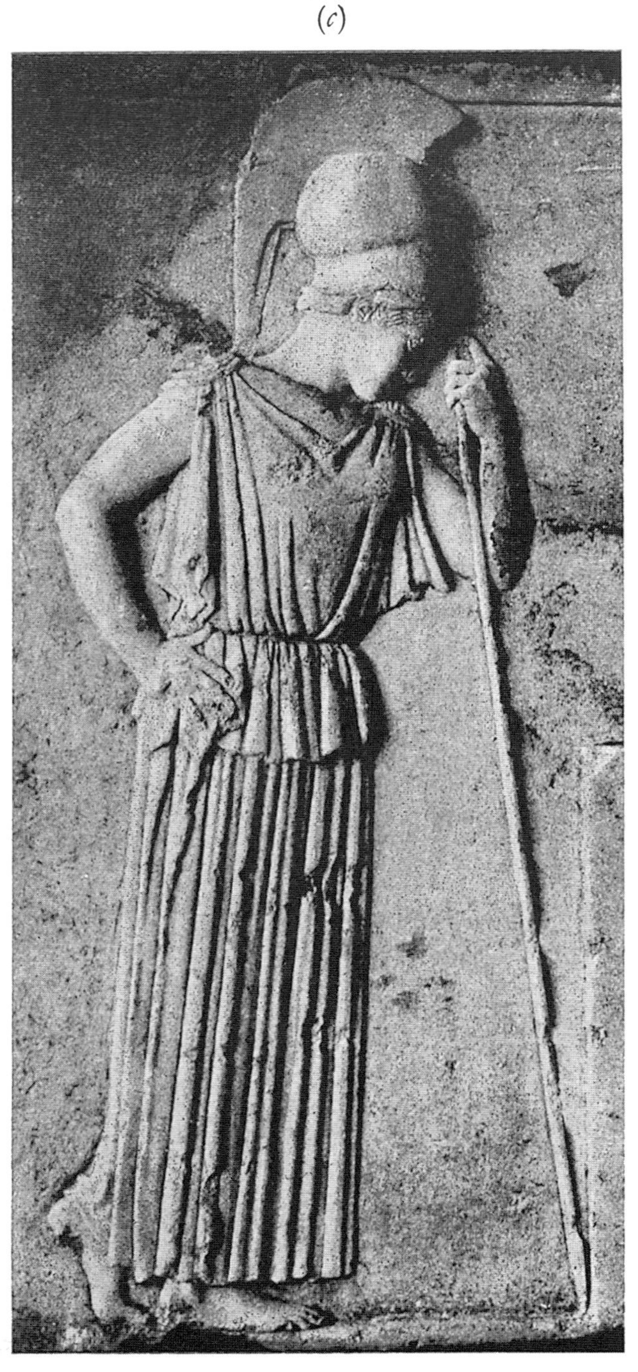

(*a*) The short folded Tunic (see Fig. B, No. 2), showing free and closed arm-holes. (*b*) The same short folded Tunic worn with a girdle.
(*c*) The simple basic Tunic of Fig. A, No. 1, in wear.

(*a*) (*b*)

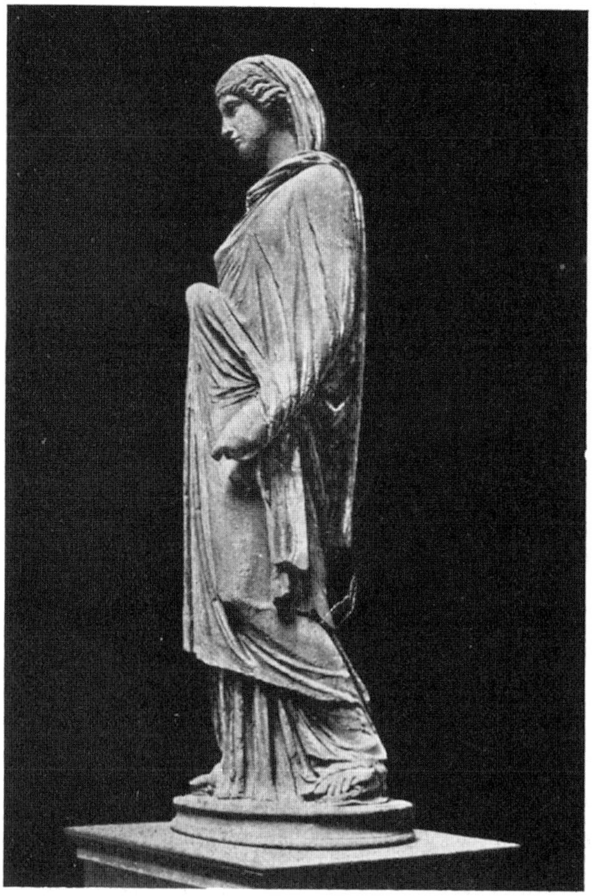

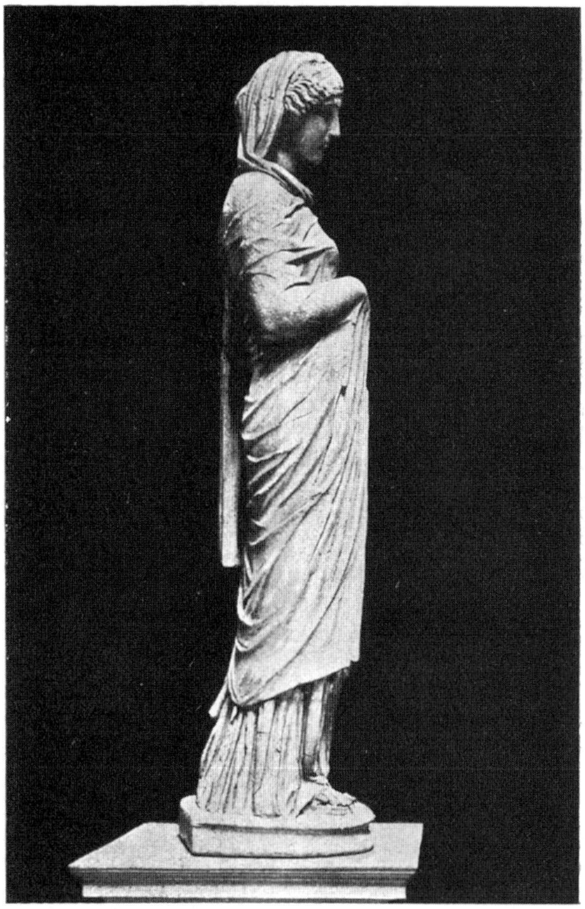

(*c*) 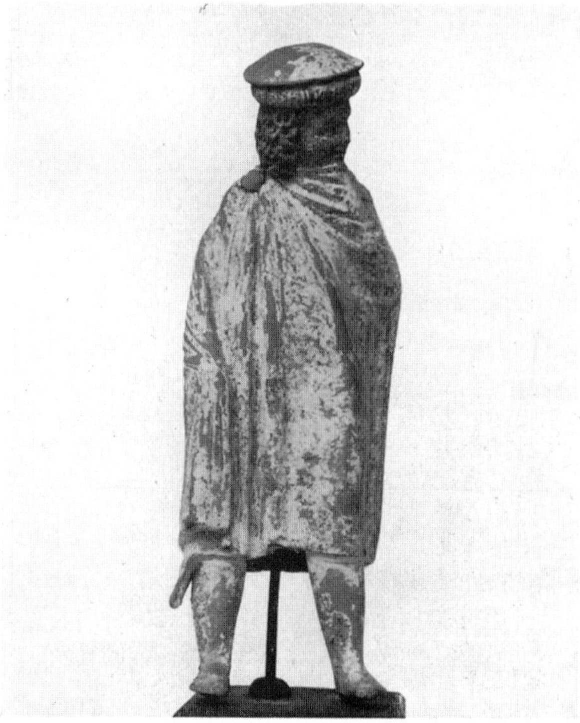 (*d*)

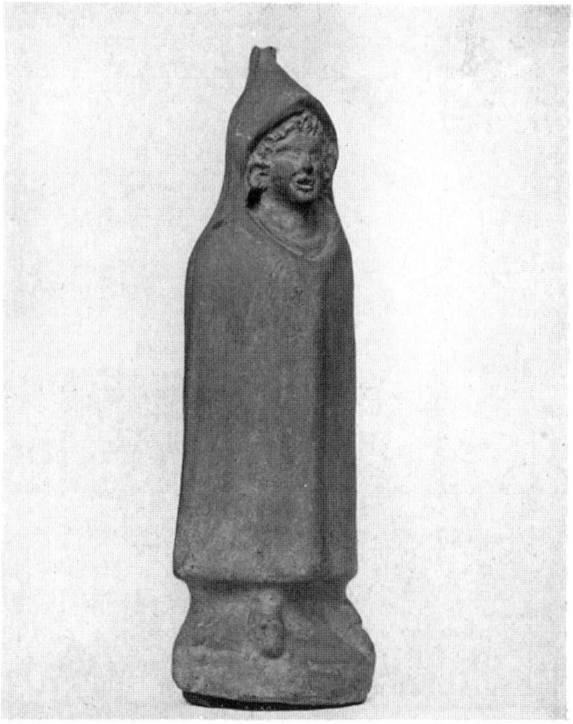

(*a*) and (*b*) The beautiful effect of simple drapers. (*c*) A similar cloak to that on Fig. D, No. 2. (*d*) The hooded cloak (see Fig. D, Nos. 8–12).

(*a*)

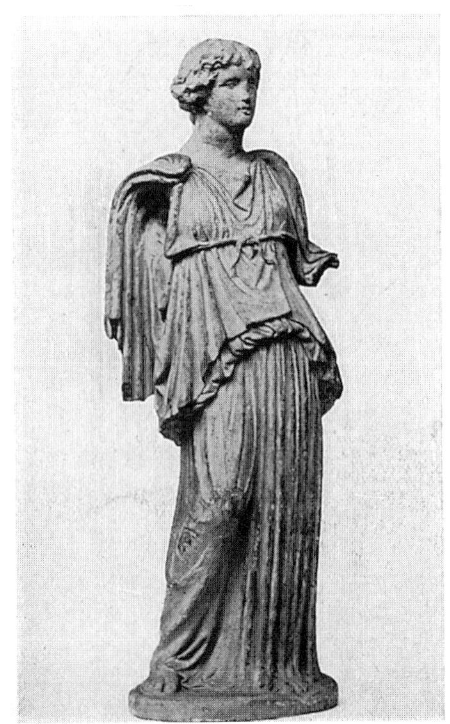

(*b*)

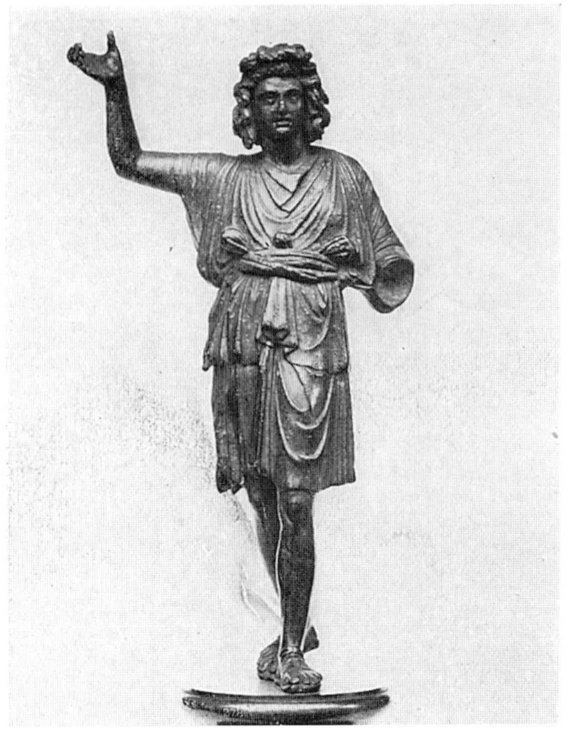

(*c*)

(*a*) This drapery is entirely the result of careful folding and arranging; the pieces of material are plain straight lengths of cloth. (*b*) A tunic bunched up by waist wrapping. (*c*) Large single squares of material skilfully worn.

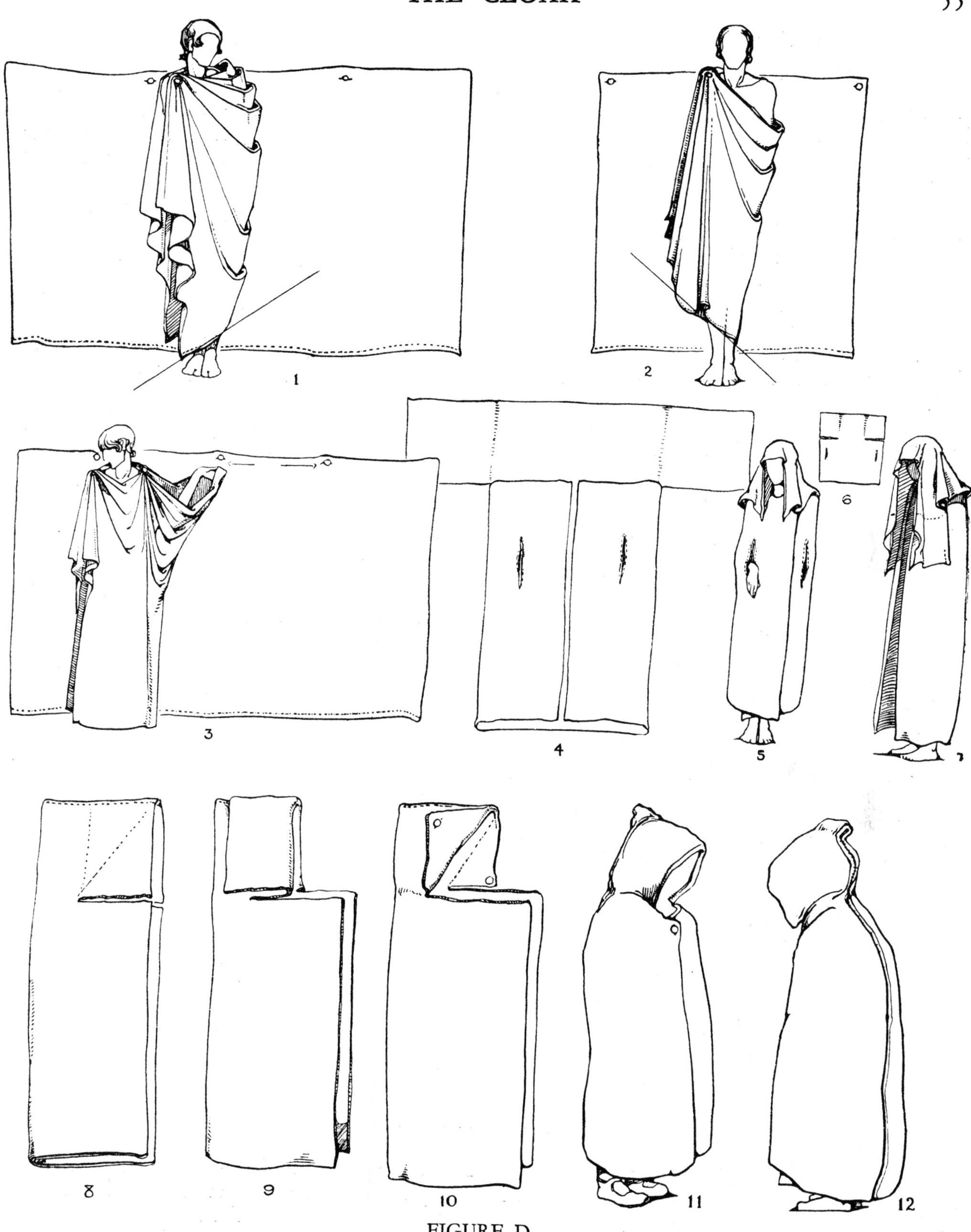

FIGURE D.

1. Cloak with fastening set in towards the neck. 2. Cloak with fastening at the corners of the cloth. 3. Cloak with two fastenings at the neck, involving folded sides. 4–7. A folded cloak capable of very varied treatment. 8–12. The basis of the hood shown in a hooded cloak (see also illustration on p. 53).

but all designers should have that underlying consciousness of essentials that these draperies show so well.

The two main divisions of Homeric dress were the single garment worn next to the skin, and the outer garment for protection or appearance. The Chiton was worn long or short. When long it was composed of a single piece of material fairly wide width and about 4 yards long, and the illustrations and diagrams show its various uses and adaptations.

One of the Greek figure drawings reproduced in this book is by Lord Leighton. This master left minute instructions. He advises dressing the model in a simple bag about 2 yards square, sewn up at the sides, but leaving spaces about 15 inches long for the arms, and a similar space for the neck. (A pattern of this will be seen on page 46.)

This dress was kept in place by thin bands crossing over the chest and passing round the waist—the band being placed over the head with a long loop hanging down the back; the two ends crossed on the chest and passed back below the breasts. These two ends are then threaded through the loop at the back and brought again to the front of the body, and tied.

After this cross-piece was put on, the folds of the drapery were drawn out between the bands, often purposely, though the same effect would be obtained had the model moved about and exercised sufficiently.

When trying this we should recommend the student to arrange the model with only the very simplest waist girdles, and it will be seen at once how any action tends to loop up the straight folds over them into broken curves. It is a well-known trick to obtain that crinkly effect seen in this master's drawings. The whole garment should be wrung out in water and twisted into a tight rope lengthways. If the folds are wanted very tight, strain the material, twisting it very tightly, and leave it until quite dry before undoing the twist; but if lighter creases are required, shake it out while still damp.

This wetting and setting of drapery should be practised by all students, but used with very great care, as it may induce the most terrible artificial effects. The student need go no further than the family clothes-line on a windy day to study the difference between wet and dry drapery, and it may help him to appreciate the more subtle difference between clinging fabrics which have this watery quality, and the dryer fabrics with their more buoyant folds. (We recommend a material of ordinary double width. We believe 2 yards too wide.)

The outermost Greek garment, the Himation, worn by both men and women, varied in size and shape and position according to the weather. The photographs of it in use explain it very well, and we certainly recommend the student to make it up and study it for himself.

All essential character of lines known and used by the designer will be found in these simple forms. " Straight lines convey a feeling of power, dignity, stability, calmness, nobility. Curves are the life and joy of an arrangement. Restrained curves are always beautiful; curves may be used with freedom in clothing to be worn on occasions of gaiety. Simplicity in masses is an element in good design. All decorative detail must be kept subordinate and should be consistent in feeling with the idea of the whole" (Laura I. Baldt).

EGYPTIAN COSTUME

It is impossible to cover the subject here. From the tight shoulder-strapped tube to the intricately-folded ceremonial costumes, there is hardly anything that the student will not find of the utmost interest and service, but the four diagrams of the use of the scarf suggest some useful ideas and illustrate the tremendous variation possible with the most simple material. In the first a single piece of material is drawn tightly round the figure and fastened on the left shoulder, leaving the right breast bare (Diagram No. 1); carried out in this material, it is one of the most useful arrangements for the study of drapery, as it shows the dominating factor of the form actually creating the drapery. The two ends of the scarf are drawn through a waistband (No. 2); in the Greek you expect them to be knotted in front. No. 3 shows the shoulder-scarf plain-knotted in front.

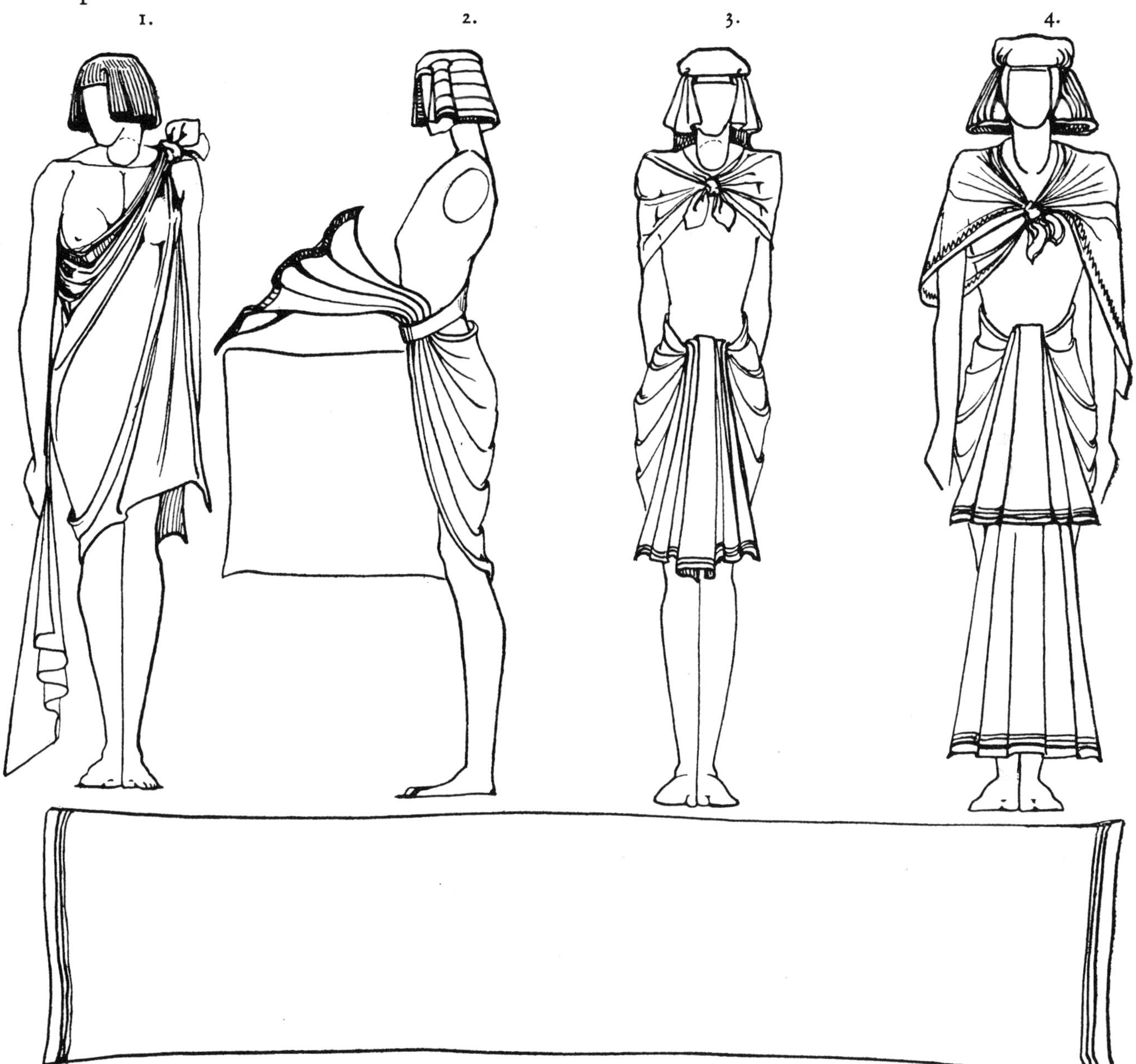

In No. 4, the scarf-making hip-drapery is put on unevenly, so that one end hangs longer than the other, and the shoulder-scarf is knotted end to end, forming a curious sleeve effect.

Attendant slaves would wear nothing but the loin-cloth, though this oblong piece of stuff could be adjusted in various ways. It was common wear for everybody, and the diagrams show its adjustment into long regular folds. The Egyptians also wore a skin-tight chemise, sometimes little more than a strip of material tied on to the figure, sometimes a tube upheld by shoulder-straps. Of course, the ceremonial dress was most intricate; far beyond the scope of these short notes. It can be well studied at the British Museum, and whole books have been written on the subject.

The costume of the Assyrian women consisted of a long tunic and mantle, and the adjustment of both may be studied in bas-relief at the Museum. They seem to have loved ornament, and hair, arms, and ears are covered with jewels.

ROMAN COSTUME

May we say it amplified the Greek? The most typical Roman departure was the toga. Again experts differ as to the cut, some making it quite square and some believing that the form was curved. It was a particularly voluminous garment, difficult to adjust, and difficult to wear by persons unaccustomed to the dress. Its form was entirely dependent upon the spontaneous throw of its folds, which were held in place entirely by their own weight. Perhaps the simplest form of toga for the student is roughly semicircular. To adjust this the garment was held behind the figure by both hands outstretched, the rounded edge downwards. The left hand side was then gathered on to the left shoulder, the point, which was weighted, just touching the ground. The other half was brought under the right forearm, across the chest, and flung back over the left shoulder, so that the other point hung down behind. This is a very simple form. The larger and later toga is most complex, and a system of folds are drawn across the waist, and other folds are pulled up through these into a sort of bag or pouch, called the umbo, which could be used for a pocket. Altogether an interesting garment for specialized study.

BYZANTINE AND CELTIC COSTUME

This word to the costumier has an ecclesiastical sound. It is perhaps less interesting to the drapery student than to the student of historic costume. Many of the simpler forms of the tunic are there, but they are now ecclesiastical vestments. The alb, the planeta (a pouch with a hole in the middle for the head), the lacema, or cloak, are all elaborations of very simple form. It would be a good exercise for any student, particularly interested in ceremonial costume, to trace back some of the present elaborate Roman Catholic vestments to their original simple forms and uses.

The costumes of the races that overran the west of Europe during the first five centuries, Gauls, Goths, Franks, and Lombards, all appear very different to the uninitiated; but the intelligent student will see at once that all of them used variations of the tunic and mantle. They differed mainly in ornamentation.

For example, in ancient Gaul, the ladies' metal belts predominated the costume, the folds of which but served as a background to them, and Usanne admires the rugged splendour and strength of the costume so well suited to the wild beauty of its wearers.

Boadicea, " fleeing from the Roman rods," probably wore far less costume than she wears in her chariot on Westminster Bridge. It was probably the tunic held in place by barbaric jewellery, and the material Scotch tartan plaid, since this was the homespun of all Celtic tribes, though it probably bore little relationship to the brilliancy of colour and finish found in modern regimental uniform.

A characteristic of all early English dress is the ornamentation upon the fabric itself. Of course, it must be only from written descriptions that we can gather what it was like, but English women seem to have been specially skilful, as Anglican Opus was the name given on the continent to rare work of this sort, and Adhelm, Bishop of Sherborne, writes in the seventh century of the admirable art in weaving and embroidery among the English women.

ENGLISH HISTORIC COSTUME

Very many books have specialized on this subject. Any fashion designer requiring knowledge of some special period, should have no difficulty. We also recommend our students to visit the National Portrait Gallery, and to study the statutes and laws governing cloth and cloth-working for the period that he has on hand. This last is more important than the more superficial workers understand. The width of the cloth necessitating one or two workers to a single loom was often a matter of legislation. The material itself, its weight and colour, were matters of minute legislation. The historical worker must indeed cut his coat according to his cloth.

When the turn of a sleeve, or a 2-inch loop of braid might convey that the wearer had £10 a year of her own, no husband, and was over forty, it will be seen that attention to details is extremely necessary.

Let any student who has period work to do study the history of that period thoroughly well; only thus will he be able to create that wonderful, unmistakable sense of atmosphere that marks the true artist.

The Saxon gown was a long robe, with loose sleeves and a girdle. Later, it was laced up to fit the figure, and your practical girdle becomes ornamental; the sleeves develop fantastically, till the close of the eleventh century they are long, knotted extensions dangling from wrist or elbow. On the whole, up to the end of the fifteenth century, simplicity of form and long folds prevail, though the Norman love of finery was responsible for the introductoin of many extravagant ideas. At one time shoe points became so long that they bowed out in front of the foot in a semicircular curve that had to be fastened up to the knee. It would have been impossible to walk upstairs, especially the winding mediæval stairs, in such monstrosities. The long rich mantle of this period is very typical. It is a period of long lines. The hair was allowed to hang loose if long enough, otherwise it was braided into artificial elongated plaits. Even the lines of the wimple were simple, and seem to add to the effect of length. This period well demonstrates the extreme magnificence compatible with fundamental simplicity. When Henry III. confirmed the honour of knighthood on William de Valence in 1247, he wore material called Cloth of Baldekins. It was woven with a weft of gold and richly wrought with figures of beasts and birds. And elsewhere we read of a simple sheepskin coat, but the skins were checkered diamondwise of black and white. The skin side was dyed bright green and patterned with silver.

We recommend the student of drawing who wishes to study historic costume rather for the enlargement of his own ideas than for its historical significance, to take one particular garment and study its evolution through the centuries. For example, the hood, a simple structural example of which is given in the pictures, develops in the most extraordinary way until, during the reign of Richard II. a fantastic transformation turns it into a hat.

This happens as soon as some adventurous person, instead of pulling it over his head, thrusts his head in through the face opening—the cape of the hood flapping down over one ear, and the crown of the hood (which by then had grown a long tail) flopping down over the other. The cape part was then piled up over the top of the head, and the tail part twisted round to fasten all tight. The result was a most distinctive head-dress, popular for more than a century. We have shown you the beginning and the end of the story of the hood. Study it for yourselves and then you will have learnt something of the first five centuries of English history, and a great deal more about the natural evolution of costume.

The reigns of the Lancastrian kings during the first part of the fifteenth century are perhaps the most well known and most vaguely used for costume of all historic periods. The chief feature of this costume was the head-dress of the woman. The net-caul of the Richard II. period was retained, but superimposed were all the various horned and steeple-crowned head-dresses so well known, and often so carelessly used. This period, too, shows a very definite waist-line, and there is often another horizontal line at the level of the knees. Thus, if the head-dress be high enough, the whole figure appears divided into four fairly equal parts. The reign of Henry VII. gives that distinctive costume which we associate with the house of Tudor. Broad felt hats and plumed bonnets of fur or velvet now replace the hood, and the works of the painter Holbein should be studied by all students of English costume of this period. The so-called dog-kennel, or diamond-shaped head-dress, is another good example of a very simple form carried to a very elaborate finish, and the student who has worked out the sequence of the hood may well follow it by the sequence of this plain cap. Let the student take a large, plain, white whimple or head drapery and fold back one side quite smoothly and simply over a piece of stiffening, about 4 inches wide and 20 inches long. Bend this stiffening lightly around the face, with the long, loose piece of drapery hanging loosely over the back of the head. You will find that the creases, or bends, come almost automatically, one in the centre and one on either side, a little set in above the ears, and these creases will vary automatically with the shape of the face, and give you a very good outline of the dog-kennel head-dress, and a very helpful guide for your further study. Holinshed tells us that Anne of Cleves, the day after her arrival in England, wore a French hood after this English fashion, and that it became her exceedingly well. During Elizabeth's reign we have one of the most bizarre developments of the wide skirt, the great wheeled farthingale, the making of which is explained in the diagrams. The later portraits of Queen Elizabeth are most interesting from a designer's point of view, whether he approves, or not, of the costume.

The masses of skirt, sleeve, and torso are interesting, and the decoration of the radiating lines of skirt, farthingale, and collar are worth much study. The whole decorative scheme, framing the face and shoulders, has curious unity, despite its extreme elaboration. During the reign of the Stuart kings, the character of the costume subtly changes, and with the accession of Charles the First marks a very picturesque epoch that may be well studied through the works of Vandyke and his school. With the restoration of the house of Stuart Dame Fashion living in England develops a dual personality. The Court beauties may be studied in the works of Sir Peter Lely and *Pepys' Diary*, and the Puritan costume, although so simple, requires quite as much study to get it right. The demure little Quaker Girl of musical comedy is as far from the real truth as the ludicrous austerities of the would-be humorous. The Puritan costume could be a plain working-man's everyday suit, or a very dainty refinement of quiet design and exquisite material. With William of Orange comes a curious tall frontal head-dress. It was called a commode, and rose a tower of frills three or four stories high.

The frivolous, fascinating eighteenth century is the century of powder and patches, of hooped petticoats and piled hair. Sir Roger de Coverley expresses the difference between the old and the new style, between the farthingale and the hooped skirt. " My grandmother appears as if she stood in a huge drum, whereas the ladies now walk as if they were in a go-cart."

THE PANNIER

The typical Watteau shepherdess effect, the picturesque milkmaid, or the voluminous silken presence of your elderly fairy godmother, the fitted bodice of the first diagram, with its straps across, is taken from an eighteenth-century model, where the front of the corsage was straightened out across a delicately shaped and curved wooden base (see page 62).

The skirt of the pannier costume, which frequently looks quite terrifyingly elaborate, is usually quite simple. The diagrams show how perfectly straight pieces of material gathered in straight lines across the graduated intervals can be bunched up about the waistline in most effective folds. If another straight piece pendant from the shoulders and swinging clear of the back is caught in with the skirt folds, even more complicated draped and trained effects may be obtained with most reassuring simplicity.

We advise any student, before making one of these costumes, to buy several pieces of cheap dressmaker's lines and experiment for himself.

The side-pieces of the Georgian costume were definitely dependent upon the waist and hips in contrast to the Elizabethan or the crinoline effects; they were side-pieces only, the figure from front to back remaining slender, so that a number of figures wearing this costume give the curious effect of having been run through the mangle and having been pressed out sideways.

The history of the French Revolution would be interesting ground for any student wishing to specialize. The complete change in the costume is so marked, and there are so many artists who have shown it so well—Vernet, Carle and Horace, and many others.

The Incroyables and the Merveilleuses are well known, and the classic revival would be recognized by every one. And for the student there are all those smaller matters of red caps and tricolour stripes that make the history of costume, indeed, the history of its wearers. It will make your studies real and alive, and will show you how to understand these things.

THE CRINOLINE AND BUSTLE

That invaluable support of so many ideas deserves more study than it gets, the artist being frequently content with a bounding, billowing bundle. He attaches it to the waist-line, but the subsequent soft explosion sadly lacks the steadying influence of its true understanding.

The crinoline itself was a separate affair, worn below the dress, and over which the folds of the dress swung themselves freely, so that a definite movement right to left, not only sent the crinoline-cage swaying about the wearer, but would definitely move the folds from side to side across the circular hoops below (see page 65).

The crinoline is dependent from the waistline only, which gives it very different character and movement from the Elizabethan corset-supported skirt, or the panniered and padded width of the Georgian dress, where the movement depends on the hip-bone.

The arrangement of the hoops, when sitting, is shown in the diagram (page 65), though the inevitable piling up of the material at the back of the figure gave rather more short-waisted effect (and helped to create the impression one always gets of your crinoline lady being like a dainty little bantam hen trying to accommodate rather too many eggs).

The upright but slender-waisted corset explains a good deal, and contrasts forcibly with the mid-Victorian corset shown. Whereas the crinoline lady had of necessity a centralized upright carriage, the bustle produces a definite tilt forward, the feet coming definitely to the front, and the main weight of the skirt being carried well out behind. To develop this upright, rather strutty carriage, and perhaps to counterbalance the weight behind, the supplement (or improvement) was frequently fastened on in front, which further emphasized the forward thrust of the figure with the flattened back and the upright carriage of the head.

This style is more interesting for the study of the effect of clothes on form and carriage than for its beauty of style, though some of the later Victorian fashion-plates will show how very charming " Figures, Faces, and Folds " could be at this period.

The stiff Elizabethan corset of leather had side shelves of leather fixed immovably above either hip. It encased the ribs firmly; so the tilt of the artificial hips was dependent on the thorax rather than the legs, which legs trotted freely below their inflexible leather hip-pieces. (When your Elizabethan lady fainted she had to faint all in one piece; her legs would collapse under her, but there was no " giving " at the waist, as above the billowing Georgian panniers or the delicate bend of the slender waist above the swaying crinoline.)

MATERIALS

The principal materials used for clothing are wool, cotton, flax, jute, silk, and hair.

Fur, leather, indiarubber, and other materials hardly enter into the making of dresses, and we mention them only in passing.

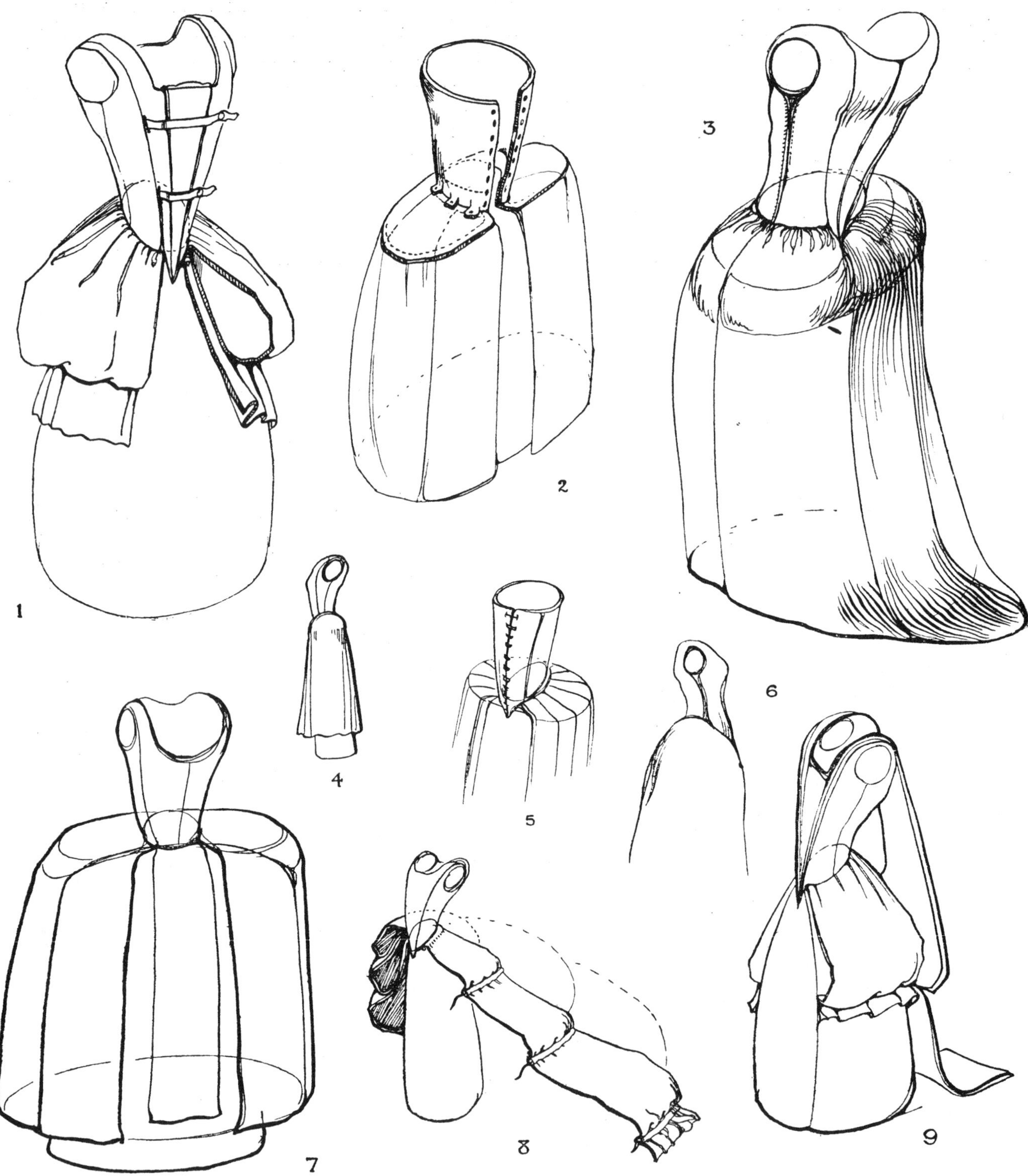

1. The Georgian dress with side panniers. 2. The leather corset of the Elizabethan era. It encases the ribs firmly and dominates the outline of the hips with great precision. 3. The circular waist centralized between the padded hips is well shown, and the bodice was shaped rather by the figure beneath than its superficial bony structure. 4. The construction of the Georgian pannier. 5. Another variant of the stiff Elizabethan corset. 6. A side view of the dress shown in (3). 7, 8, 9. Variant types of Georgian panniers and hooped skirts.

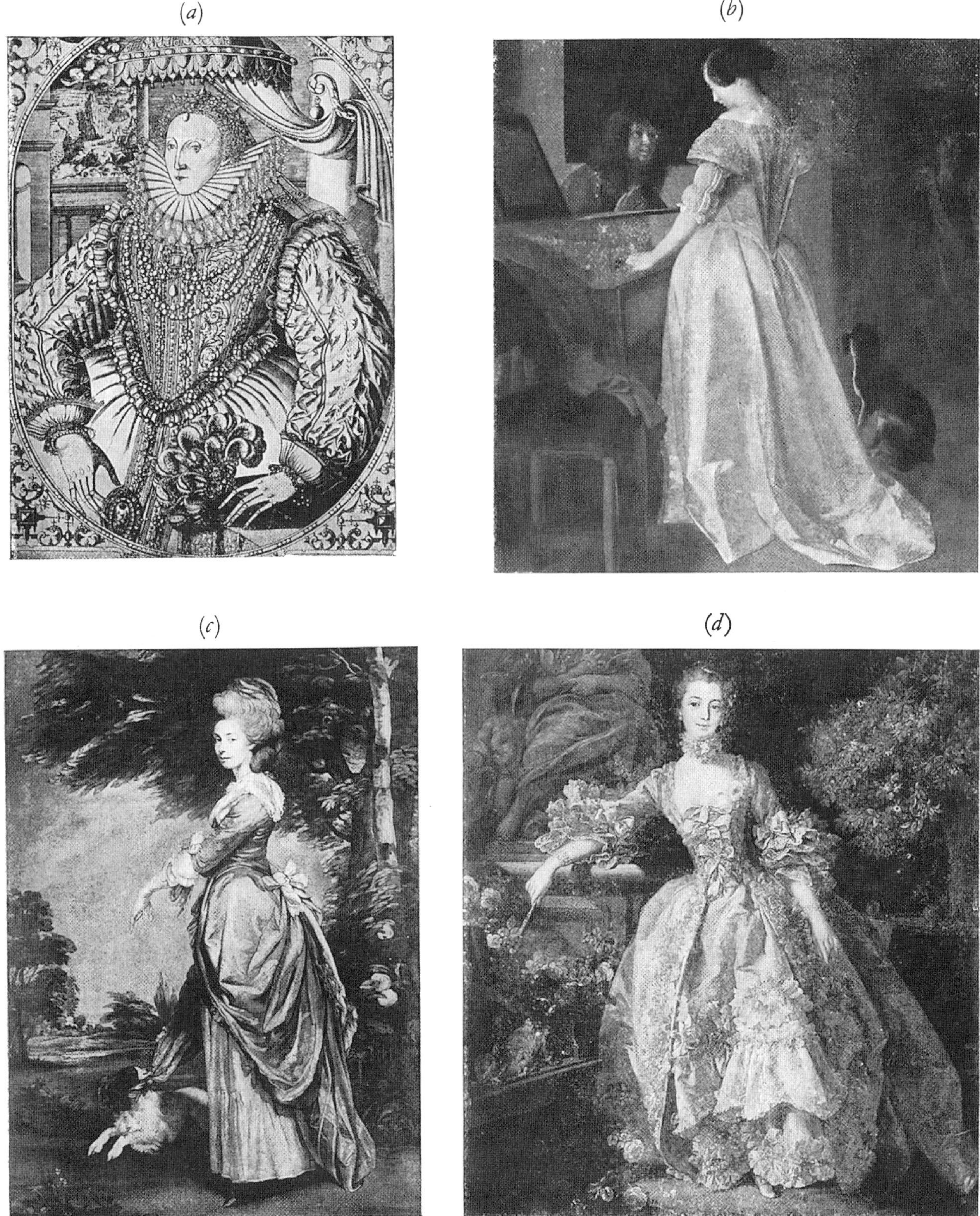

(*a*) Queen Elizabeth, a contemporary portrait. (*b*) Dutch, 17th Century.
(*c*) From a Mezzotint after Reynolds. (*d*) By Boucher. This picture shows how easily the outer skirt can be looped into a pannier effect.

(*a*)

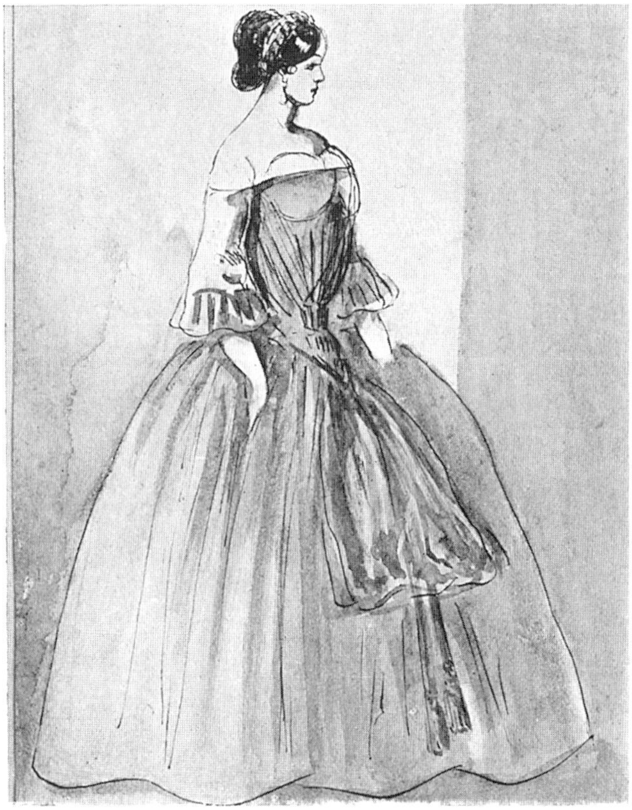

(*b*)

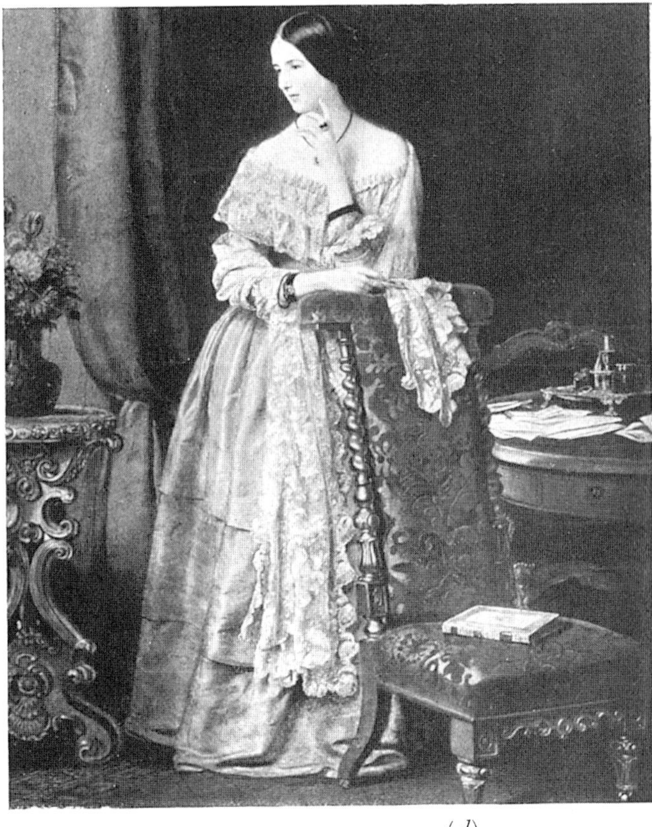

(*c*)

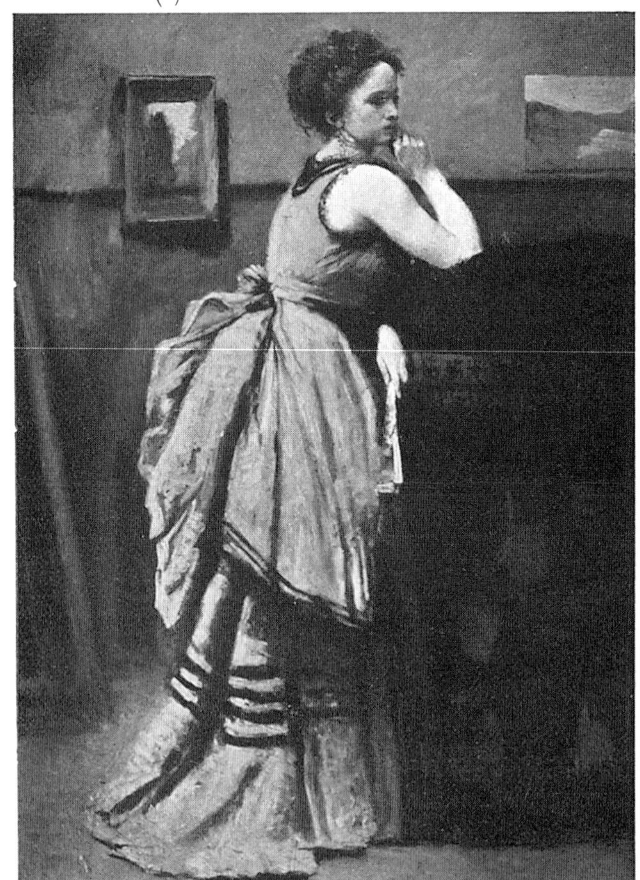

(*d*)

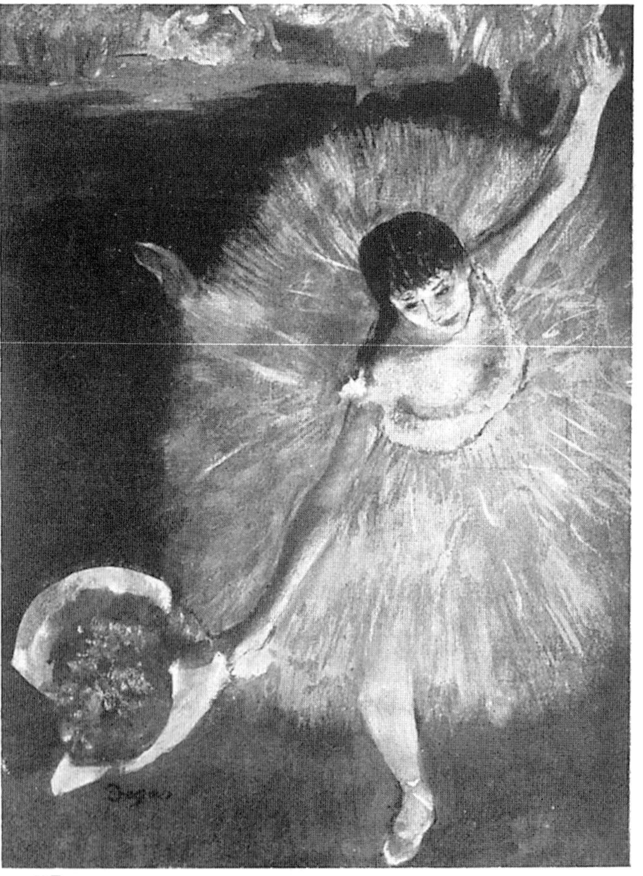

(*a*) By Constantin Guys. (*b*) By Sir W. C. Ross. (*c*) By Corot. (*d*) By Dégas.

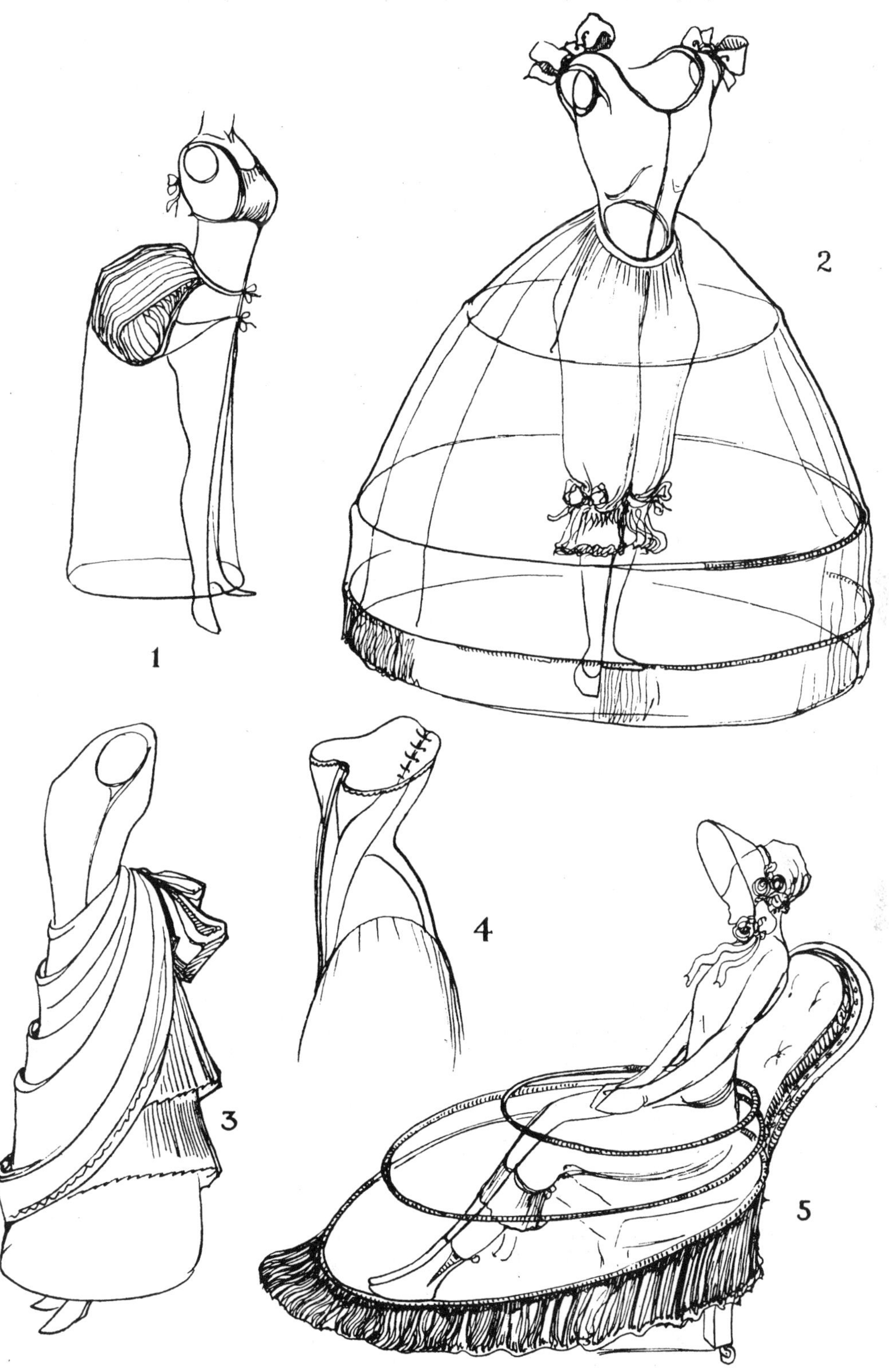

1. The bustle and supplement in place. 2. The cage of the crinoline pendant from the waist. 3. The forward lilt of the figure, with its apron-effect drapery. 4. The corset-line of the bustle period. 5. The folding forward of the crinoline-hoops when seated.

Woollen and worsted materials are manufactured from the fleece of sheep, llama, goats, and other animals.

Woollen clothing dates from the earliest times, and we know that the woollen fabrics of the ancient Jews and Greeks had a reputation of excellence among the peoples of the ancient world.

The introduction of woollen cloth into England is attributed to the Romans.

It may be surmised that felting wool was antecedent to wearing it. Even nowadays, in some parts of Russia, the peasants have a primitive method of wetting and beating the wool until it forms a compact thin layer which can be cut or shaped as required. There is also a tapa cloth made from wood fibre.

Fabrics made entirely of cotton are of comparatively recent origin, and were only introduced into England at the close of the sixteenth century by the Protestant refugees from the Netherlands. At first, cotton fabrics were made with a linen warp, and as early as the eleventh century, church vestments were in use which had a cotton weft.

Flax is manufactured into linen. Jute is made into a kind of linen, and sometimes used to adulterate silk.

The use of silk is very old, and on account of its lustre and excellent adaptability it has remained in favour ever since it was first introduced.

Of recent years the manufacture of artificial silk has become one of the leading industries of the world. It was natural that such a valuable material as silk should have tempted the speculator. With collodion the chemist has succeeded in imitating the thread woven by the silk-worm, and now we find artificial silks placed side by side with the genuine article in our foremost shops.

The hair of horses, camels, goats, etc., is used to stiffen and strengthen certain materials.

Under the general name of woollens one comprises fabrics made from wool, from wool and cotton, and from wool mixed with hair.

Yarn that is intended for diagonals, corkscrews, etc., is combed as well as carded, and the wool is often treated beforehand to give it the necessary degree of softness for combing. Cloths made of these yarns are called worsteds. This is also a matter dependent upon the wool staple.

WOOLLENS AND WORSTEDS

Among these, Habit Cloths are noted for their compactness and mellow texture. The right side is glossy, with the nap (the woolly substance on the surface of the cloth) running down.

Meltons (about 54 in. wide) are made in heavy and light weights. Only the latter can be used for dresses. To do justice to the heavier ones, they must be tailored, and there is much distinction between a tailor-made and a draped garment, the former revealing an architectural effect, achieved by cutting and padding, in which the clothing conceals rather than reveals. The best Meltons are smooth and closely woven, and less glossy than habit cloth. Neither the twill (when the warp is raised one thread and depressed two or more threads for the passage of the weft, the fabric presents an appearance of diagonal lines) nor the nap are conspicuous.

Covercoats (about 54 in. wide) have a bright finished surface and a distinct nap, which runs down the finished garment. The cutter must always head the way of the cloth; it is not altogether a question of nap, but of tension also.

Vicunas (about 47 in. wide), though finely twilled, have a rather dull surface, with only light nap.

Serges (about 44 to 54 in. wide) are either woollen or worsted, the former being soft, the latter more springy. When twilled, they are of closer and firmer texture.

Tweeds (44 to 54 in. wide) are light or heavy, and range from the rough homespun to thin and smooth fabrics, and may be plain or twilled.

CASHMERE (about 47 in. wide). There are various kinds of cashmere. Usually both sides are twilled, but some of the best qualities are so made that the twill is invisible.

NUN'S VEILING (42 to 47 in. wide) is a loosely woven fine fabric with a dull surface.

MOUSSELINE DE LAINE (about 31 in. wide) is very thin. Its surface is dull, and usually printed on one side of the material only.

ALPACA (about 47 in. wide) is a glossy, springy fabric, not easily crushed, though some of the modern makes are pliant.

MOHAIR and LUSTRE (about 47 in. wide) resemble alpaca, but are usually inferior in quality and appearance.

FLANNEL (28 to 54 in. wide) is more or less fleecy, but mellow and comfortable looking. Several modern makes of flannel are now unshrinkable and sold under special names. A fabric very much in use.

Other woollen fabrics comprise MERINO, which resembles cashmere; LLAMA, a plain single-width material; CREPONS, thin and puckered, rather fanciful.

French woollen materials which have acclimatized themselves in England are GABERDINE, CAMELOT, REPS.

SILKS, COTTONS AND LININGS

Of actual silks, a large number come from the East. Oriental love of splendour is proverbial, and Indian muslins date from very remote times. Silk gauzes come originally from Gaza, in Palestine.

The best known silks are:

GROS GRAIN (about 22 in. wide), not very glossy, but substantial looking, with a visible cord; there are fine and thicker varieties. Gros Grain looks the same on both sides. The heavier varieties are known as CORDED SILKS.

OTTOMAN SILKS (about 22 in. wide) are thicker and heavier than corded silks, and also brighter and more glossy; they are used in the making of heavier garments, such as mantles and jackets.

BENGALINE (about 22 in. wide) has a worsted or cotton weft, and looks like Gros Grain or Ottoman.

CHENÉ (about 22 in. wide) is a thin, plain, crisp silk, alike on both sides. Its peculiar and blurred appearance is due to a design being printed on the warp before the weft is woven in.

GLACÉ (about 22 in. wide) is rather papery, but looks bright and effective while it lasts. It has a modern effectiveness—like all the crisp taffeta silks it has the wrapping and fluting effect of a paper material rather than the soft effects of a loom product.

PONGÉE (22 to 30 in. wide). Plain or printed, rather dull, but soft and pleasant.

CHINA SILKS (22 to 30 in. wide) resemble Pongée, but brighter.

TUSSORE (24 to 36 in. wide) is made of raw unbleached silk, is soft, and has an agreeable lustre. Tussore and Shantung silks have a warm finish of their own. Tussore is now used more for the colour. The same silk is dyed many lovely colours, in spite of difficulties with oil in the fibre.

SARCENET (about 20 in. wide) is a plain thin silk, chiefly used for linings.

MOIRÉ ANTIQUE (22 to 26 in. wide). Watered silk. Is like Gros Grain on the right side and plain at the back. The moiré pattern is due to a process of moistening and hot pressure.

BROCADE (about 22 in. wide) is thick; the floral pattern is slightly raised.

BROCHE (about 22 in. wide) is made on a similar principle as brocade, but less thick, and the designs are smaller and woven on the surface of the silk, not above it.

SURAH (about 22 in. wide) is bright, thin, and soft, and has a marked diagonal twill, similar on both sides.

SATIN (about 22 in. wide) is bright, brilliant, and smooth on one side, and dull on the other.

SATIN MERVEILLEUX (about 22 in. wide) is twilled. It is soft and resembles Satin, but is not so bright.

IRISH POPLIN (about 24 in. wide) is a pleasant-looking, though not too lustrous fabric, corded selvedge to selvedge. Only the warp is silk, the weft being fine worsted.

VELVET (18 to 20 in. wide) is made of silk, and the material is so rich that only the best qualities should be used.

PLUSH (18 to 24 in. wide) is velvet with a much longer pile (the nap of the material when it is regular and closely set).

Many varieties of silks are imported into this country, and the following varieties are widely known :

FOULARD, DAMAS, CRÊPE DE SOIE, GEORGETTE, TAFFETAS, CHARMEUSE, etc.

Materials made of cotton and linen embrace FLANNELETTE (about 27 to 36 in. wide), which has a fleecy surface similar to flannel, but without the latter's substantial appearance.

VELVETEEN (about 24 in. wide) is soft and heavy, and has much character for certain uses.

SATEEN (about 31 in. wide) is soft, and models the figure well. It has a bright glossy face and a dull back, and is used for dresses and for linings. This and velveteen are useful for trying out fancy dress and stage effects, where velvet and satin will ultimately replace them.

POLONAISE (22 to 24 in. wide) resembles Surah, is twilled diagonally, and is mostly used for lining skirts.

PRINT (about 31 in. wide) resembles sateen, but is undyed at the back.

MUSLIN (36 to 40 in. wide) is thin and more or less transparent. The finer varieties are soft and silky.

COTTON CREPONS (about 27 in. wide) are usually clever in design and effect, and, like silk and cotton crepons, their texture is puckered.

GINGHAM and ZEPHYR (about 31 in. wide) have both sides alike, and are supple and light in appearance.

HOLLAND (33 to 54 in. wide) is a thin linen fabric used for dresses.

French and foreign cotton and linen fabrics are numerous, and the following names will be familiar to many readers :

MADAPOLAM, NAINSOOK, VOILE DE COTON, TOILE DE LIN, BATISTE, LINON, ORGANDI.

ITALIAN CLOTH (about 54 in. wide) is a mixture of wool and cotton. It resembles Sateen, and has a glossy and a dull side ; it makes good linings.

DRESS DESIGN AND FASHION DRAWING

SINCE history and ethnology furnish us with innumerable documents from which we can derive inspiration, the adornment of men and women by means of garments has largely become a matter of research, adaptation, predilection; but there is still plenty of room for the exercise of discretion and individual taste and fantasy.

Every woman wants to be up to date and wear the latest. If she knows what styles and colours suit her own particular build, complexion, and beauty, she will exercise a judicious choice in the selection of her raiment; and if she is cultivated and keen on dress, she will not mind the trouble of going to the storehouse of the present and the past to discover there the design which will suggest her garment.

To make it easier for every woman to narrow down her choice and also to help the unimaginative, battalions of dress designers and fashion artists are engaged by stores, dressmakers, manufacturers, and publishers, to think out and represent graphically garments that will appeal to women. Are the men and women who are thus employed equipped for their task of clothing and beautifying mankind?

What should the dress designer, if he or she wishes to live up to his or her trust, know and be able to do, before he or she assumes the responsibility of launching the fashions?

Fortunately, it is not given to any one to exercise so strong an influence as to be able to mould the taste of a whole nation or period. Usually subtle influences are at work, and ideas spread from shop to shop and from brain to brain, until they reach the brain of the dress designer. In this manner he becomes the receptacle of prevailing views; he digests them, gives them cohesion, and by assimilating them with his own ideas, develops them further and gives them the reality of new creations.

The great force and superiority of Paris over other centres of fashion consists in the active interest and enthusiasm of a whole population of dressmakers and dress enthusiasts, for in France almost every woman is skilled with the needle and can cut her own dresses, so that an elementary form of dress design is more or less practised in every home, and in Paris especially there are very many influences at work to exchange and disseminate opinions on dress which reach the dress designer.

The feminine garment is based on the materials, the cut, the draping, and the making up.

The materials consist of the dress fabric, the lining, and the accessories and trimmings.

To understand materials well takes a lifetime; new materials are constantly brought out by the ingenuity of the manufacturer, so that the woman who takes an active interest in dressmaking has to enlarge and revise her knowledge as long as she lives.

Whereas the study of materials is only a matter of application and keen observation, the question of *cutting* is much more complex and inaccessible to the uninitiated, even to many of those who can cut out their own dresses. There is a vast difference between understanding a paper pattern and using it intelligently and cutting a garment from special measurements and ideas which the cutter has in his mind.

In one case it is mainly a matter of adaptation, checking, adjusting, and trimming; in the other a matter of calculation and visualization. The expert cutter must be able to see his garment, so to speak, on the flat cloth, take woof and warp of the material into account, gauge the behaviour of the cloth when made up, and generally to conceive the whole pattern in his head, measure it on paper, trace it on the cloth, and ultimately cut it out.

A person who can do this may be likened to a pianist who can play any tune out of his head, perhaps without being able to read music. But a real musician should be able to play without notes, and to play still better with the score before his eyes. In the same way the perfect cutter relies on his imagination, but he does not neglect exact measurement and prepares his work most carefully.

Draping is a vast science. The Greeks and the ancient peoples whose notions of cutting were not so advanced as ours, and who cut most of their garments on the square principle, derived their finest effects from draping.

When looking at the complicated folds of the garments in many of the ancient statues, we notice how varied draperies can be. In mediæval times a number of garments were worn which depended on draping for their effect and beauty, and many of the unlogical and unhygienic fashions which have been produced throughout the ages have only been redeemed by the dignity which the art of draping conferred upon them. Oriental peoples and numbers of primitive peoples understand the art of draping themselves.

Good draping is a test of ingenuity, skill and taste, and deserves the patient inquiry of the would-be dress designer.

Although all materials follow the same laws of gravity and certain principles which we have referred to in the chapter on "Drapery" apply to all of them, there are differences of detail—differences not only due to texture, but to cutting. It depends on the shape of the pattern, and depends whether the material is cut on the straight or on the cross, is folded woof-ways or warp-ways or cross-ways; in each case the folds behave differently. The differences will not impress the superficial observer, but they are full of meaning to the expert.

Making up is probably just as difficult as cutting or draping, for there are right and wrong ways of assembling the various pieces; there is good and bad stitching; many fanciful stitches and finishing touches may enhance the beauty of a garment, if absent they may diminish its attractiveness.

Unless he is a genius and capable of replacing practical experience in all departments of dressmaking by a vivid imagination, the dress designer who is worth the compliment of his title should be a cutter, an artist in draping, and be able to use the needle cleverly.

He should know the history of costume, should have visited museums, making a speciality of dress and costume, and actually handled many a curious and elaborate dress, analysed and, perhaps, even copied those parts which intrigued him mostly.

But this is not all; he should have good notions of the fine arts, understand design, and possibly a good deal of geometry.

The human form should be very familiar to him. There have been various periods in the history of costume when a physical abnormity or a ridiculous fancy of some exalted and influential person determined the trend of fashion. Unnatural garments, like the farthingale and tight-laced corset, were not the work of designers, but of humourists or maniacs, and have only been copied by fools.

To make up for them there have been many sane periods in the history of dress.

The growth of education has gradually compelled women to admit comfort into the realm of attire. Once again it is being realized that the human frame is beautiful, and that instead of concealing its graces, dress should on the contrary help to reveal them, while leaving the body all its freedom.

The notion that material, cut, and draping have a beauty of their own is right, and should not interfere with the other important notion that physical beauty governs the styles which are to be worn. Occasionally there is a clash between the two views, but as a rule they complement each other and harmonize.

In working out his ideas, the dress designer is fond of resorting to contrasts: glossy materials alternating with lustreless ones, vertical stripes set off against horizontal ones, straight lines opposed to curves, as the V-shaped neck and back of the evening gown, giving emphasis to the roundness of the shoulders and bosom; colours that differ, areas that differ.

Harmonies keyed to the dominating features are another means which the dress designer uses: short sleeves to exhibit beautiful arms or long ones to show up lovely hands.

Light and shade provides the designer with powerful effects: the skirt that shades the knees and legs, the cape that shades the bust, the hat that shades the eyes, the folds that produce a wide range of tones from light to dark.

With these and so many other means at his disposal, the dress designer is still dominated by the construction of the human body. Bearing in mind the great variation that exists, he must take into account the things that are common to all, though hardly any of his creations will be generally applicable to all.

Nevertheless, he must obey the economic law and pay more attention to the normal average than to any particular type of person, and it will help him considerably if the person on whom he bases his design schemes belongs to the normal average, to that majority of the public whom he wishes to serve.

Besides having knowledge, ideas, and taste, the dress designer should be a man or woman of the world and move in the best circles. It is there that he meets those elegant people who wear their clothes with natural charm and utmost distinction, and whose whole bearing and even conversation will suggest to him many new creations.

The theatre, the cinema, the races are sources of inspiration that have been overrated. The dress designer must, of course, keep his eyes open and neglect no occasion of seeing or learning something that will set his brain working, but his own fund of knowledge must be greater than all that he can pick up by chance and enable him to assimilate new ideas rapidly.

Naturally the fashion and fashionable papers, especially those patronized by the upper classes, will supply him with valuable data.

To be a successful dress designer is to have reached a responsible position in the world. In many cases the material reward is great, and no pains should be spared to maintain such an exalted status.

Whether the fashion artist or the dress designer is the superior artist is really a matter of opinion; probably the perfect fashion artist would also be an excellent dress designer and *vice versa.*

In any case the fashion artist should know quite as much as the dress designer, and at the same time he should be an artist of the first order. But usually the fashion artist knows too little about dress design; he has acquired a certain routine of doing figures, line and wash, and he can copy backgrounds; discretion is one of his necessary assets, and if he is gifted with imagination he will immediately rise to a higher level of achievement.

As the dress designer, the fashion artist seeks inspiration in the fashion magazines and shops, and he gets about a great deal to see *what* is worn and *how* it is worn. A certain flair and chic are also part of his equipment. But the fundamentally sound fashion artist, to be true to his title, should know how to draw and paint the figure in isolation and in groups, to compose an interesting picture, to think out a new pose, or to endow hackneyed poses with a renewed power and originality.

He must be able to draw and paint with every kind of tool—pencil, pen, brush, chalk, etc.—and be fluent and live in his handling.

When the fashion artist is employed by the shops, his work may be twofold: he may have to draw from actual dresses and supply sketches for circulars and catalogues, or work in collaboration with a dress designer and evolve fashion designs which are submitted to clients or used to guide the cutter in preparing the patterns.

Journals and magazines who employ fashion artists, expect them to design new dresses for every new issue. Often these publications are called upon by advertisers to reproduce some of their models, and they entrust their fashion artists with the execution of sketches representing these models.

Fashion artists are well paid, and one would think that the best talent would be attracted to join their ranks. But if one looks through the magazines and catalogues one is surprised to see so much inferior work.

There are only a few good English fashion artists, and hardly any are outstanding. The

French and Americans seem to produce the best fashion artists, probably because they are recruited from the ranks of the painters and illustrators, having had an academic as well as a practical training; they are therefore more complete, more versatile, more expert, more adequate, and their production is more decorative, more effective, and more true than that of their British confrères.

The tendency to separate fine art from applied art is still too great in this country. Commercial and fashion artists confine their activities to specialized work, and the painter gets only isolated chances of doing commercial or fashion work. A certain amount of overlapping would be advisable. It would bring freshness where there is at present too much routine and repetition.

Art never loses from contact with the realities of life, and applied art gains enormously from rubbing shoulders with the highbrows.

Good fashion art conforms to all the laws of academic and modern art, and should have an eye on posterity. As it is, and for practical reasons, much of the indifferent kind will survive and be referred to in the future. Under the circumstances there is no reason why superior fashion art should not be edited again and again for the benefit of collectors, book lovers, designers, and historians.

NOTES ON DRESS DESIGN

Let the designer first consider and formulate to himself exactly what he wants to do, whether he is to develop and show up, as well as possible, the beautiful points of some individual—that is, use his material only to bring out the personality so that the material is subservient to the wearer—or whether he is using his wearer merely as a clothes-prop for his material, trying to get a uniform effect.

Having considered what he wants to do, let him then consider the material most suitable for the personality and its requirements.

He should be careful to eliminate artificial effects which are due to unsuitable combinations of materials; the most extravagant combinations can be used, but they take the hand of a master and the income of a revue star not to look ridiculous.

The occasion on which the dress is to be worn is important, as there are definitely grave or gay, hard-working or laughter-loving materials.

The designer must be capable of dealing with the slow statuesque beauty of the heavy folds, or enjoying the delicacy or the dainty smartness of a modern dress arrangement.

Having decided exactly what he wants to do and selected his means of expression, just as any artist would collect any material to hand, let him study the lines he is aiming at.

Upright and horizontal lines make for steadiness and emphasize proportions. This will be seen in uniforms where epaulets are used to make uniform the varying shoulder widths and stage effects of lines running across.

Uniforms will standardize most varying proportional figures, so that they all look like a row of ninepins. Where upright and horizontal lines are well placed in the individual, their beauty should be developed to the utmost, and no attempt should be made to obliterate the characteristics of the figure.

But beauty is not only in this upright and horizontal arrangement of lines. Diagonal and curved lines are equally valuable, since they have a joyous unity of their own.

It is as wrong to force a figure whose beauty obviously depends upon curves and slanting lines into a perpendicular uniform for the sake of fashion, as it would be wrong to make a waist on one of the Caryatides.

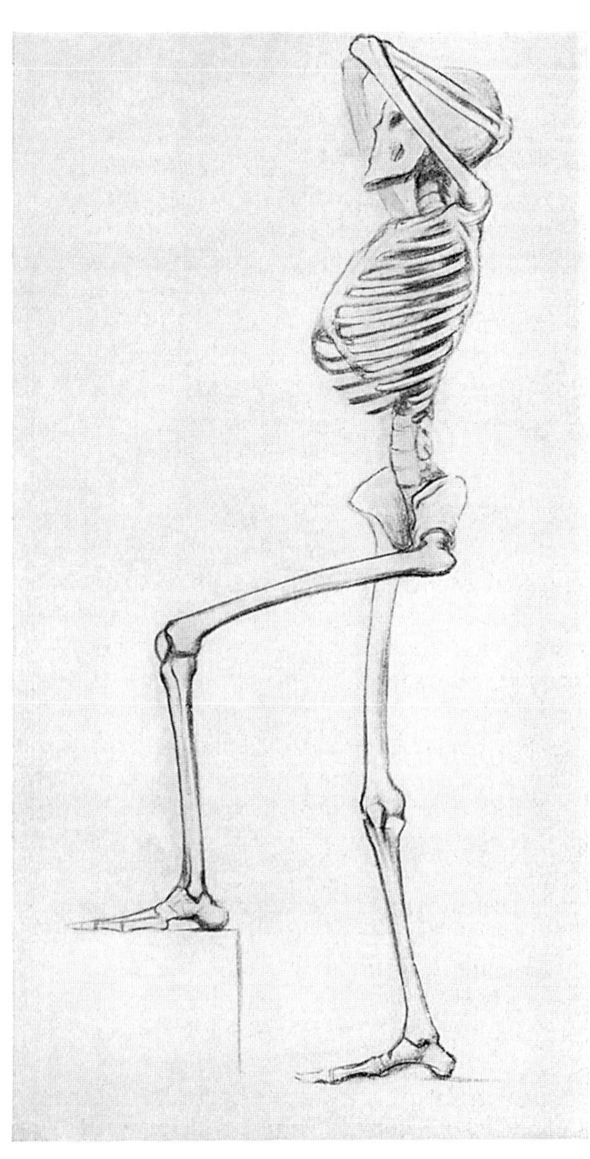

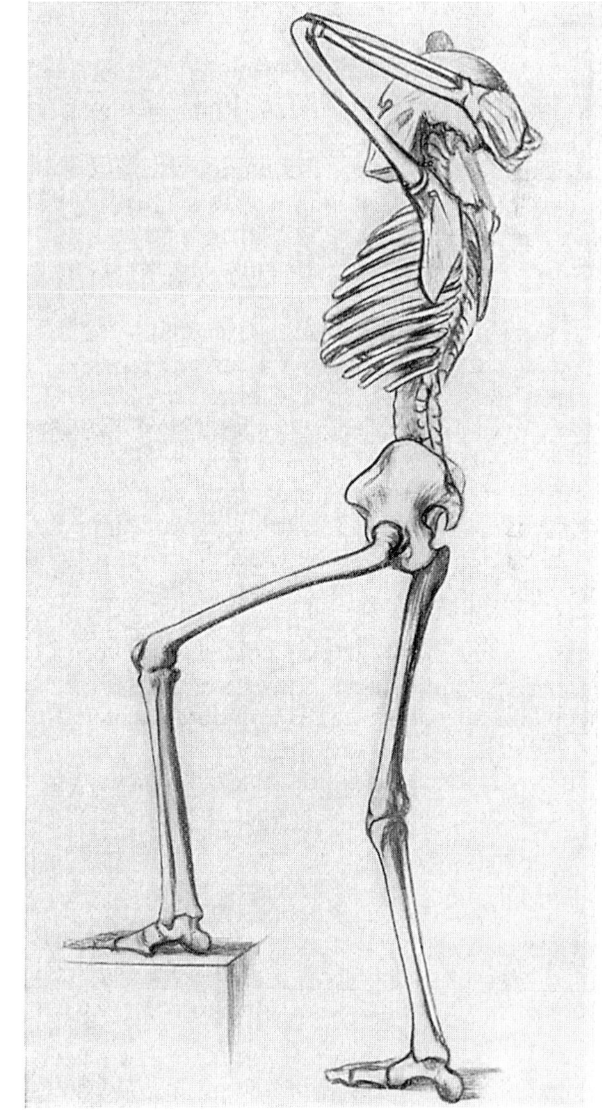

Profile and three-quarter views of the Skeleton in the same pose.

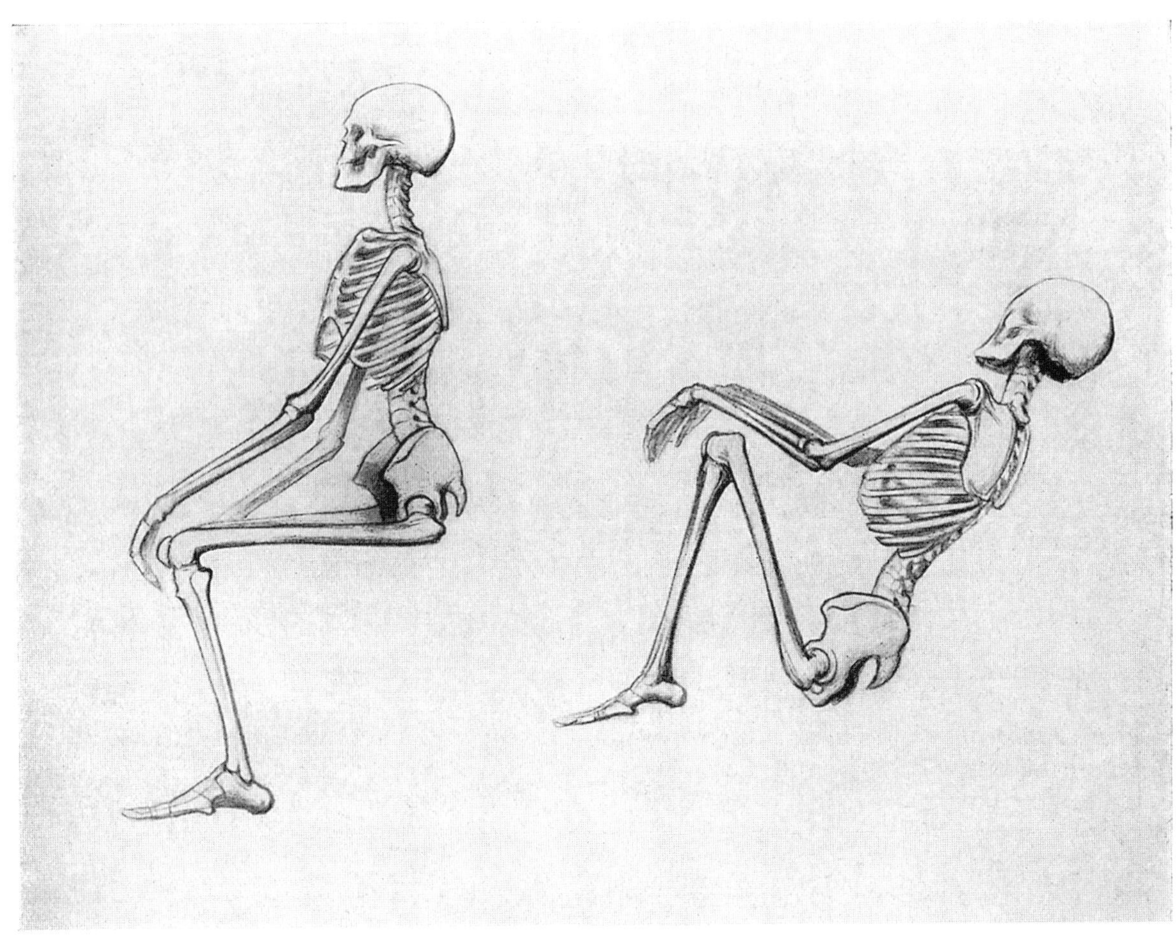

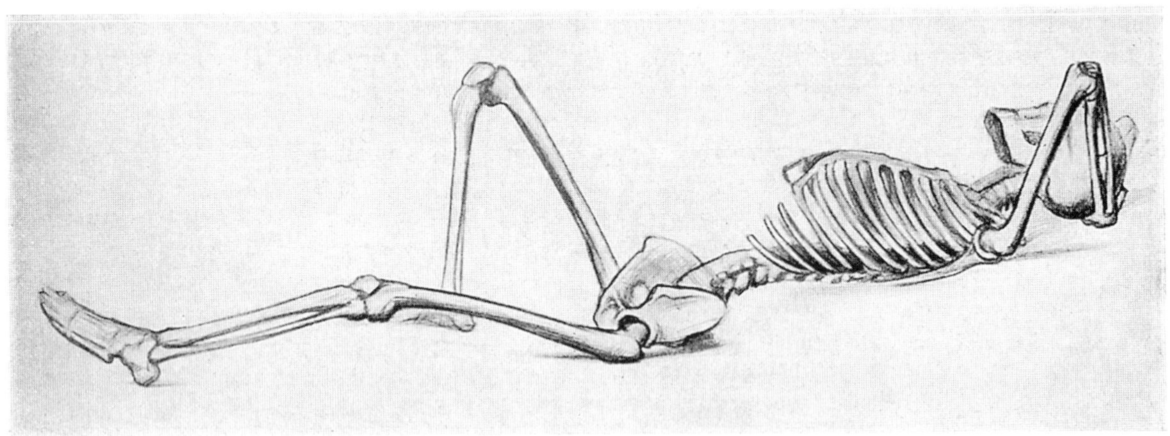

Sitting and Reclining Poses of the Skeleton.

THE PROFESSOR OF ANATOMY

THE Professor of Anatomy who takes his stand upon the opposite page is an experienced person who has led a hard life for many years as Chief Instructor of Anatomy to Students. He shows the marks of long and hazardous work, but in spite of a certain amount of wear and tear we were very glad to secure the services of so experienced a lecturer.

His position in this book is similar to that which he holds in the Art School, for he stands beside the model throne—always at hand to explain a pose, to reassure the new student with basic facts, and to interest the advanced anatomist by details of joints.

As every student knows, there is often considerable difference between the male and female skeleton.

The man's figure is heaviest about the shoulders. The weight is predominated by the powerful thorax. In the woman's figure the thorax is comparatively light and the hip bones wider in comparison.

That is the main difference.

A comprehension of this difference is essential to understanding the make-up of the entire figure.

As with our study of the figures, so let us first consider the matter of balance.

If you have a weight at the end of a flexible rod (a punch-ball raised up from the floor is a good example of this), the curves of that rod as it sways backwards and forwards under the weight will be fairly simple and direct. It will bend to the right or left, backwards or forwards in one simple curve.

This is the principle of the man's balance.

If you have a weight half-way down your flexible rod, and a smaller weight nearer the top, you will get a far more complicated system of curves. The smaller top weight will tend to hang back or swing forward behind the main weight, so that this rod is far more frequently bent in a double curve than the rod which had the main weight at its end.

This is the principle of a woman's balance.

Let the student look for it in all smaller movements : ask a man to put his hand down on the table and he will put it down—flat down—quite firmly, with the arm straight, and probably with the inquiry, " What for ? " Ask a woman to put her hand down on the table and she will probably lay it down quite gently, sometimes pressing upon the finger-tips only, sometimes resting the palm slightly upon the table. Quite frequently her elbow will remain bent. The whole movement suggests resilience rather than force.

All this is a matter of weight adjustment, and it is interesting to contrast the woman's more delicately adjusted poise with the man's definitely arranged balance.

Now let us consider more the structural differences, for it is upon fixed points in the bony structure that you must base your measurements. We have spoken of the comparative difference in *size* between the shoulders of the man and woman. The woman's skeleton is comparatively smaller across the shoulders (and you must measure the distance carefully between the two acromion processes, otherwise the development of the deltoid muscle may confuse you). When you have taken this measurement, across the shoulders, compare it with the measurement across the hips (taken very carefully between the two iliac crests).

These two measurements are particularly important to the dress designer, as upon them depends the entire " set " of the figure. You will see at once that wide shoulder bones and narrow hip bones will give you straight lines running up and down between hip and shoulder. If the shoulders are narrow the lines will bend outwards towards the wider hip. (Some of the photographs in the " Drapery " section of this book illustrate this very well.)

Another proportion for the dress designer is the actual shoulder measurement from the acromion process to the pit of the neck, and remember that this *is* a shoulder measurement, and must always be taken, as well as the more obvious dress measurement, from the acromion process to the base of the neck.

When you are taking this measurement notice, too, the " set " of the acromion process; where, in standing, it is brought forward level with the front of the neck (giving a hollow-chested, round-backed figure), or set well back (giving the straight shoulders, rounded chest and flat back).

Study the side view of the model in all the photographs, and draw a line downwards from the mastoid process of the temporal bone.

Another result of the main structural differences in the male and female skeletons is in the " set " of the legs and the lines stretching upwards from floor to hip. At the floor end, the bones of the two legs are held fairly close together, delicately upheld upon the arches of the feet. At the hip end, there is a strong ball and socket joint, into the pelvis, under the overhanging iliac crest.

If the hips are wide there will be a considerable outward curve, but if the hips are narrow the legs will probably seem fairly straight.

The knees, when standing, are fairly close together. Therefore, this curve, or this straightness, must be looked for chiefly in the thigh bone.

In an ugly, but descriptive phrase, a woman tends to be more knock-kneed than a man.

Consider this point carefully, for the stripe down the outside of your soldier's trousers will be likely to hang in a very different curve upon the principal boy in your pantomine.

Another difference from the same cause (*i.e.* contrast between thorax and hip) will be seen in the hang of the arms. Let every dress designer consider carefully those measurements we suggested across the shoulders and across the hips. You noticed how the contrast between these two measurements made the side lines between shoulder and hip slant downwards? Notice now how the arms swinging freely from the shoulder to hip parallel these lines.

Thus, in a boyish build, where the hips are narrow and the arms hang straight, the hands will tend to touch the thighs when straight. The wider hip again tends to give a more complicated curve.

NOTES ON THE SKELETON

The Skull.—This should be drawn and considered from every angle.

It is difficult enough for the student to classify for himself the variously shaped heads which he draws, but if he will consider a line passing across between the ears as a pivot upon which the head tilts *up* and *down*, and the base of the skull where it sweeps inwards to the neck as the line upon which the head *turns*, it may be a help. For the rest, a line taken from ear to ear over the top of the skull, and two others round the back of the skull, and forwards across the forehead (following the lines of a Greek bandeau), he will arrive at some standard.

The Eye Sockets.—The square bony structure around the eyes should be followed with inquiring finger from close to the bridge of the nose through and along under the eyebrow hairs, rounding the corner by the temple to the thin lower side at the outer edge of the eye, back again towards the nose upon the lower ridge, which is the upper part of the cheek.

The Nose.—The small bony structure which gives the nose its start in life is tremendously important.

The Zygomatic Arch.—Here again it is the bony structure which makes the beauty and interest of the type. It is the spread of this arch which so models the face. The wide, rather high cheek bones of the Slav type show this bone very well.

THE JAW BONES.—Oh ! Is it unnecessarily obvious to emphasize the necessity for their matching the rest of the face ?

THE MOUTH.—It is extraordinary how a change in the shape of the lower jaw will entirely alter the appearance of otherwise similar heads. You all know the thrust-out jaw of the strong and silent man, who advertises collars and fishing tackle, and figures so nobly in melodramic magazines, and the reticent, receding jaw, beloved of the humorist.

Don't overdo these things, and remember when you are drawing the mouth you must begin by drawing the curve of the teeth below. The very finest shaping of this curve is important.

THE ELBOW.—Mechanically speaking, a hinge joint with locking attachment. It is the humerus bone that widens out to give the changing front and side view proportion, and the head of the ulna and radius bones are set into a rather complicated joint. Several drawings should be made of this joint to understand it thoroughly. A mnemonic aid to help you to sort out the complicated anatomy of the forearm is that the bone which holds-on to the humerus (the ulna) has its round head at the wrist, and the bone which holds-on to the wrist (radius) has its round head at the humerus.

THE KNEE-JOINT.—Mechanically interesting, and complicated by the patella or knee-cap in front.

Balance yourself on one leg and watch the knee of that leg, and you will see this small knee-cap bone quivering and moving continuously.

Structurally this bone is a thickening in the tendon which passes across the knee-joint from the muscles of the thigh and is inserted below the head of the tibia. Without it one feels this tendon must surely groove too deeply the joint over which it moves. It is an integral part of the joint.

It fills in the space left when the leg is bent backwards, or lifts upwards and outwards as the front muscles of the thigh strain upon the tendon holding it.

A STANDING POSE

We spoke, in the Introduction, of the value of a thorough knowledge of the skeleton in steadying your work. The basic facts of construction and proportion that no amount of exercise or changing movements can alter should lie always quite firmly in your minds.

Notice, then, in the illustration (p. 74) where the main masses of bony structure occur. THE SKULL, the bones of which lie always so close beneath the surface. THE BACKBONE—for almost its entire length, deeply embedded in the body. THE CAGE OF THE RIBS—that light, strong basket, which can be seen so easily, changing and swaying with every breath. THE SOLID PELVIS —whose shaping is so important. The long THIGH BONES—with their reassuring straight lines. The bones of the knee-joint—and you may draw this knee-joint again and again and find it more interesting every time. The massing of the ankle bones—and the rippling, spreading grip of the toe bones

Upwards, the arm and shoulder bones are so different in character. The shoulder blades are thin light plates with complicated shoulder pieces. The bones of the arm compared with those of the leg seem so light. The bones of the forearm that turn round upon each other and make the anatomy of the forearm so interesting, and the clustering bones of the wrist, and all the delicate bones of the hand and fingers—if you know these well, you can see them distinctly below the skin and behind every intriguing curve of the hand.

A SIDE VIEW OF THE SAME STANDING POSE

Compare this carefully with the first back view, and notice for yourself which bones and joints are comparatively circular, and which change considerably when seen from another view.

To impress the fundamental facts of proportion, measurement of the bones is to be recommended. Dividing the figure into four, with the measurement from ground to base of knee as a single unit, is well known. Certain of the Greek figures have the legs half the entire length of the figure, in others slightly less. Legs and arms too long (especially if they are thin) give a curiously fibrous impression; on the other hand, any shortening of the legs and lengthening of the torso will produce a stunting, clumsy look.

The arms are easily measured upon yourself, and should also be considered carefully in comparison with the general size of the trunk. Too short arms have a helpless look (all the wax dolls of childhood suffer from this defect). Too long arms, far from being entwining and graceful, will give a sinister, gorilla look.

Measure very carefully, then, all the long straight bones of the body, and do it again and again. It is only thus you will arrive at a *certainty* of proportion. It is useless to imagine or believe that such and such a length is correct, or such another size is the only right one.

A good working knowledge of proportions taken from the Antique will steady your mind, and give you a standard that will help you to appreciate variety among your models.

A STRAIGHT FORWARD SITTING POSE

This should be studied, together with the following leaning pose, in order to appreciate the altered tilt of the pelvis.

Also look through the photographs of the various sitting poses in the " set " taken from the standard models.

They have all been arranged to help the student to realize their great differences.

The backbone is firmly wedged into the pelvis—not immovably, but quite firmly, so that the slant of the pelvic bone seems to " start off " the curve of the lower part of the back. Thus, in this sitting pose, where the pelvic bone is tilted deliberately forward, the backbone starts off with a strong inward curve. The fixed backbone of the skeleton luckily shows this very well, but you must try it for yourselves to understand the difference in pose that results from your backbone being more flexible.

Another thing to notice is the forward carriage of the ribs and the upward tilt of the head.

Those ridiculous little figures that hawkers have set bobbing and dancing along the edges of the pavement show this action with amusing clarity. It is a matter of balance. If you swing their little tin ribs forward, automatically their little tin heads swing back. Take a deep breath and fling out your own chest, and see if your chin does not rise and your head tilt back with an automatic movement. Curve the backbone outwards, drawing back the ribs and lowering the sterum, and your chin will sink down upon your chest in dejection. All this should be studied in the sitting movement.

A LEANING POSE

We have imagined away the inclined plane against which the figure leans. It must be a hard straight surface so to flatten the back. Even a skeleton would sit very differently among the cushions of a soft armchair. Again, you must realize that the backbone of the skeleton is stiffer than your own, and allow for considerable curve when you see the same pose taken by a living model. You will find for yourselves, when you lean back, that the lower ribs and upper part of the lumbar spine tend to hold most of your weight rather than the shoulder blades, which only come into play when sitting more stiffly against an upright support.

It is a matter of great individuality, this sitting down.

Have you ever noticed how some particular make of chair seems to influence all its different sitters ? And yet, no two people ever take a similar pose in the same chair.

Some people manage to curl up and look comfortable on the most uncompromisingly straight-backed "Windsor." Their very adaptability would upholster a stool of penitence, or belie the treacherous ease of the dentist chair.

There are other people who never manage to look comfortable. They always seem supported upon inadequate, uncomfortable angles. To ask them to lean back is like entreating the Leaning Tower of Pisa to take a rest. They will sit grimly upon the extreme edge of a chair, and by their own inflexible straightness of back imply a moral support—invisible, perhaps, but invincibly rigid.

A RECLINING POSE

This pose is excellent, not only for its general outline, but also for a specialized study of the joints. The patella (knee-cap), as the hyoid bone, are difficult to reconstruct in the skeleton, as they are held in position by cartilage and tendon, and must, therefore, have your special study upon the living model. The principal matter for the student to notice is the curve of the backbone which, in a living model, would follow the sweep of the support. Remember, this Professor of Anatomy has arranged to give his lectures in an erect standing pose; and no amount of reconstructing padding between his vertebrae would permit him to bend forward.

So the wisest thing for the student to do is to try this pose himself, and then he will learn the importance of this stiffening of the backbone. Held stiffly, the lower ribs are comparatively high, and the iliac crest tilted forward—let the backbone sink, and the lower ribs will subside also, and the pelvis turning backwards will give quite a different tilt to the abdomen.

Again, as in the standing pose, it is the massing of the uncompromising bony structure which is so important—the skull, the cage of the ribs, and the long straight line of the limbs.

Between these the flexible flesh will alter and change with every movement; but bones will not bend, and legs and arms must tell of their uncompromising straightness between their joints. The barrel of the ribs will not subside because you have altered the position of the body. The hip bones will tilt from side to side, but they will not alter their shape, and joints, however delicate and slender, must be of convincing workmanship in the figure beautiful.

FLEXIBILITY

The rigidity of the mounted skeleton is of steel screws and brass wire. There is none of it in your live model.

If you have played with kittens, puppies, or babies of any sort, you will know the soft, gristle-like quality of many of their bones, and know how these gradually set as the growing thing develops; and given this reminder, must follow out for yourself the effect of environment upon the various stages of development—the smooth, easily grown bones, those well developed, with beautiful lines, and the twisted and warped ones; and you must learn how to understand these things, for there are times when the young, growing bones can be wrongly twisted and bent, and sometimes it is one part of the body, and sometimes it is another which must give way, and bend under the strain; and sometimes it is the very lightest bones which should have been most delicately beautiful that are hurt; and sometimes bones seem to have grown thick and coarse in self-defence; and the bones of the whole body and the movements of the body are dependent upon the work they were made for and the work they have had to do —thus helping to accentuate the differences of build and proportion in the various individuals.

NOTES ON THE STANDARD POSES

THE following poses, properly understood, should form a good working basis for the construction of almost every position required by the artist or designer. We have spoken elsewhere upon the matter of personality, so only remind the student here of its importance, knowing that once he has realized this it will be always present in his mind. But the fundamental meaning of any pose is a matter of feeling and comprehension.

The mechanical copying of outline or painstaking construction by anatomy can produce only a working model, a dressmaker's dummy; a thing of padding and strings, proportionate, perhaps, but definitely lifeless and unalterably dull.

Therefore, consider the following series very seriously, not so much for positions and attitudes, but as a course of instruction planned for your careful study, a series of examples, the understanding of which will vivify every pose you desire from them.

THE STANDING POSES

See page 89 (*b*), (*c*), *and* (*f*)

First, let us consider the standing poses. Stand yourself, erect and alert; do not tighten any muscle, but " sense " them all; as you are standing still—but not at rest—you are quite definitely active, and if normally fit and healthy a few moments in this pose will produce a feeling of expectancy, the whole body being vibrant with suppressed movement.

It is this pose that precedes action. Notice how instantly from this position you can spring away or turn suddenly in any direction; it is a specializing of this pose that gives the ready or start attitude of almost all swift actions—the dive, the leap, the dance. Before any movement, collect a definite realization of the erect, alert, standing pose.

Now—let us study the pose. First, the balance: the body is upright; the weight, even and symmetrical upon either side of the central line, is evenly carried by both feet; the pressure of it will be felt upon the ball of the foot, so that the toes grip against the ground and the heel is tense against the upward pull of the tendon Achilles. This tendon terminates the muscles of the calf, and their tension is continued upwards through the ham-strings, and the long taut muscles of the thighs, bracing the level pelvis which supports the trunk.

The pit of the neck will plumb slightly forward between the feet, the head slightly raised and thrown back, and the straightened arms will lightly press against the sides. You have realized the balance? Now, to comprehend the muscle action that makes this balance possible, stand upright in this pose, and you will soon know for yourself which muscles are doing the work, and remember that what applies to you personally does not entirely apply to others, for no two people will feel the strain in precisely the same way and at the same moment.

THE FLEXED POSE

See page 89, (*a*)

Easy standing pose, one leg slightly flexed, bending forward at the knee.

To study this pose, stand upward; hold up the head, and let your hands swing freely against your sides; see that both your feet are evenly placed level upon the floor. The weight should be even between toe and heel, and there should be no definite strain upon any particular muscle. At this stage, both legs are doing an equal share of the work. Now loosen the muscles of the right leg, and while definitely keeping weight upon the right foot, bend the right knee slightly forward and notice the result: the whole trunk has inclined slightly forward, turning to the left. Because the weight is still fairly even between the feet, there will be little or no change in the horizontal lines of the body; the pelvis will drop very slightly only, that small distance which marks the difference in *length* between the straight and the slightly bent leg; the shoulders may remain quite level.

The first noticeable thing in this pose is its mutability. When you kept the tense standing pose, you began to ache; when you keep this flexed pose, you begin to move; therefore you understand for yourself that this pose is more a matter of balance than physical strain. Balance is a matter of weight adjustment; your weight was originally between both feet. Now, it is easier to support weight on a straight leg than upon a bent one. Therefore, in this pose you will feel the tendency to readjust your weight. Your straight left leg will take more than its half-share; then the muscles of the right leg will slacken off duty. This will allow the leg to bend still more, the forward dropping of the knee over the right foot will tend to put the pressure on to the toes of that foot; the heel may even be slightly raised from the ground, at any rate it will feel very little pressure of the body, and as the left foot and leg take over the entire support you will sense the tilting of the pelvis and complete alteration of the pose.

THE BENT-LEG POSE

See pages 90 *and* 91

A standing pose, with right leg bent, and weight completely carried by the left foot.

This third pose is the complete development of the second; as the movement of pelvis and shoulder-girdle in their horizontal planes are determined by the twist of the body, so their perpendicular movements up and down are governed by the balance of the body, the distribution of its weight over and between the feet. In this pose the weight is definitely held by one foot only, the horizontal lines of the figure are altered; they now slant at a definite angle to the ground, the central line of the figure is bent and altered to accommodate the new conditions.

This pose usually involves some definite action; try it for yourself, and notice how spontaneously the hands and arms take action with the general movement. The model has placed one hand upon her hip; while waiting for the camera and practising the pose, her arms were constantly moving.

It is the pose of the thrust-out hip and slanting shoulder. It may effect a certain air of bravado, but exaggerated it is the almost grotesque pose of the washer-woman standing with a huge bundle under her arm, or the fisher girl resting her basket on her hip bone.

It may be the weary pose of people who have been standing too long, or the graceful prelude to a bend. It is a pose capable of infinite variety and of great service to the student.

THE TENSE SITTING POSE

See page 97, (*b*)

To study the tense sitting pose for yourself, find some firm chair or seat of exactly the right height to support your body, with knees and hip-joint bent at right angles so that the thighs are level. The feet should be firmly placed upon the ground and the head held erect. The hands will firmly grip the edges of the chair, and this may or may not raise the shoulders slightly according to the length of your arms.

The pelvis will be tilted forward, giving an inward bend to the base of the spine, and the cage of the ribs will be so carried that the lower border of cartilage will be outlined below the surface. You will feel the shoulder-girdle held fairly high by the taut arms, and the scapulæ swing inwards towards each other across the back. Make quite sure of this and study it carefully, for, if the grip of the hands and the tension of the upper arm muscles are sufficient, the scapula will be held fairly tightly in position. The photograph shows it well, but comprehend the feel of it yourself; it is almost as if the ribs were backed by a rigid support; it is as if an invisible chair-back was flattening the whole of the upper part of the torso. Inhale deeply, and you will feel the ribs pressing against it as the sternum rises forward and upward, and the whole front line of the abdomen alters with the change of the diaphragm.

To study the muscle action, follow again the very simple recipe of holding the pose tightly for some minutes and noticing which part of you begins to ache first. You will be surprised at the pressure felt by the feet; and it is pressure, for the bent knees leave little weight upon them.

The back muscles feel the strain first, in some cases, perhaps, more quickly than in a standing pose—for they lack the pull of the deeper thigh muscles which are braced through the pelvis on to the lumbar vertebræ. Next, the elbow-joints may tighten as the arms steady the back against the sway of the breathing, and as in any pose and pressure of the arms, the fingers will numb slightly, but the action of the pose is definitely upheld by the muscles of the spine, and it is noticeable that nearly all models break " pose " by moving the feet, changing the angle of the thighs, and altering the tilt of the pelvis so that it releases the bending back and slacks off the inward pull of the muscles attached to the spines of the vertebræ.

THE FLEXED SITTING POSE

See page 97, (*a*)

This pose also depends on balance rather than definite muscular action. The pelvis is tilted backwards very slightly, so that you are sitting backwards on your tail; the heavy lumbar vertebræ are thrust outwards and a slow continuous curve of the spine sweeps upwards and inwards again, holding the cage of the ribs tilted forward vertically above the front edge of the basin of the pelvis. The shoulder-girdle swinging forwards and downwards gives a hollow form to the chest, the points of the clavicle which join the acronoid process of the scapula being further forward and the end which pivots upon the top of the sternum at the pit of the neck. The scapula, swinging forward round the back, and the folded edge of the latissimus dorsi, can be seen at the side in the photograph, and, felt for yourself, rather like a small tight shawl wrapping the upper part of your torso and tucked in under your arms.

There is little to be said about the legs in this pose; they are definitely off duty; the soles of the feet may tend to turn inward a little, further relaxing the long lines of the sartorius to the knees and the stirrup muscles, passing beneath the arch of the foot. This action is more likely to occur if you have been standing or walking for some time before sitting down; in the same way, previous work with hand and arm muscles will result in the pose our model shows so well, with elbows slightly bent and hands turned palm upwards with the fingers curled lightly inwards.

THE STRETCH

See pages 92 *and* 93

A Stretch and a Bend.—Study the fundamental movements shown in these two poses, and apply your knowledge to the understanding of all the other poses in this book which demonstrate either bending or stretching actions; the shortest distance between any two points is a straight line between them, and it is straightening of the lines which conveys a stretching movement. This is more subtle than you would suppose; it is not the muscles of the stretching arm or leg which convey this straightening, but the whole body (as always in any good pose) must convey the same movement. Try for yourself a long-reached stretch across a wide table, or along the top of a wall. Lean forward slowly and really study the movements: the fingers straighten; the arms straighten—straighten until the elbow locks backward as the olecranium process snicks back into that little hole in the end of the humerus bone.

The twisted tendons in the armpit straighten—like scapula sliding forward from the backbone straighten the hollow behind the deltoid,—but the latissimus dorsi will pull into a straight line down your side. Give one further stretch and—hasn't your leg begun to lift off the ground and straighten out behind you? And does not your foot straighten into line with your leg? And does not each individual sympathetic toe straighten in sympathy with your straightened fingers? so that from one extreme end of your body to the other you are stretched out in two different directions like the piece of elastic which indeed you are.

Now, have you realized for yourself the movement of the stretch; it is important, as of all movements it most surely sweeps together into one action the entire body. It is almost impossible to make a detached dissociated stretching movement of any one member of the body; even a baby fastened into a high chair with a strap across its tummy, reaching out for the jam, if it is too old to put its legs upon the table in front to get a purchase, will probably bend them back under the chair behind to get a balance!

Test this movement of the stretch in every way you can think of. Lift your arm forward, and thrust the palm upward (supination) and turn it downwards (pronation). You can do this quite dispassionately; the body is not disturbed, but attempt the least forward stretching movement, and you will feel the difference at once. If you attempt to hold your body aloof, you will soon find you are exerting as much force behind the shoulder against the strain as you are using your arm towards it.

Do not think this is only to be remembered when there is definite action to be studied. The simplest pose will stretch some muscles and relax others. The simple standing pose will have taught you the strain and tension of the long muscles of thigh and back, and it is the valuable little *straight* bits which you must learn to look for (the tendon Achilles, the hamstrings behind the knees, etc.) which will give your figure reality and life.

THE BEND

See page 94

Once in describing the bend, a student said that "it was the other side of the stretch," and we have yet to find a more adequate explanation. Look at your own bent finger; the back is straightened, the bones below the surface and the skin drawn tight over the knuckles; on the bent inner side are the rounded curves of the phalange muscles, with the small secondary curve in the hollow of each bend.

Now, look again at the front view of the stretching figure and notice how on one side of the torso the flesh seems stretched away, and the ribs and hip bones show thrusting under the surface, while on the other side the bones are imbedded in the soft muscles, but the bend has folded down upon them. The more treacherous the grace of the bend, the more rigidly must you adhere to the tension of the stretch that makes the movement possible—that is, if you wish your figures to bend with the resilient grace of a willow shoot in the drawing of an artist, not the accommodating collapse of a piece of lead piping in the hands of a plumber.

The difference in the movements is largely the matter of locating the bend; when as a piece of mechanism we realize the comparatively few bending areas and comparative length of our unbendably straight pieces, it is astonishing to realize we are still capable of buckling on our boots.

Analyse the most graceful poses you can find in this book, and even in those where the figure at first glance appears swept together in continuous flowing lines you will be able to trace out the beautifully uncompromising straightness of the thigh and arm bones; and the adequate bracing straightness of the stretching muscles that make the bending possible. The mechanism of the various types of bend is a matter of constructive anatomy. The hinge joints of elbow and knee, the ball and socket joint of hip and shoulder must all be studied until their bending possibilities (and restrictions) are impressed upon the student's own mind.

The spine bend in itself is most interesting; there is comparatively little movement between any two vertebræ, yet the whole together make one exquisite flexible rod. In the lower part, between the heavy lumbar vertebræ, the movement is slight; especially is this noticeable in old or unexercised models, where the lower bones of the spine and the pelvic bones have grown rigid.

A little higher at the waist the vertebræ are free and light, so a great deal of bending takes place in this region ; higher up, again, the spine holds together the cage of the ribs, and between the vertebræ doing this work there is very little movement. Above the first rib and the important seventh cervical vertebræ the thin neck bones rise flexibly, upwards to where they finally carry the versatile skull upon a delicate setting,—marvellous for its lightness and freedom.

THE REST

See pages 95 *and* 96

Never attempt the study of this pose apart from the complementary lines of its support. The very essence of the pose being its lack of tension and absolute reliance upon its underlying support, one might almost say it is a pose depending more upon the chair or sofa than upon the figure itself. Every one knows how definitely some chairs induce certain positions ; that is why, for this pose, we have chosen the uncompromising and bony " Windsor " chair, or the right angle between wall and floor. This last, perhaps, is the simplest for your own study ; you could have nothing simpler than these two obvious supports but the perpendicular wall and the horizontal floor.

Therefore, sit down upon the floor and lean against your wall, and register for your own use the infinite variety of poses that are possible.

Note in each case the angle of the pelvis, which will swing through full 90 degrees as you alter your distance from the wall and the tilt of your leaning against it. Notice too, whether ribs, shoulder-blades, or head and shoulders, carry the leaning weight of the body.

We can give you one more piece of help. When you are drawing from the model, or out of your head, and using an unfamiliar chair or sofa, draw this chair or sofa very carefully first, and plot upon it the geography of your resting model before you begin.

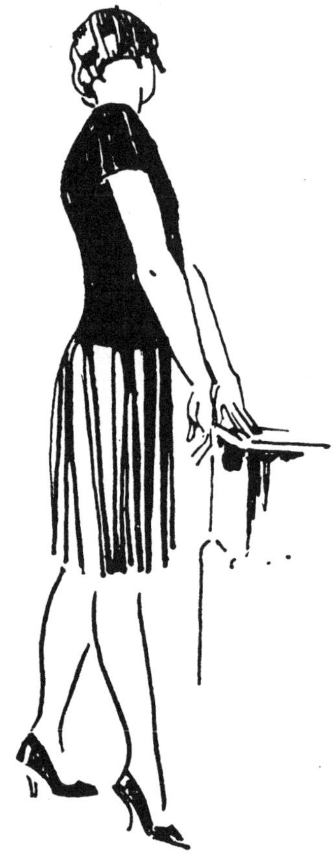

THE APPLICATION OF THE POSES

In such branches of art as the above a ready source of reference is well-nigh essential if the artist is to produce the rapid, efficient, and original work that his *métier* requires. It is not enough to depend on inspiration—to wait patiently for its appearance. This is a busy age, and the commercial artist must keep to his contract, like every one else, and deliver his work punctually if he is to be successful.

In setting out some of the purposes of this book in the Introduction, we stated that it was not in any way meant to replace the use of the living model; but for such rapid work as we have referred to above, the use of the model is not always practicable. We have therefore set about to supply the deficiency. The various hands that have aided in the compilation of the book have had some considerable experience of the requirements of Commercial Art, as has, indeed, its author. These requirements have been kept steadfastly in mind in the preparation of the standard poses which it is hoped cover a wide enough field to serve as a nucleus for reference.

Adapted from Pose (*a*) on p. 128, by G. M. Ellwood. This pose would serve equally well for illustration or advertisement.

Throughout the book we have tried to identify ourselves with the artist, and, in selecting the material and posing the models, have endeavoured to imagine immediate and frequent applications of his needs. In the accompanying sketch-suggestions are shown, by the hand of

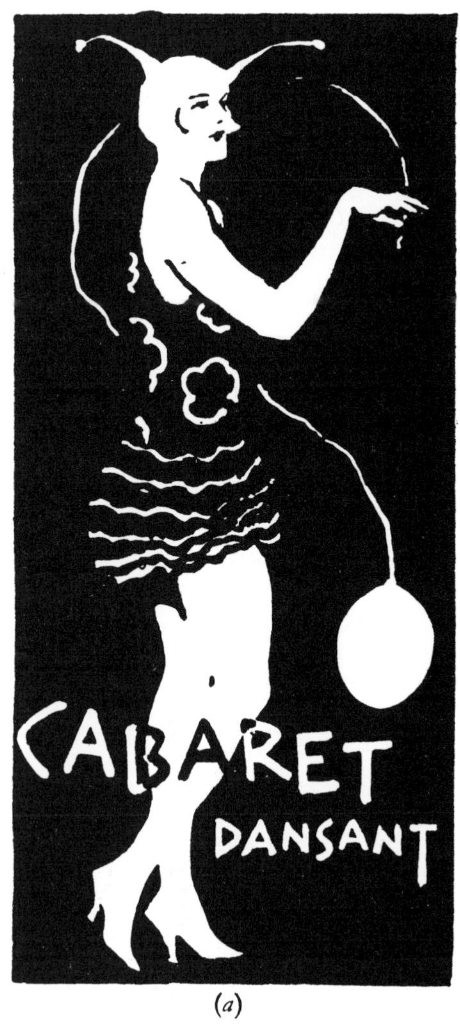

(*a*)

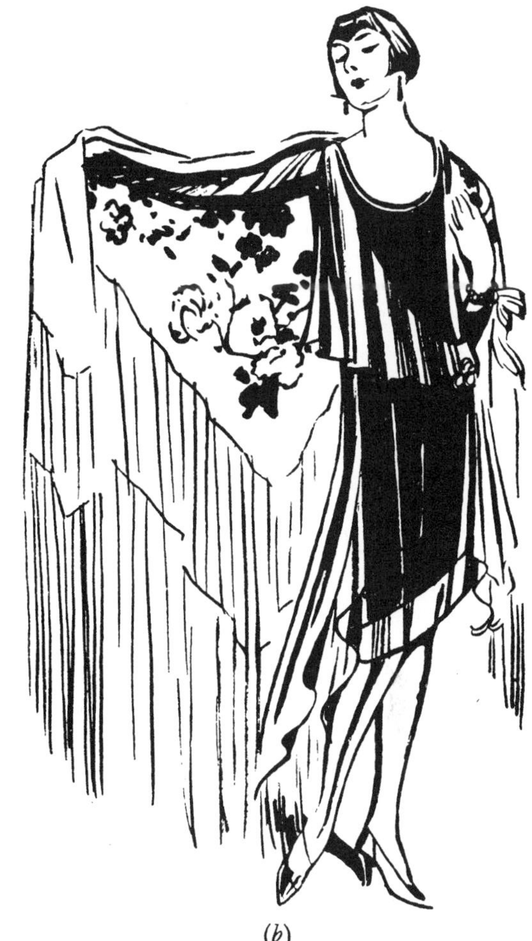

(*b*)

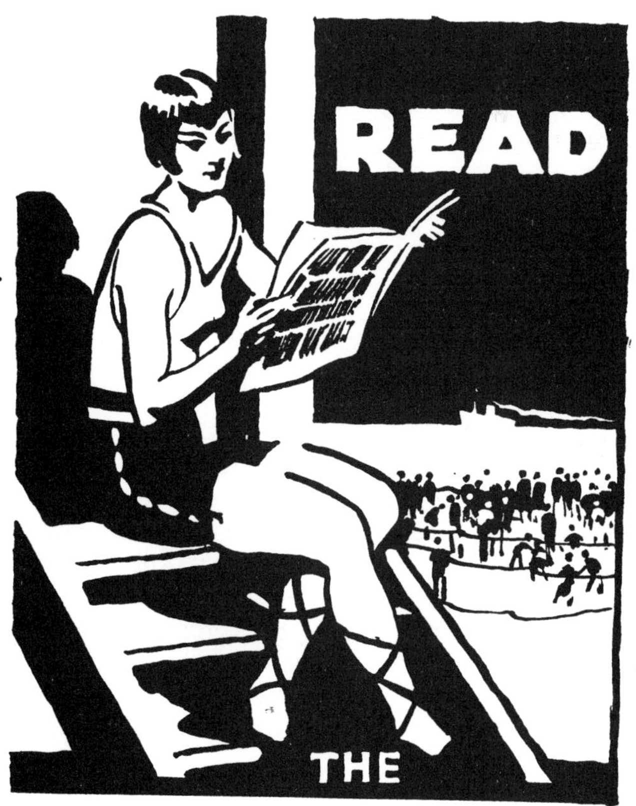

(*c*)

Some Suggested Applications from the Standard Poses.
By G. Montague Ellwood.

(*a*) A Cabaret Advertisement. Adapted from Pose on page 121.

(*b*) A Fashion Design or Advertisement. Adapted from Pose (*a*) on page 113.

(*c*) A Newspaper Poster for the Holiday Season. Adapted from Pose (*b*) on page 134.

a well-known commercial artist, some such applications based on five of the standard poses. They are rendered on bold lines, and bear the hall-mark of an experienced hand, sure of itself; yet they owe much to the aid of the camera.

The contempt in which the camera is often held is hardly justified, although it must be admitted that the triviality of its records is sometimes disheartening. What the artist is looking for may very well exist in the photograph, though hidden within a mass of irrelevant detail. To separate the essential from the irrelevant, to analyse, as it were, the detail which the photograph supplies and discard all that is outside his purpose should be one of the artist's chief cares in working from a photographic record. To do this needs the trained artist's eye or the natural artist's discrimination.

A photograph will supply the rhythm, gesture, expression, tonal values, and general harmony of a pose or fleeting movement. It is the artist's task to transfer all these qualities to the medium in use with due economy and an eye for irrelevancies. It would obviously be impossible to make a literal copy of a photograph in pen and ink, and however near to truth the results might come, they would hardly be of much artistic importance. The object of the photograph is to supply the nucleus for eyes that can perceive it, imagination that can adapt it, and a hand that can render it.

The accompanying suggestions for advertisement, poster-work, illustration, and fashion-drawing are excellent renderings and adaptations of the poses from which they are taken, and should be studied carefully with their originals. Their study will demonstrate far better than the written word ever can the general principles which should be observed in working from photographs for these styles of work. It is to be hoped that the student will try his own hand at some other of the poses with this lesson in mind. It is equally to be hoped that the practising artist will find in them that essential nucleus with which it has been our object to provide him for the ordinary course of his work.

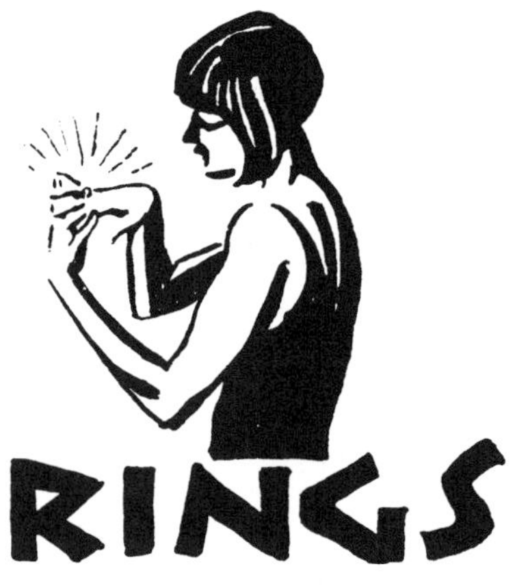

A Jewellery Advertisement. Adapted from Pose on page 124, by G. M. Ellwood.

THE STANDARD POSES

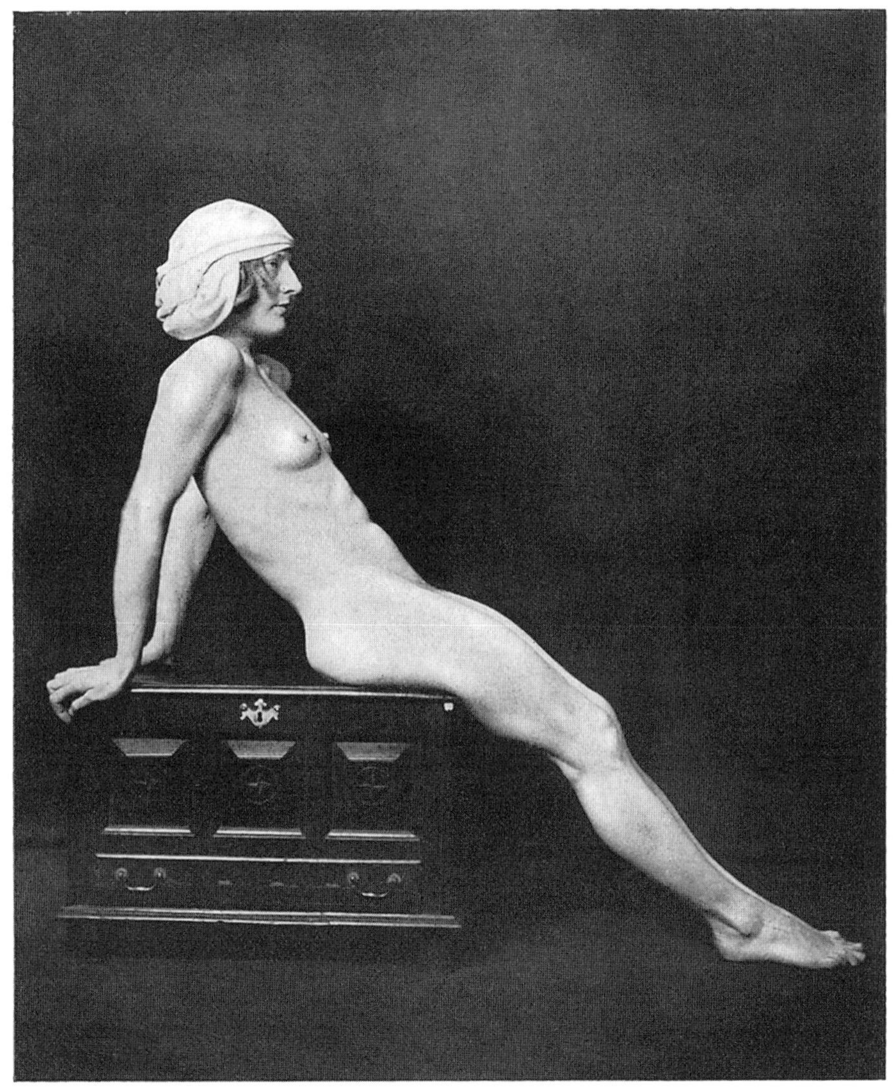

THE FIRST MODEL

A natural pose, showing the personality of the first model chosen for this series of standard poses.

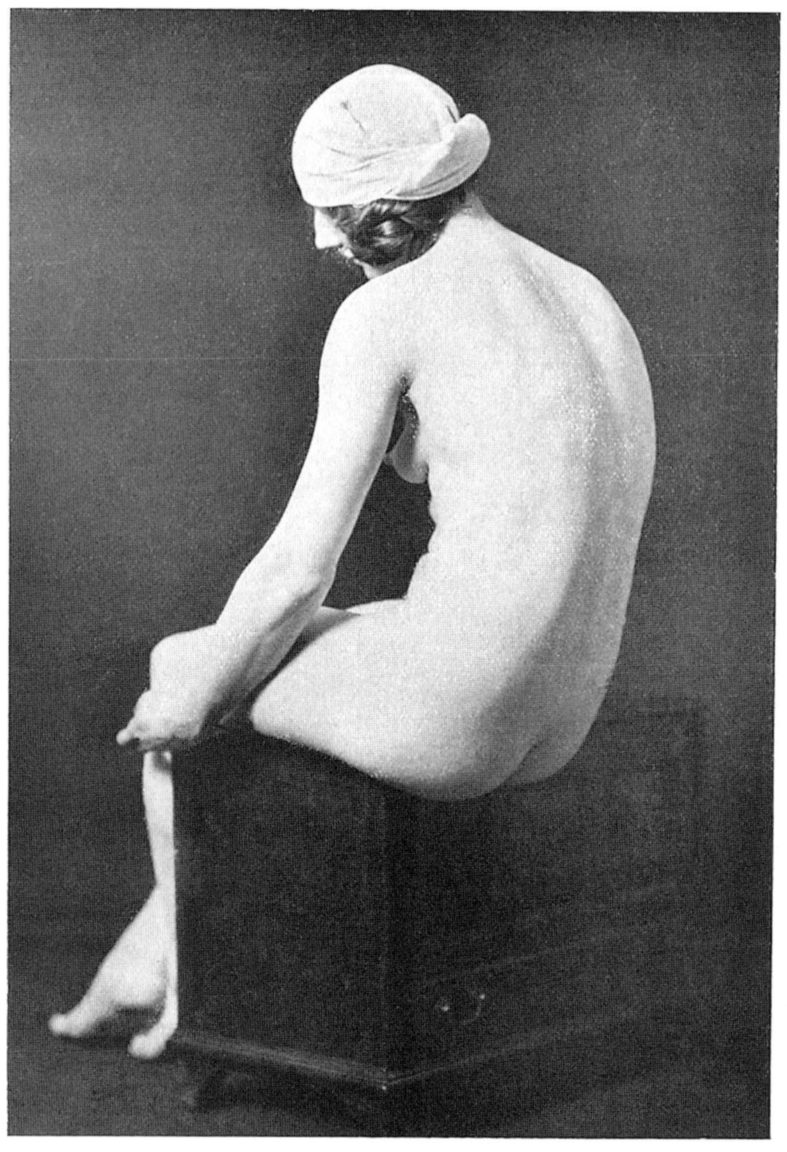

An easy relaxed sitting pose typical of the same model.

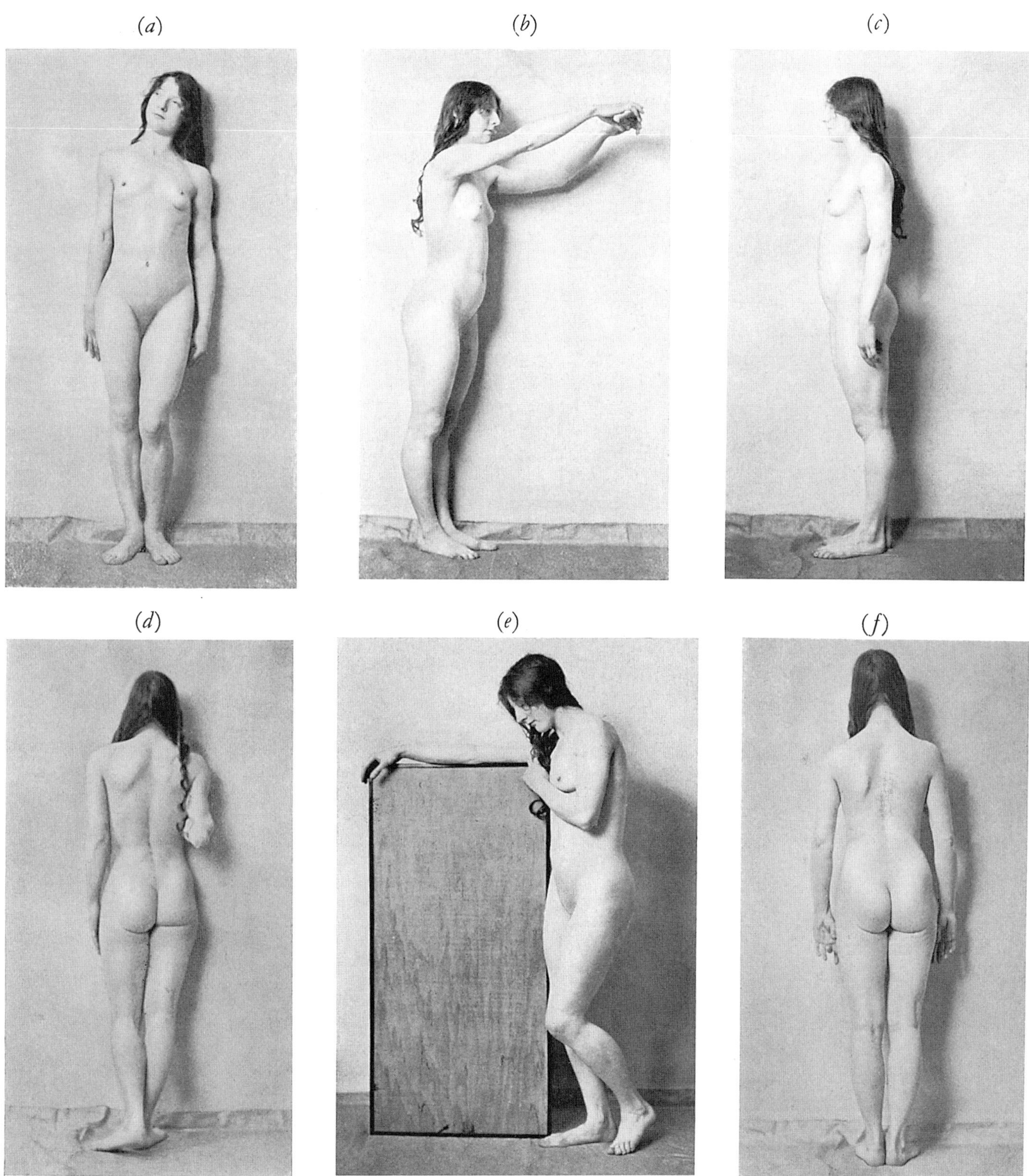

(*a*) Standing pose, the left knee flexed. (*b*) Plain standing pose, three-quarter view, with arms extended. (*c*) Plain standing pose, side view. (*d*) Back view, with left knee flexed. (*e*) Three-quarter view, with left knee flexed and right arm laid along a support. (*f*) Plain standing pose, back view.

(*a*)

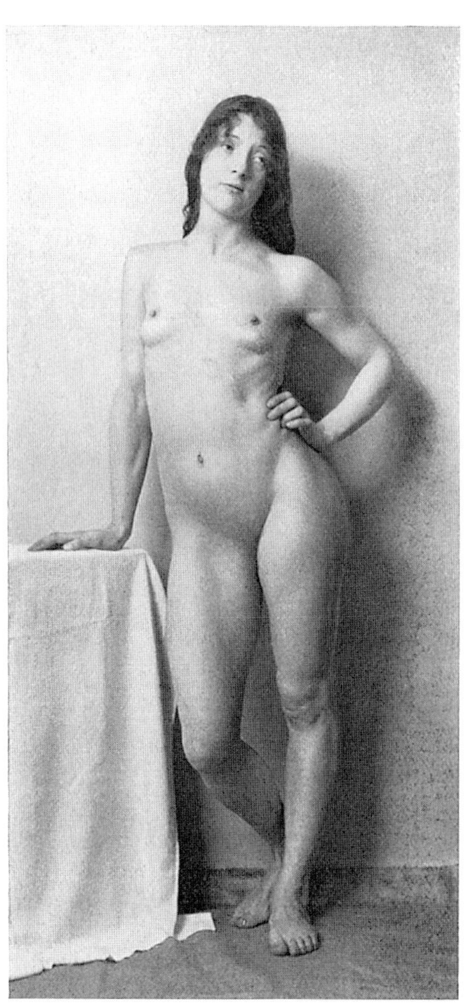

(*b*)

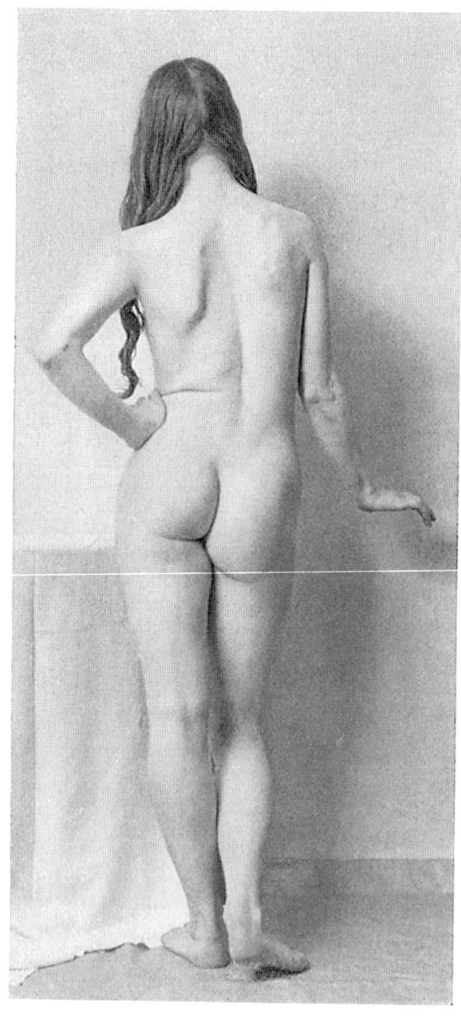

Right knee bent, throwing the weight of the body definitely upon the left leg.

(*a*) Front View. Plumb the position of the great toe and note the changed support altering the tilt of the entire pelvis.

(*b*) Back View. This shows the definite lifting of the right foot.

(*a*)

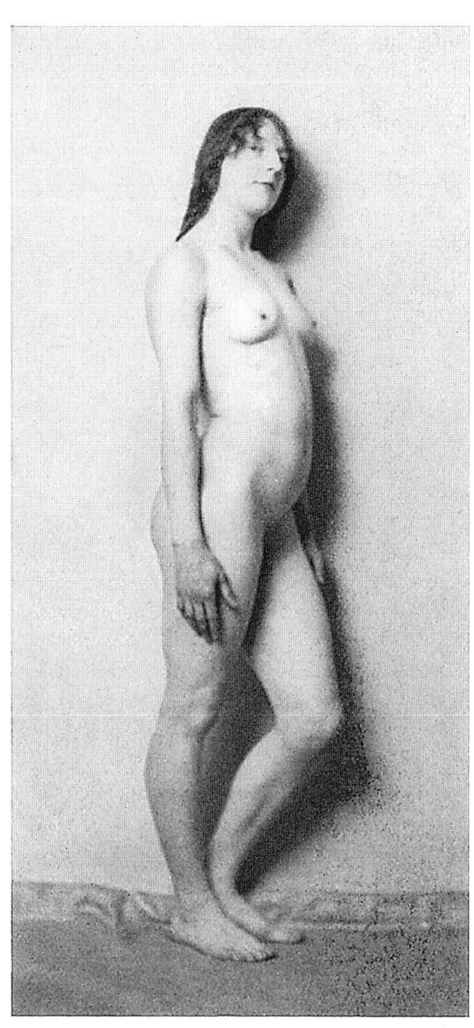

(*b*)

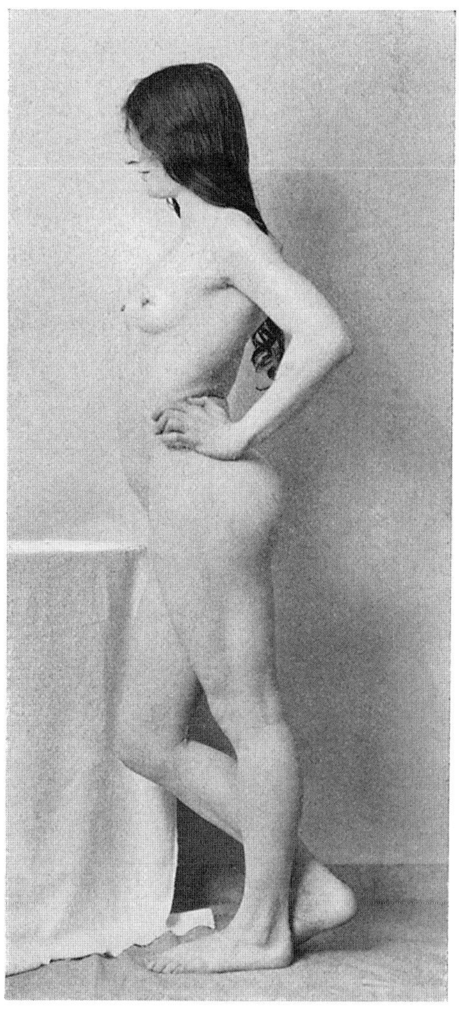

(*a*) This time it is the lifting of the left foot that drops the pelvis downwards from right to left.

(*b*) The definite placing of the weight upon the left leg and loosening of the right is well shown in this side view.

(*a*)

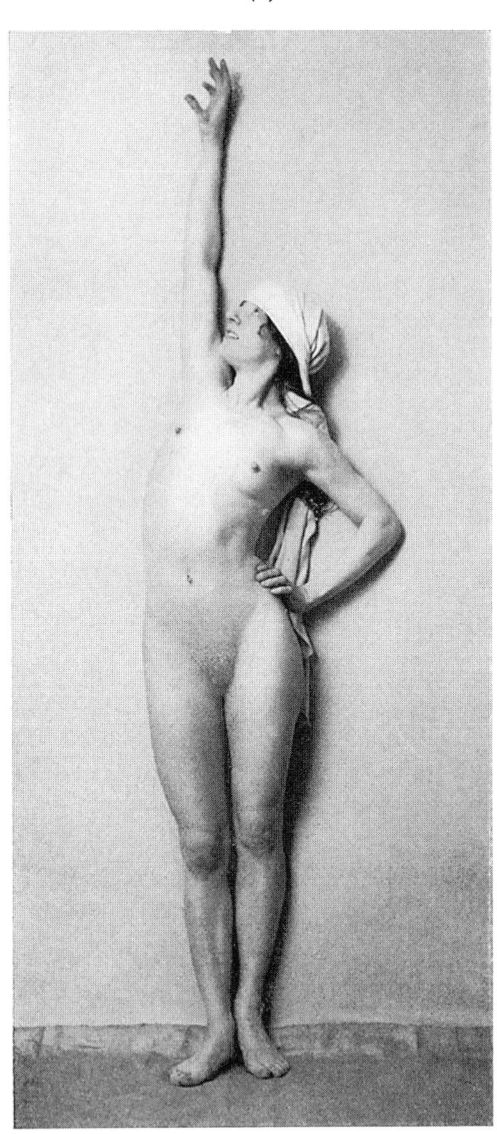

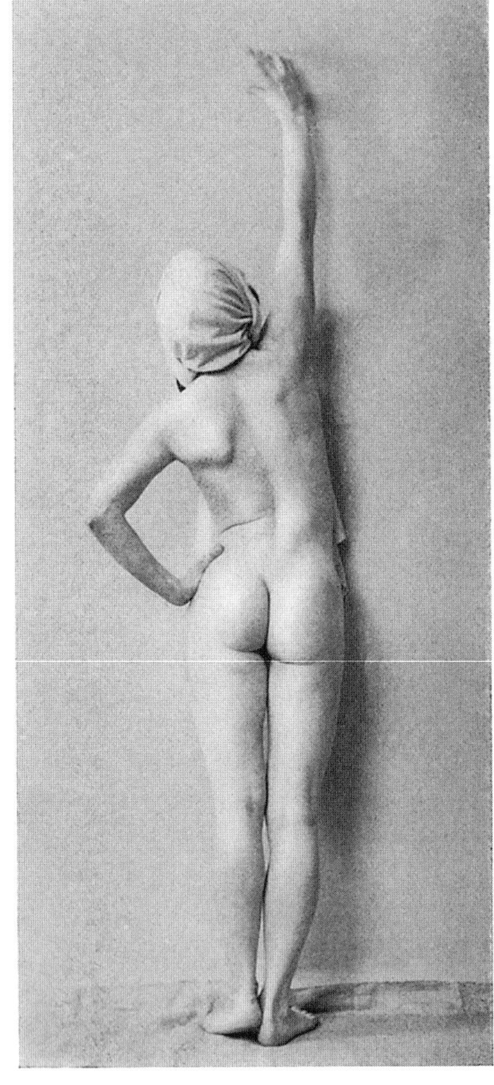

(*a*) Front View. Plumb carefully from the pit of the neck, and note the tremendous bend of the central body line.

(*b*) Back View. Contrast the tension of the right side with the folded curves of the left.

(*a*)

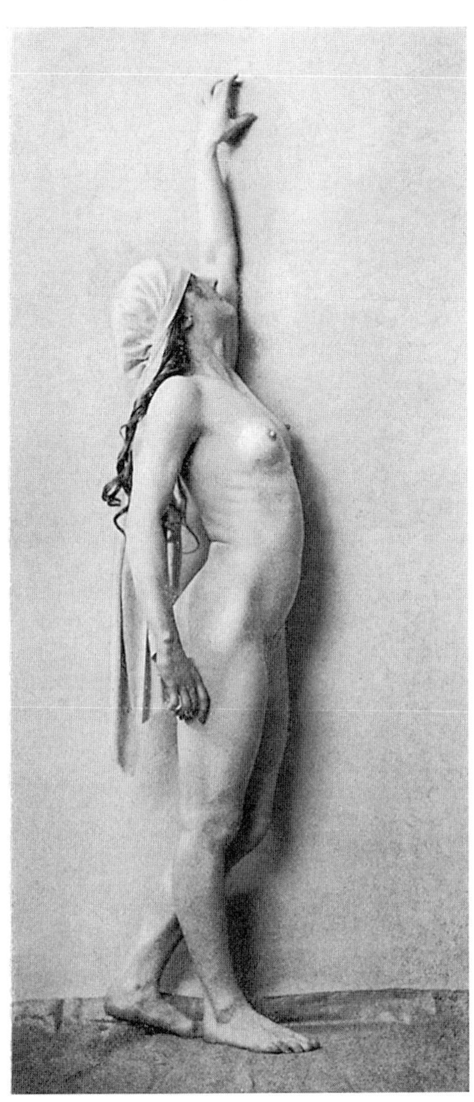

(*b*)

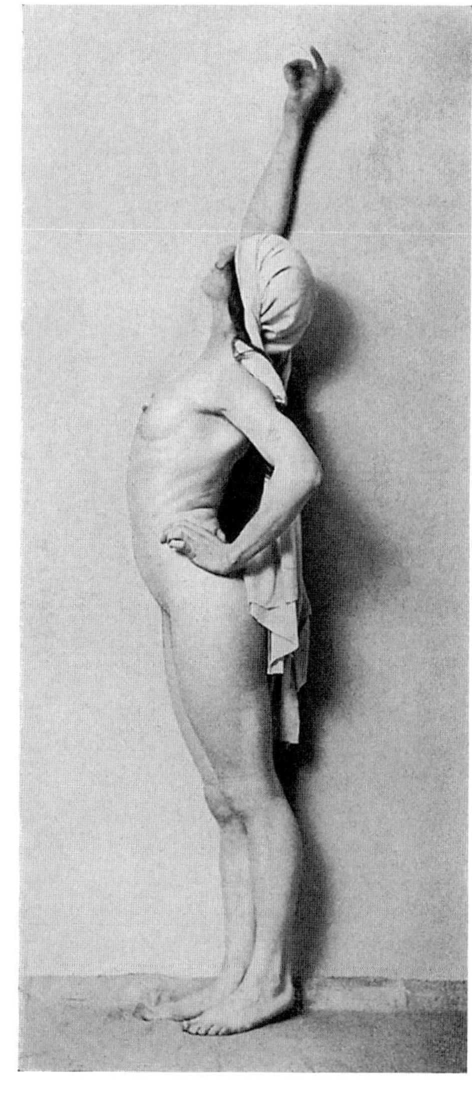

(*a*) Note the perpendicular line through the left hand, pit of neck, to the right foot.

(*b*) In this pose the model has swung even farther back, and the tension lines are shown most clearly.

(*a*)

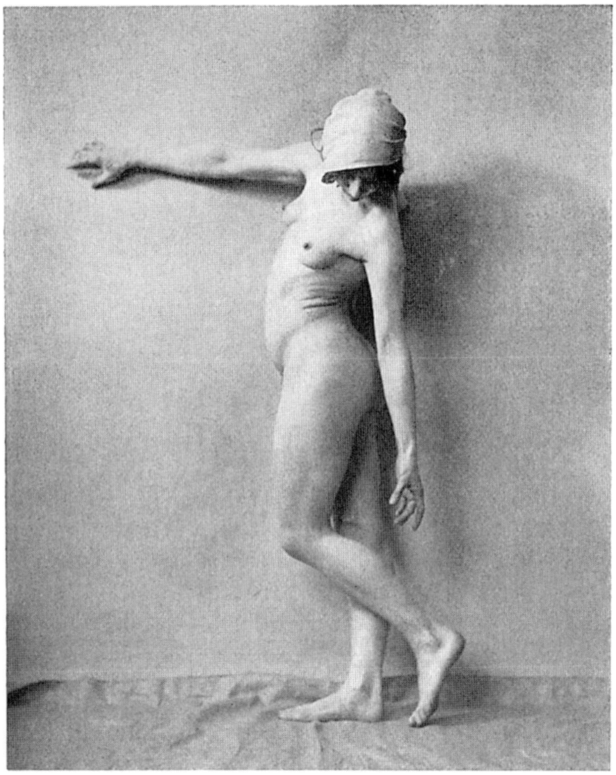

(*b*)

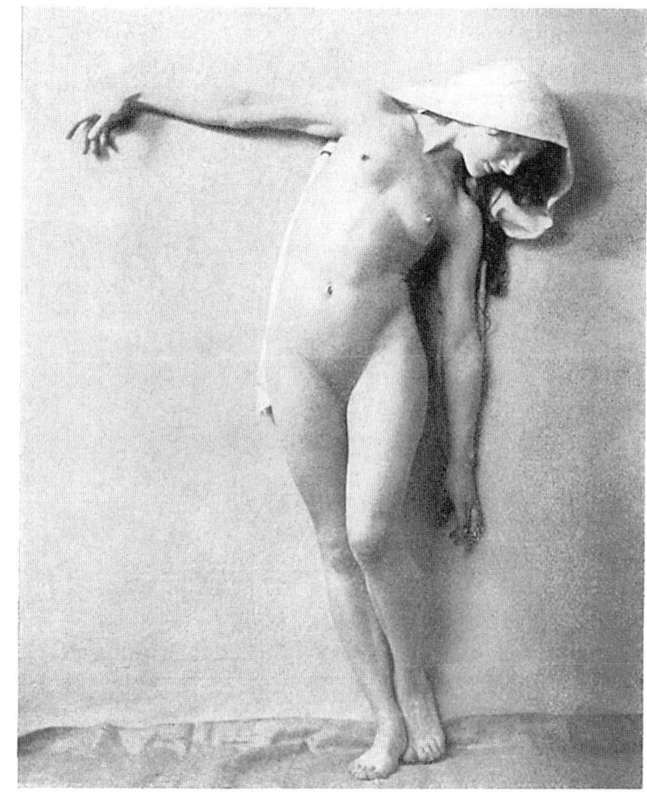

(*c*)

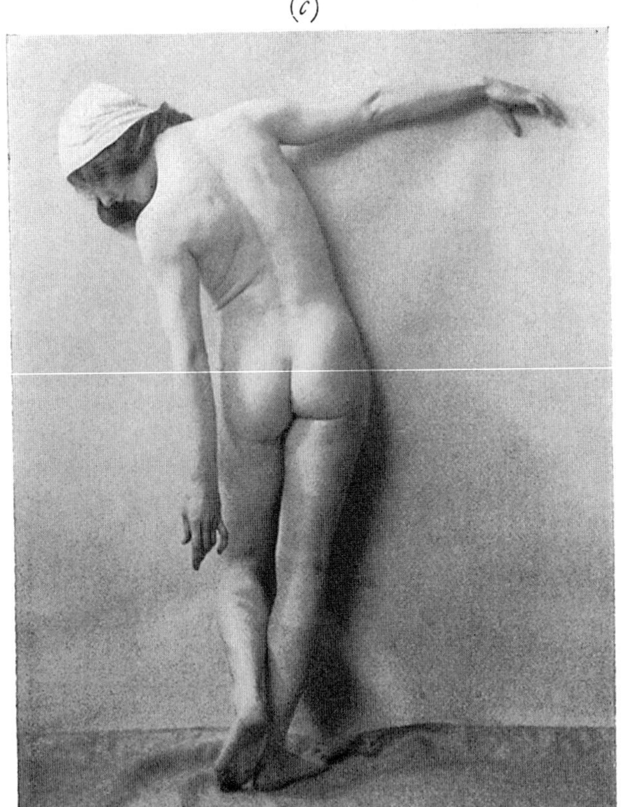

(*d*)

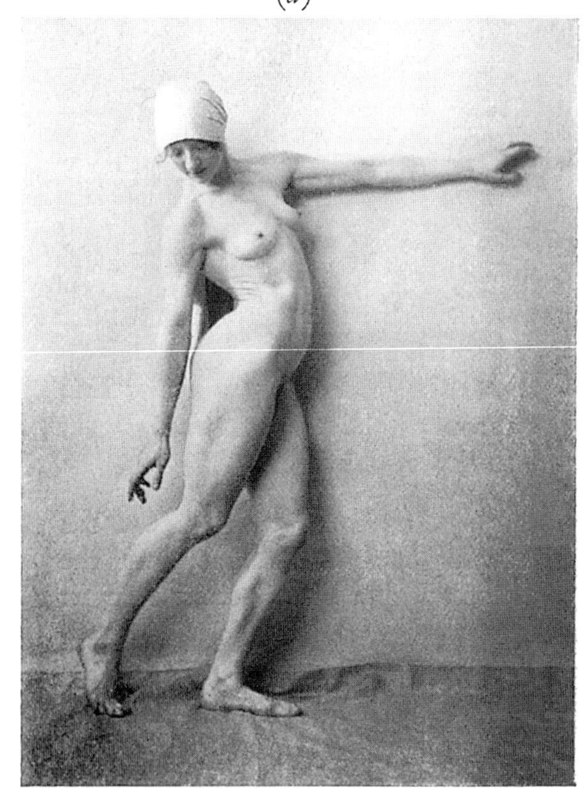

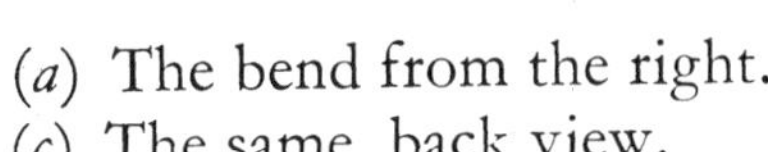

(*a*) The bend from the right.
(*c*) The same, back view.

(*b*) The same, front view.
(*d*) The bend from the left.

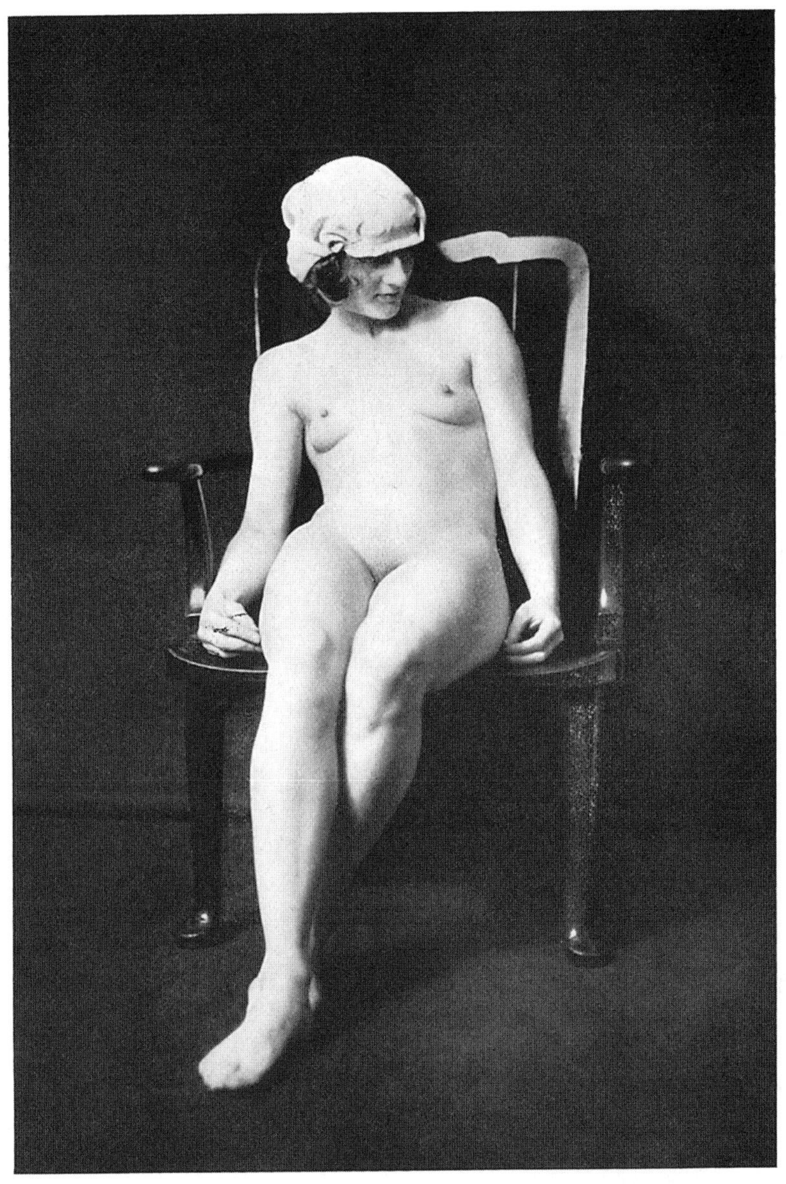

Leaning back, with the figure relaxed. A very simple, graceful pose.

(*a*)

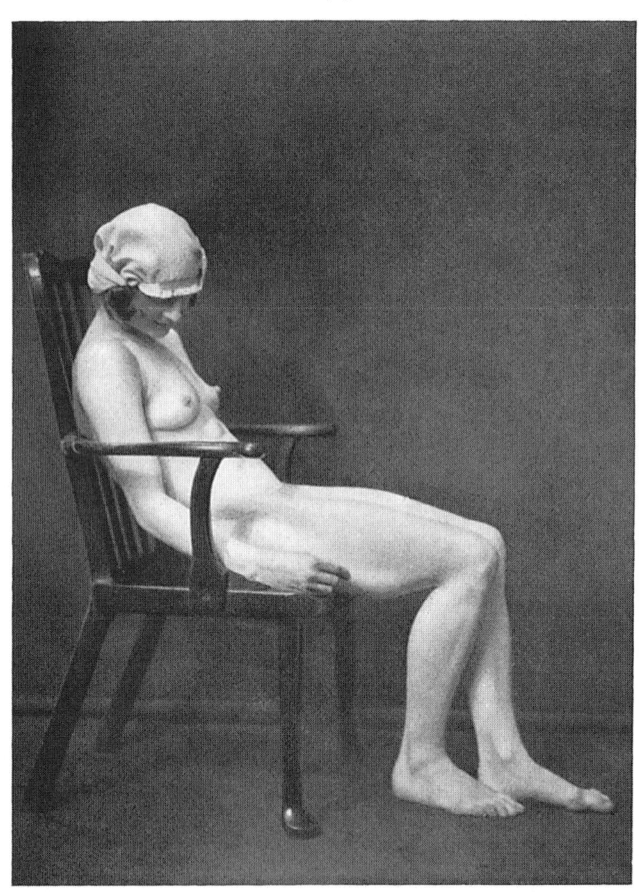

(*b*)

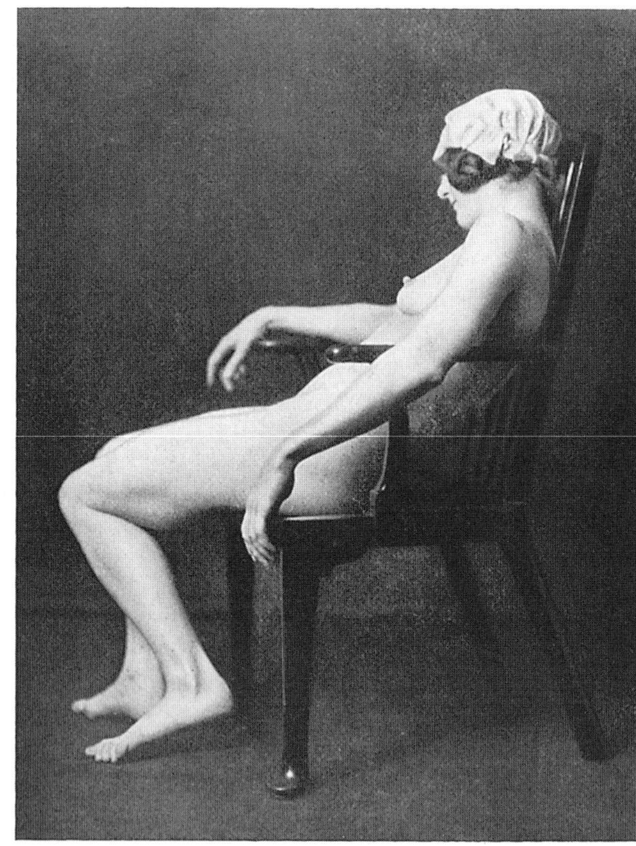

(*a*) Side View. The inward sweep of the body from neck to knee contrasts with the outer curve of the back against the support of the chair.

(*b*) Three-quarter Back View. The restful lines of the pose suggest how well it might be adapted in drawing to the wearing of the softer house-gown, tea-gown or *négligé*.

(*a*)

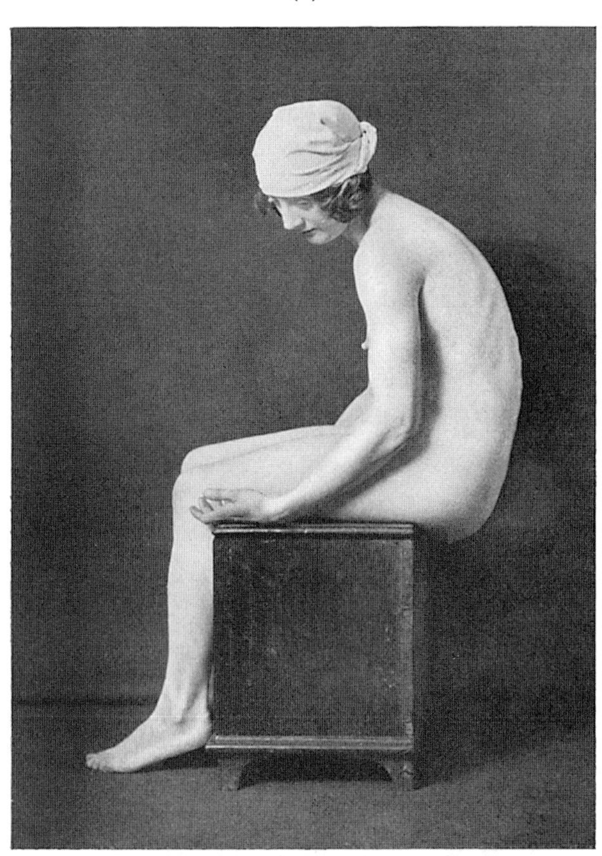

(*b*)

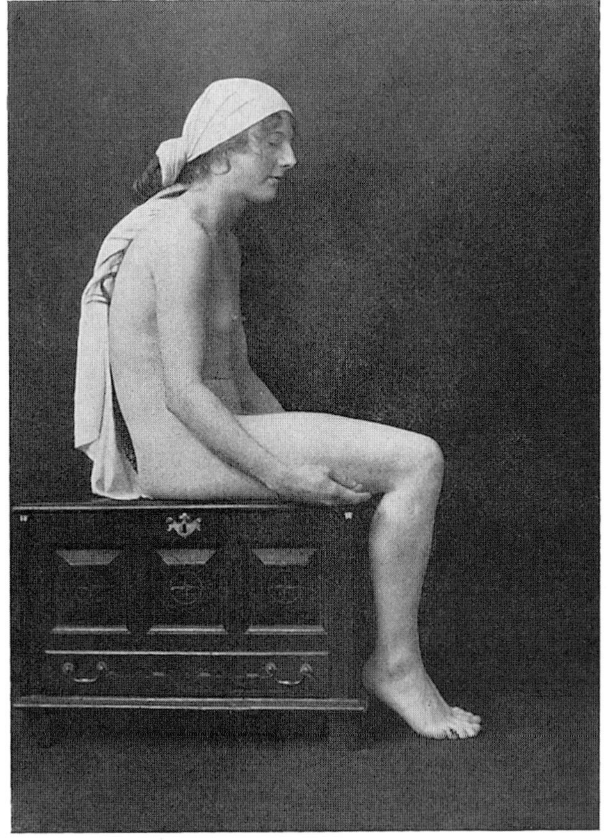

(*a*) Side View. The shoulder girdle slides forward, hiding the pit of the neck within the hollow of the neck.

(*b*) Three-Quarter Front View. The droop of the whole figure is well shown. The outline of the back should be traced carefully, and lack of all muscle furrows in leg and arm contrasted with the more active poses.

(a)

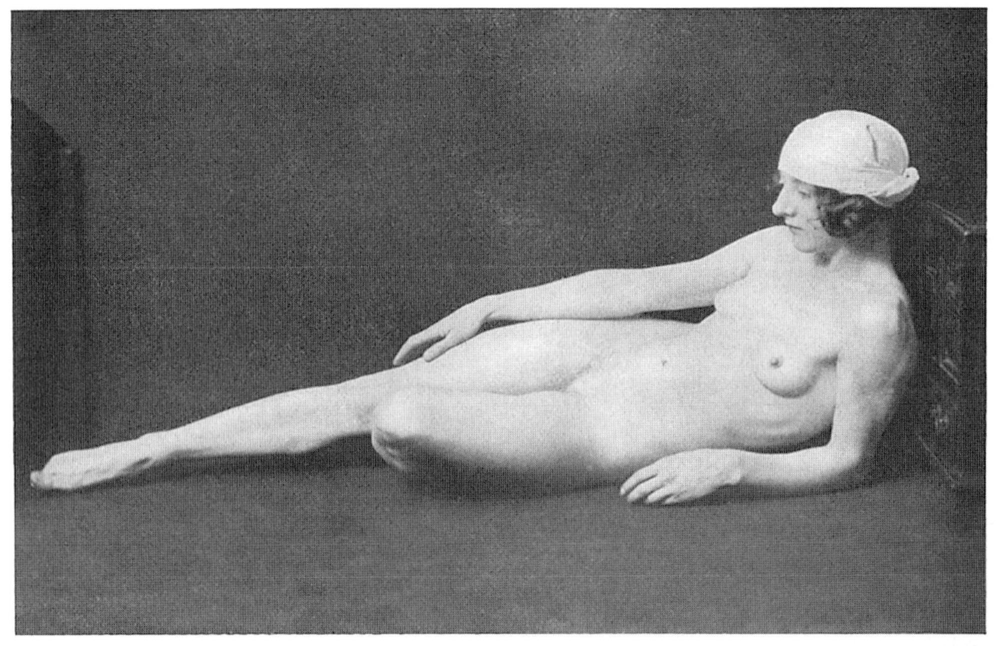

(b)

(a) Laziness. (b) Lassitude.

Every line of the body in these utterly natural attitudes is indicative of profound repose.

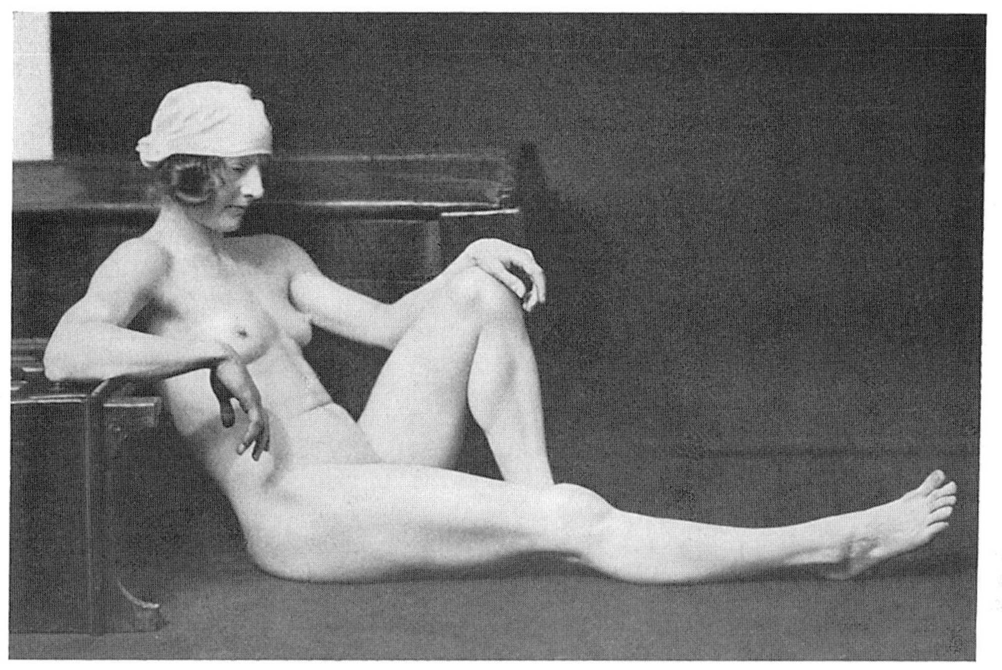

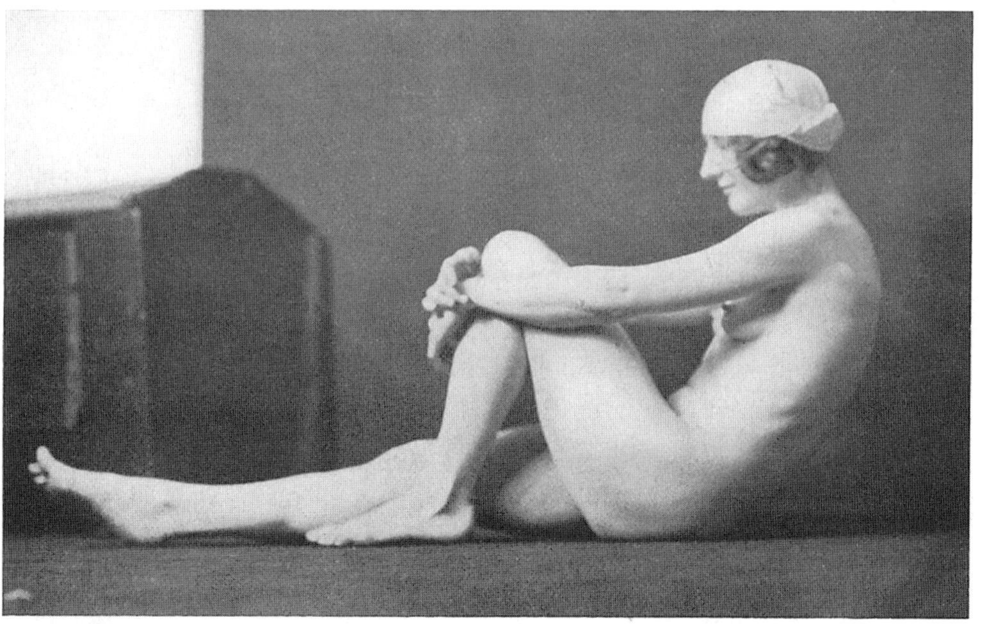

Classical attitudes which should be of great interest to the designer.

(*a*) (*b*)

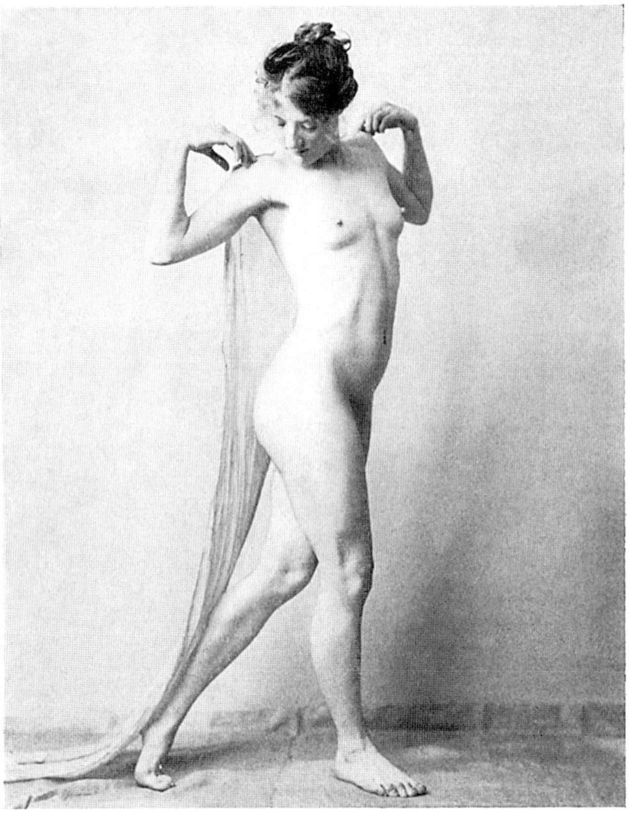

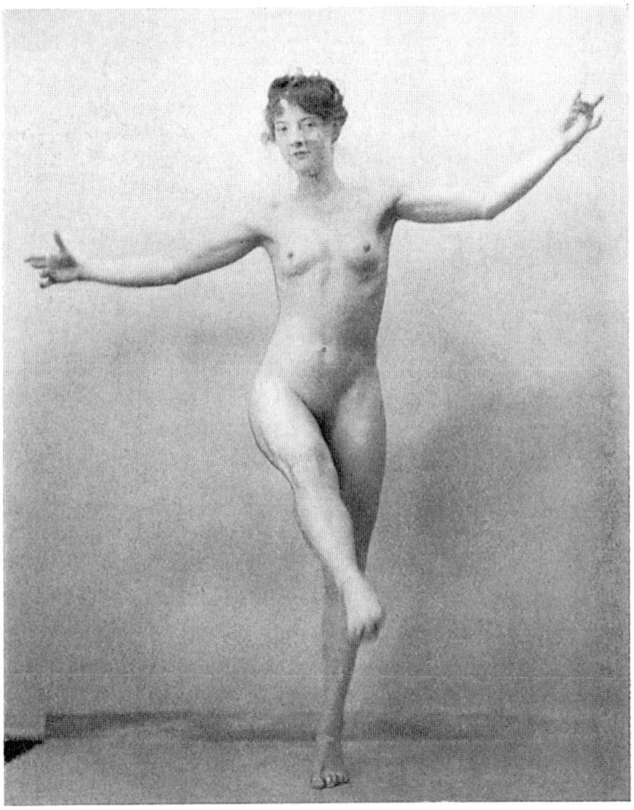

(*c*) 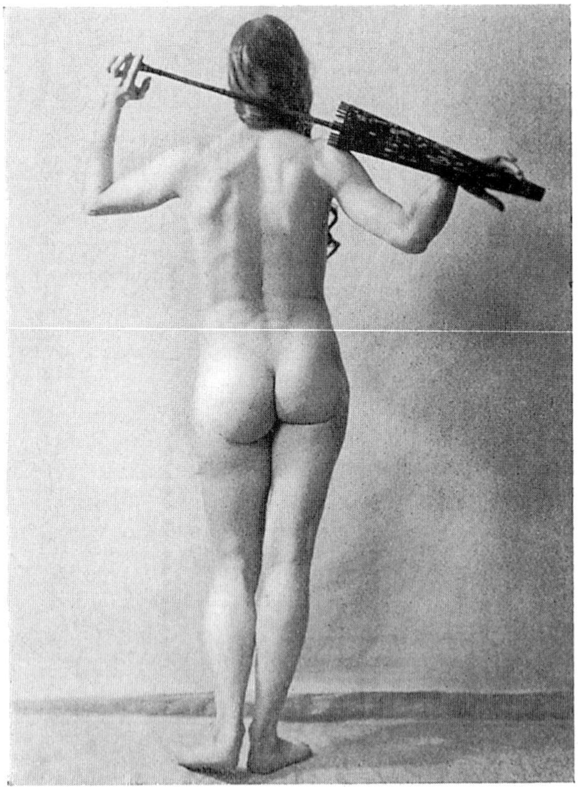 (*d*)

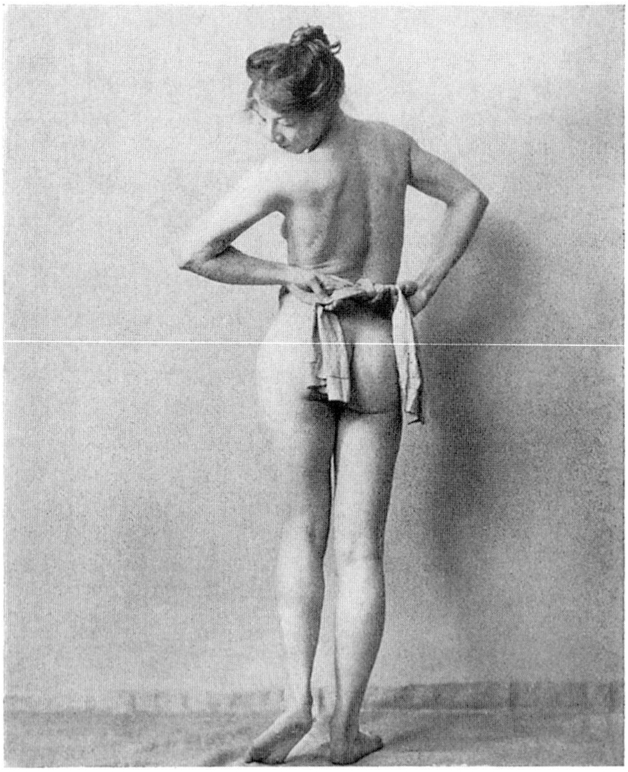

(*a*) The Train. (*b*) Balance. (*c*) The Sunshade. (*d*) The Sash.
Each of these poses is suggestive of brisk, lively activity.

(*a*) (*b*)

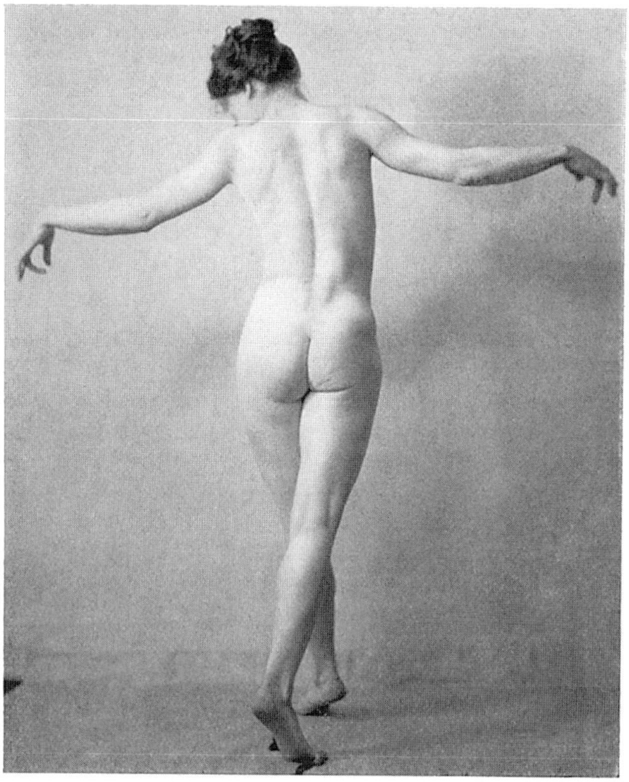

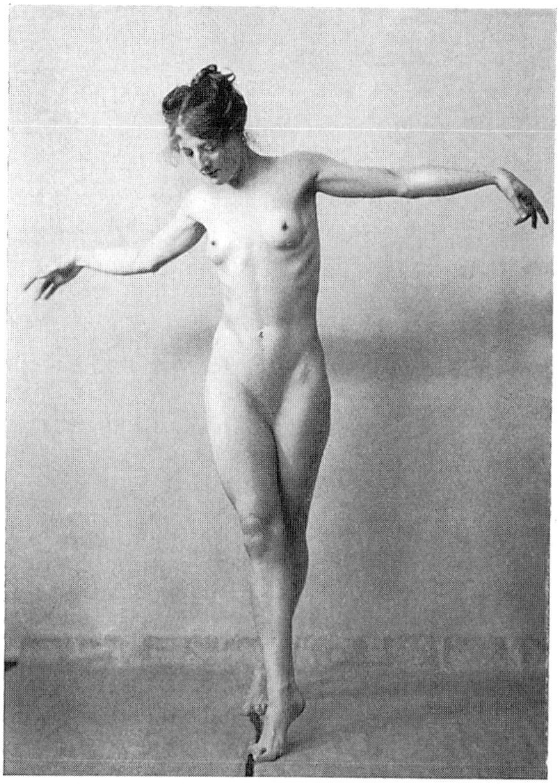

(*c*) 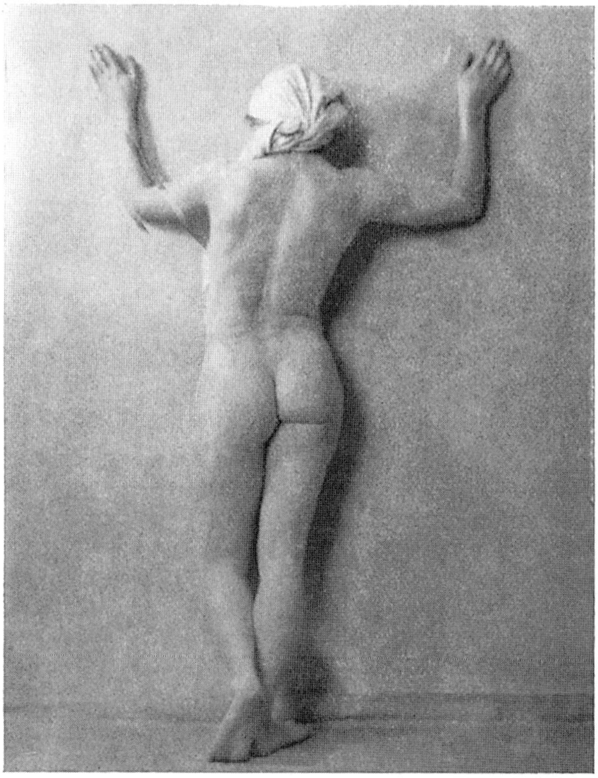 (*d*)

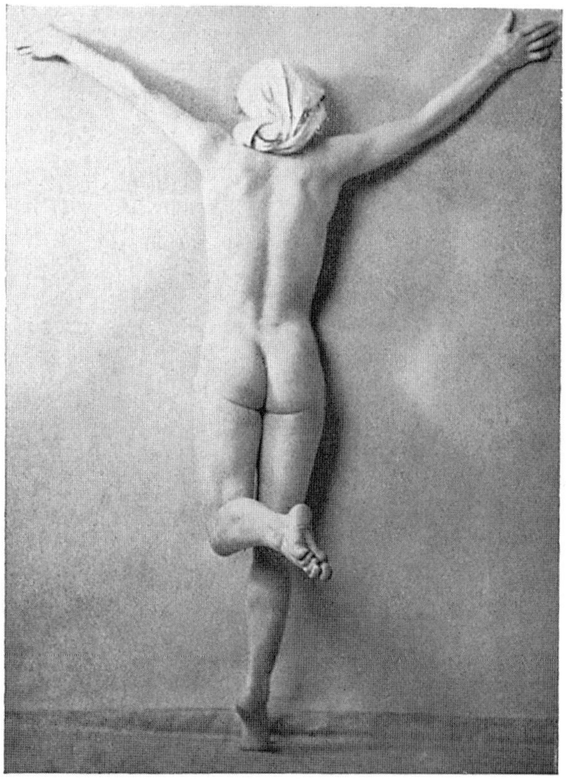

(*a*) Toeing the line, back view. (*b*) Toeing the line, front view.
(*c*) A standing pose. (*d*) A spring from the same pose.

Here again action and energy is the keynote to each pose.

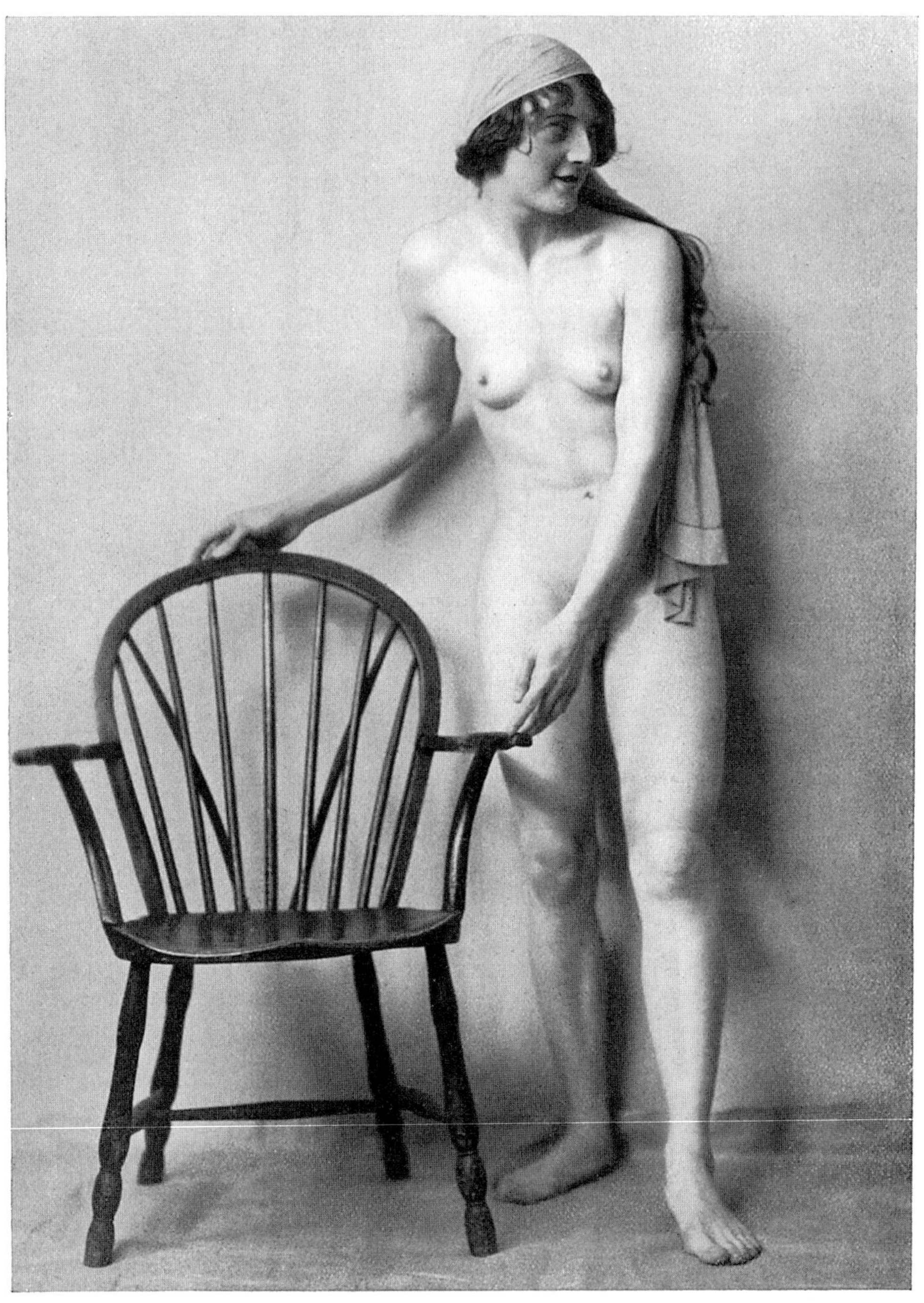

Offering a chair. A charming study of easy, natural grace.

(*a*)

(*b*)

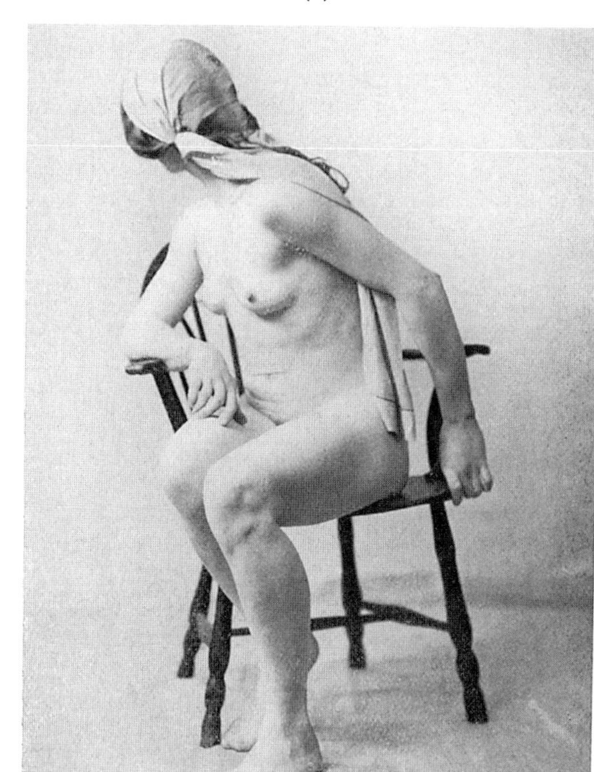

(*c*)

(*d*)

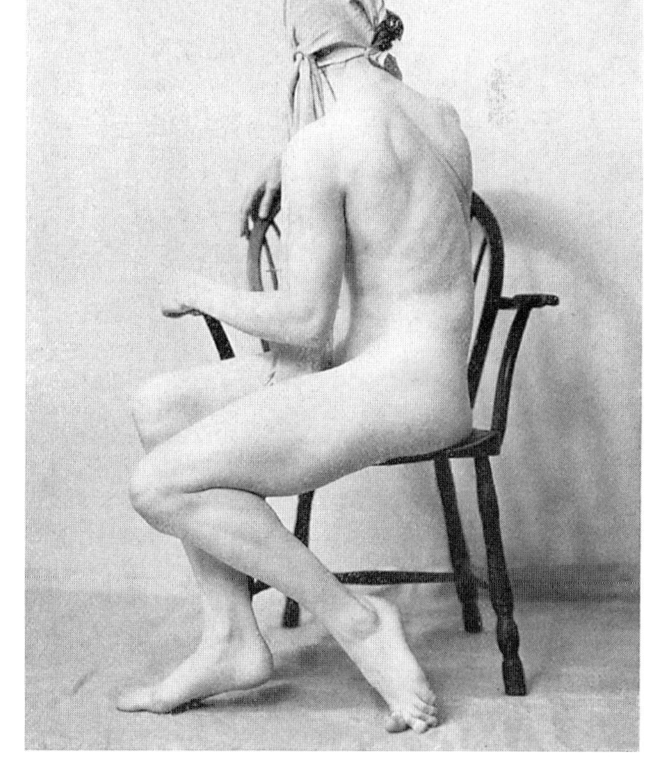

(*a*) Offering a chair, side view.
(*b*) Sitting and turning pose.

(*c*) An interesting side pose on the chair.
(*d*) A back view.

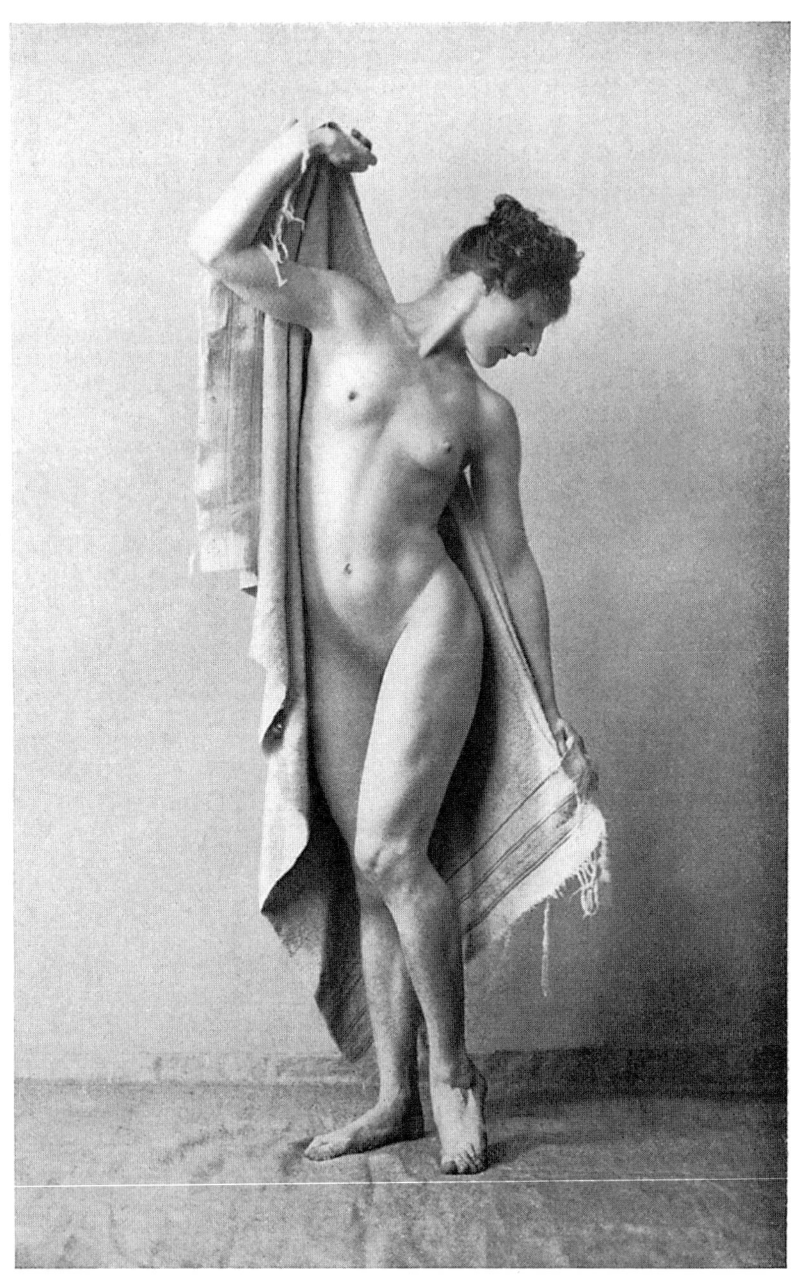

A graceful study in which the curves of the body synchronise perfectly with the falling folds of the towel.

(*a*)

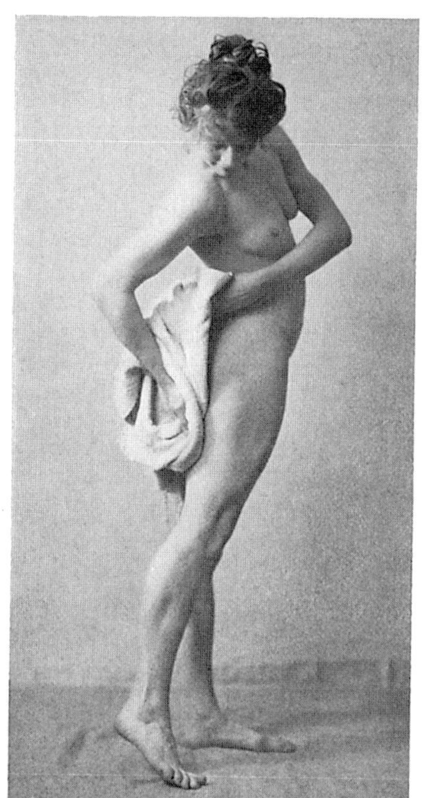

(*b*)

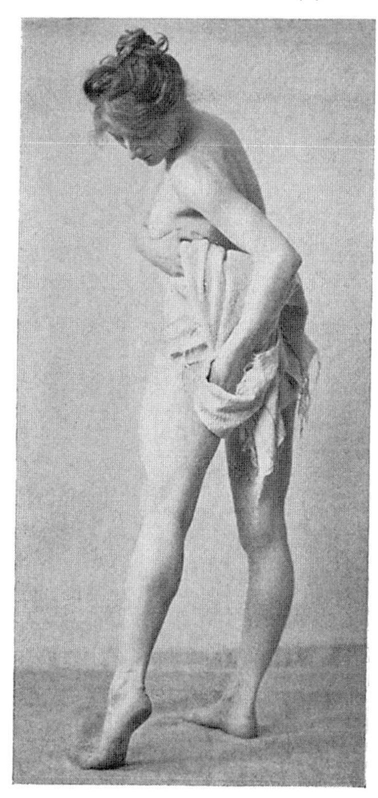

(*c*)

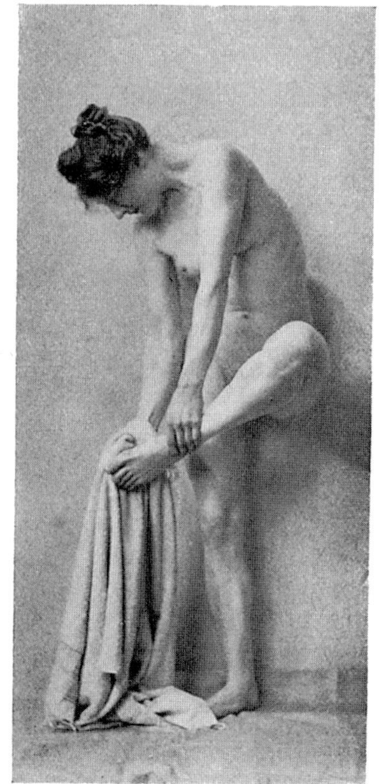

(*a*) Drying the thighs, side view.

(*b*) Drying the thighs, three-quarter view.

(*c*) Drying the feet, front view.

(*d*) Drying the feet, side view.

Interesting studies in action and balance.

(*d*)

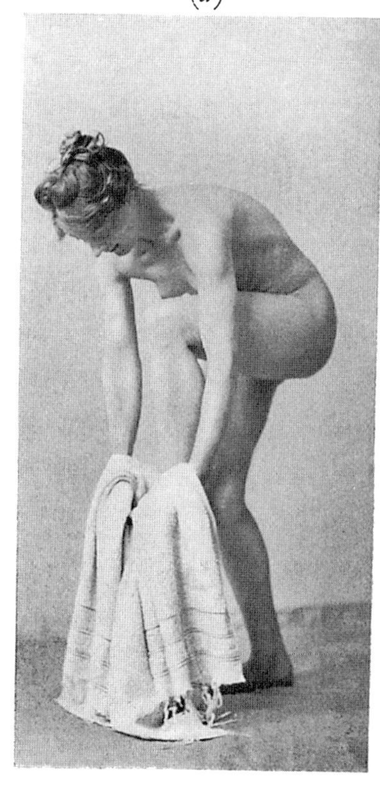

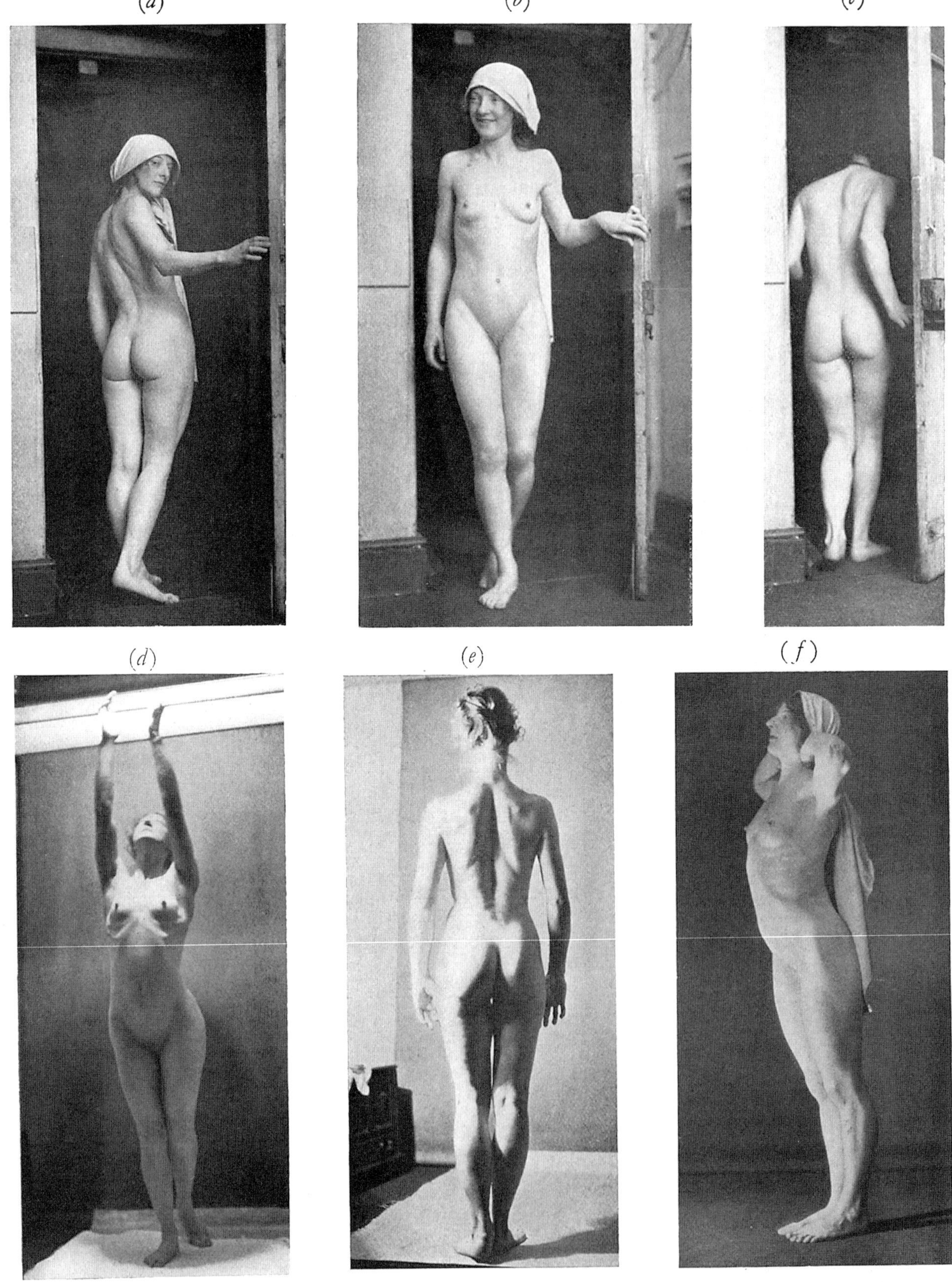

(*a*) A glance before leaving.
(*b*) The gentle entrance.
(*c*) Closing the door behind her.
(*d*) An interesting effect of high lights.
(*e*) Back view, with side lighting.
(*f*) Side view, with low lighting.

(*a*)

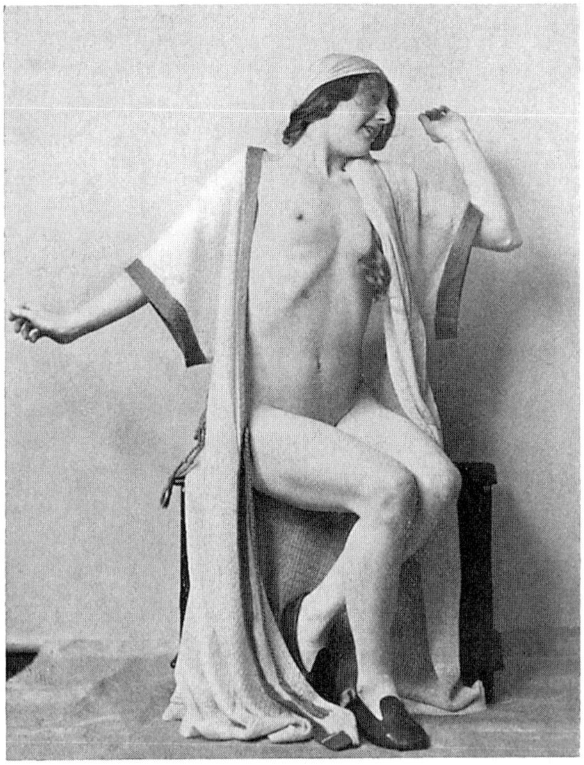

(*b*)

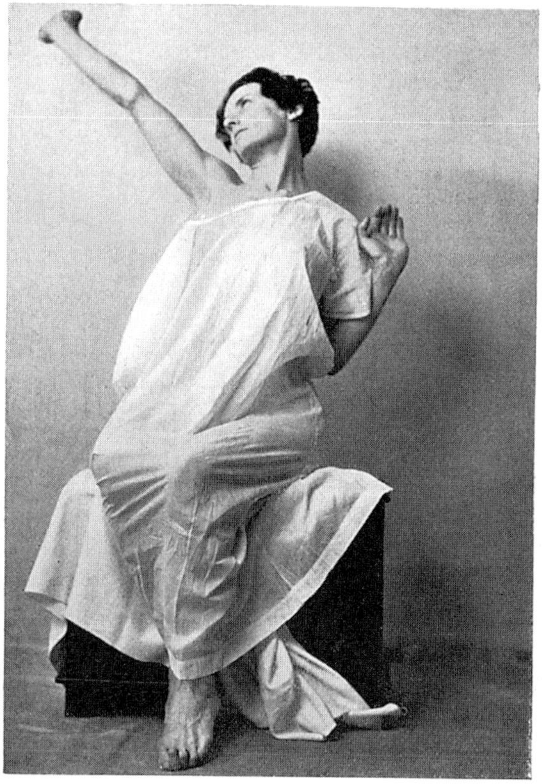

(*c*)

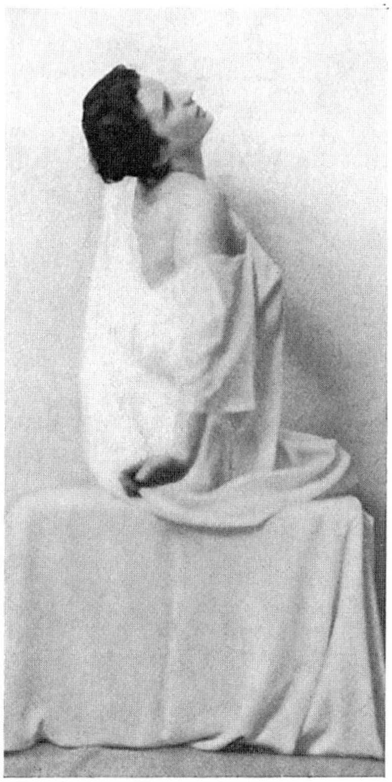

(*d*)

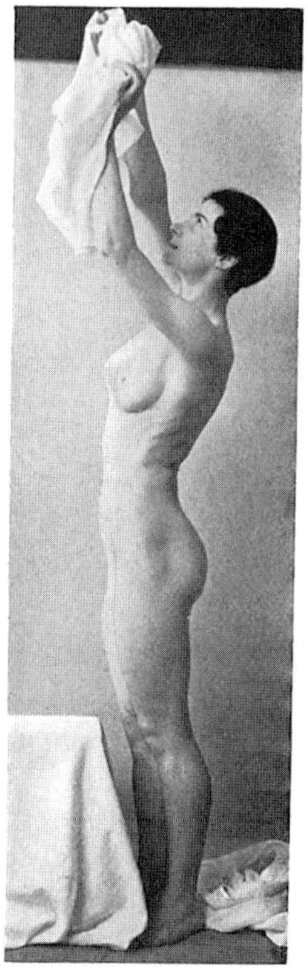

(*e*)

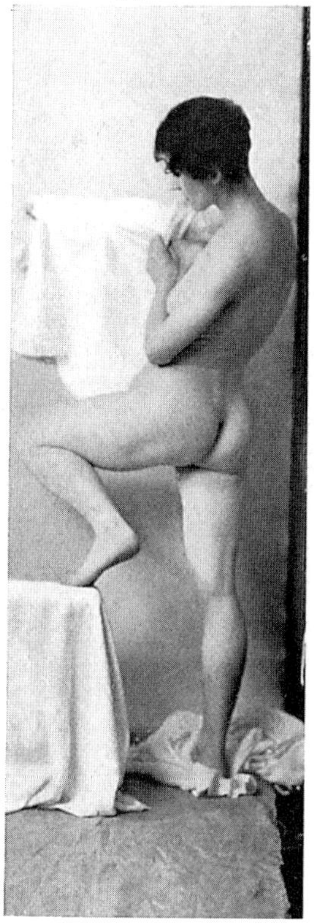

(*a*), (*b*) and (*c*) portray the natural stretching motions of the body after sleep. The light filmy robe and the thin dressing-gown form interesting studies in drapery.

(*d*) and (*e*) are useful " dressing " studies easily adaptable by the artist.

(*a*)

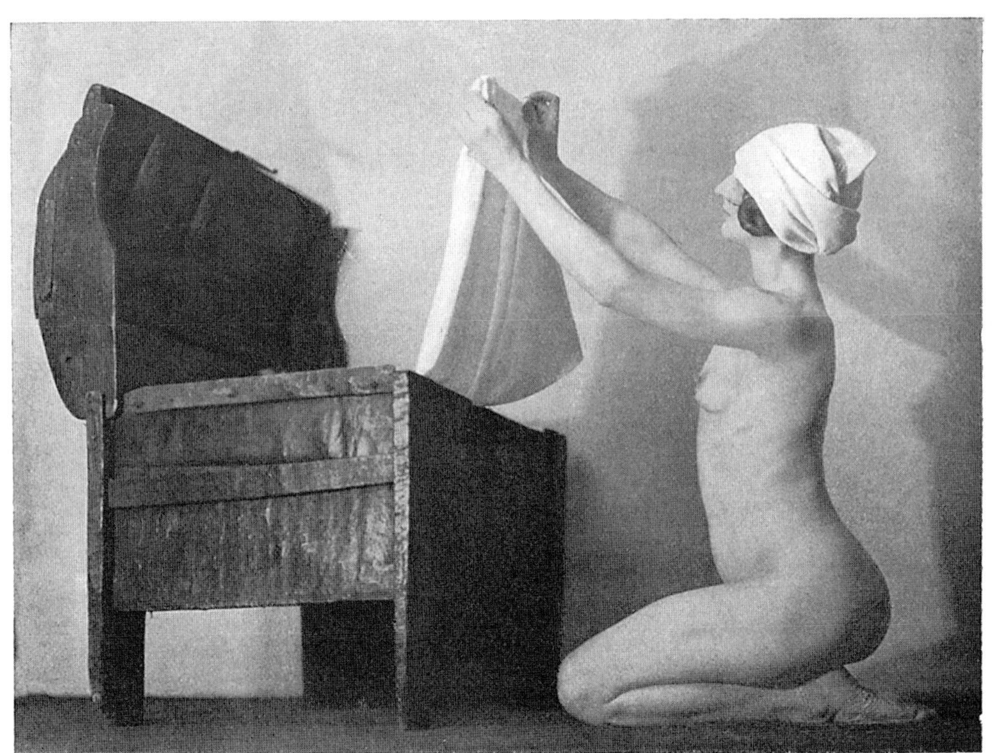

(*b*)

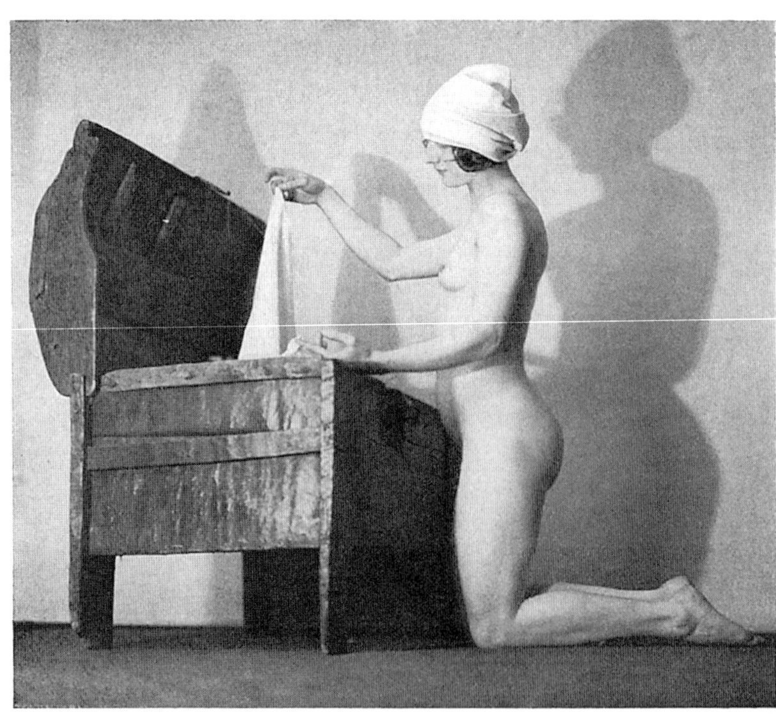

(*a*) A good pose, which forms a useful suggestion for a fabric display advertisement.
(*b*) Another fabric suggestion.

(*a*)

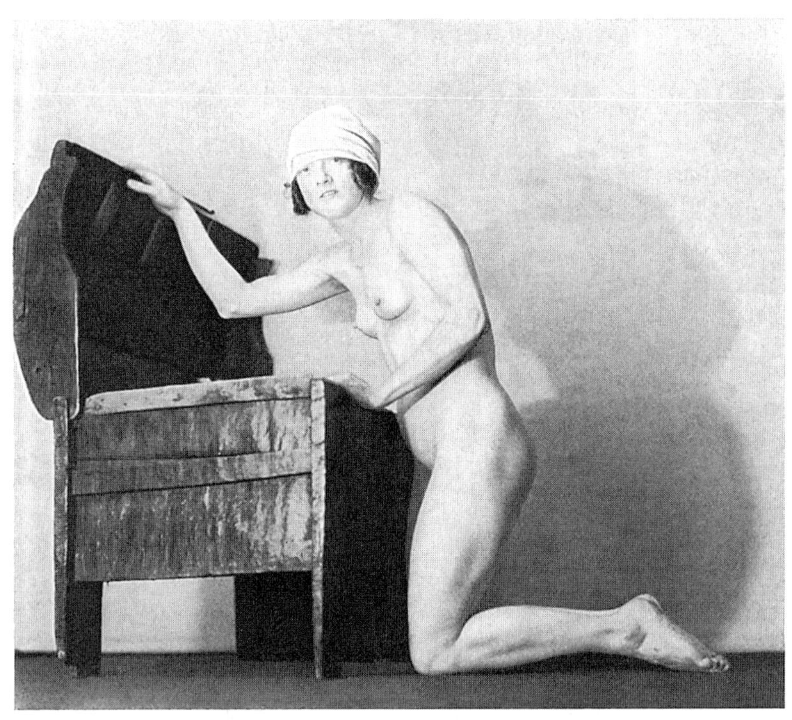

(*b*)

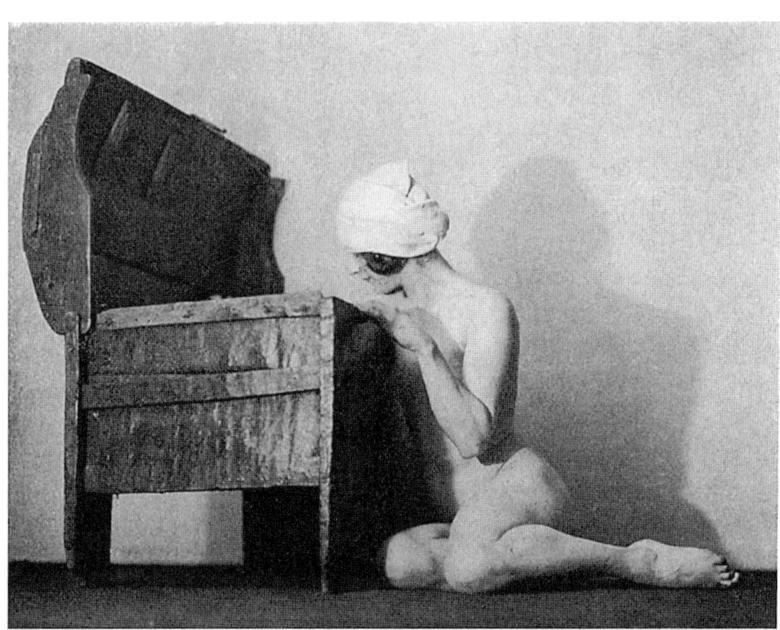

(*a*) Shutting down the chest.
(*b*) A charming pose that could be employed successfully to advertise many commodities.

(*a*)

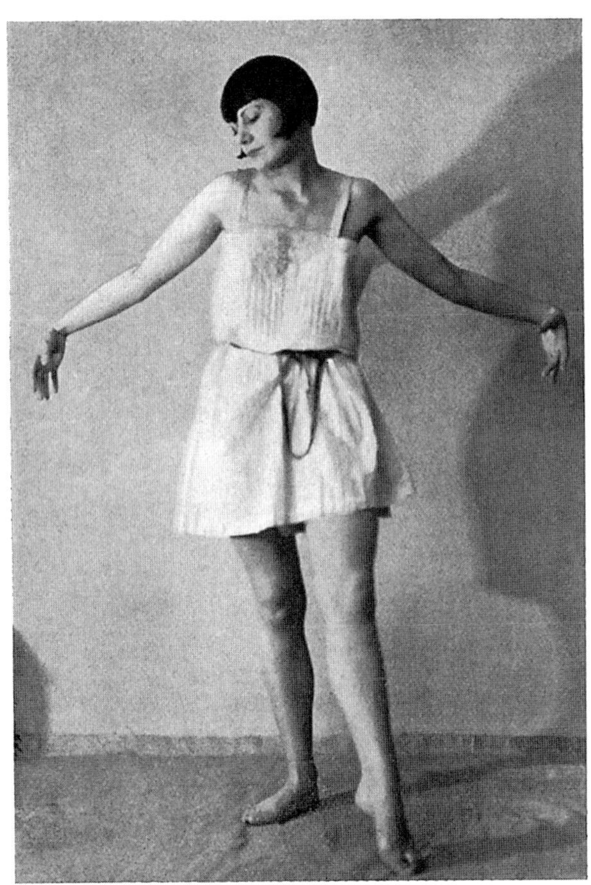

(*b*)

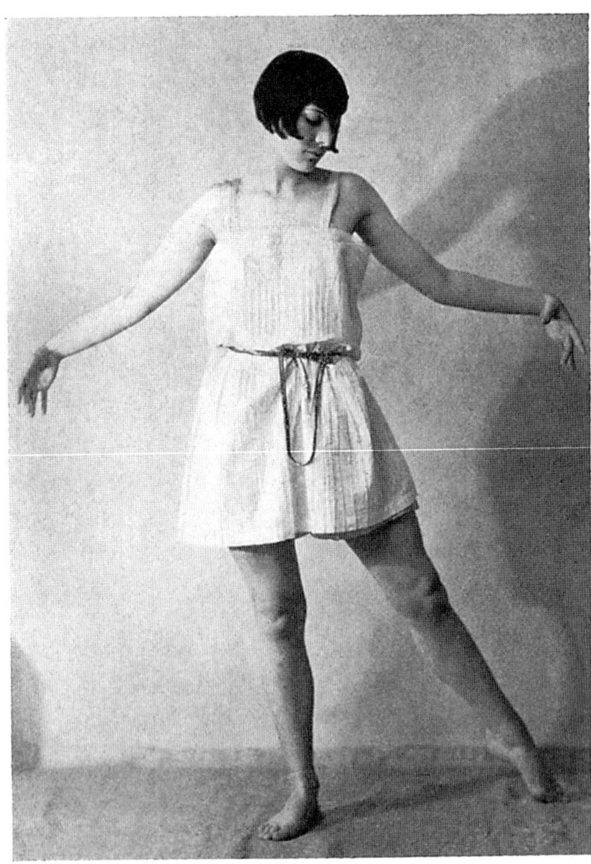

(*a*) Fourth Position.

(*b*) Fifth Position.

Poses that recall the dignified grace of the classical dance.

(*a*)

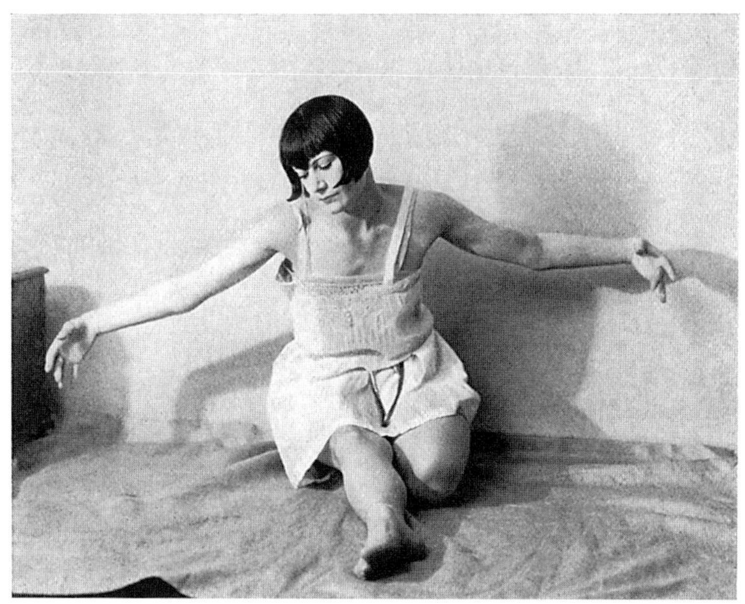

(*b*)

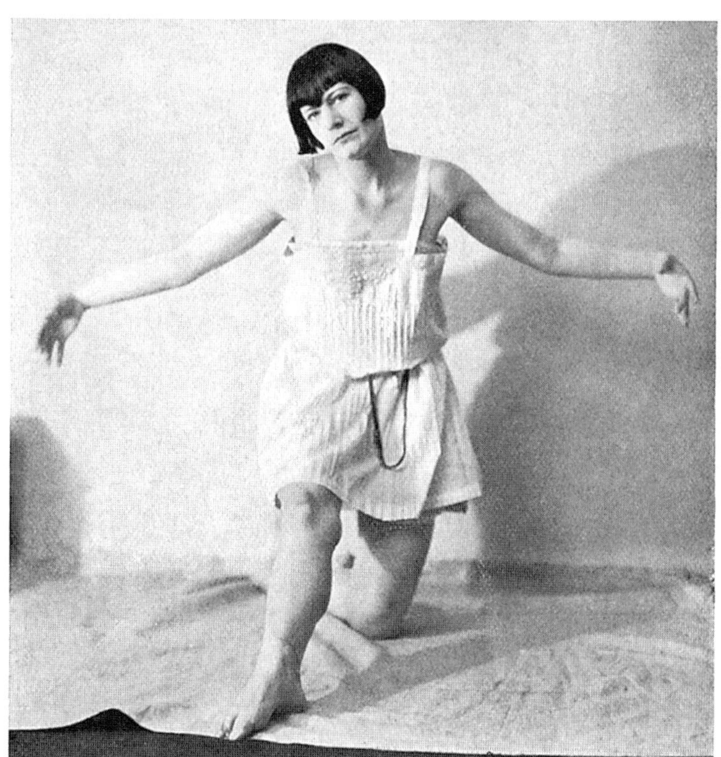

(*a*) The complete curtsy. (*b*) Sinking downwards.

Two more positions reminiscent of classical dancing that suggest perfect balance and muscular control.

(*a*)

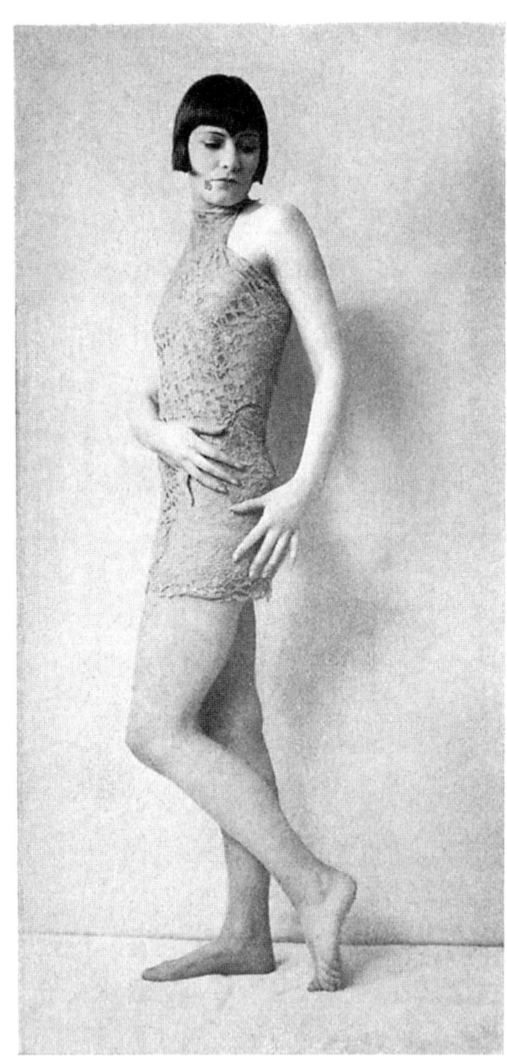

(*b*)

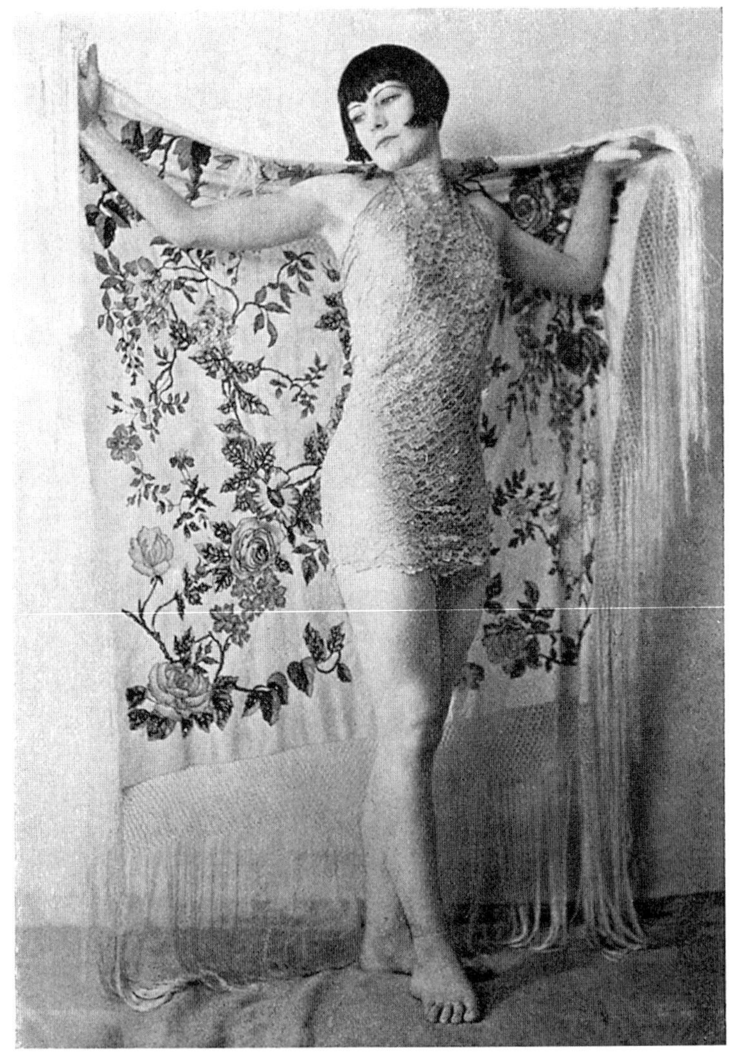

(*a*) A hesitant pose.

(*b*) Posing with a shawl.

Both of these studies could be successfully adapted by the fashion artist.

(*a*)

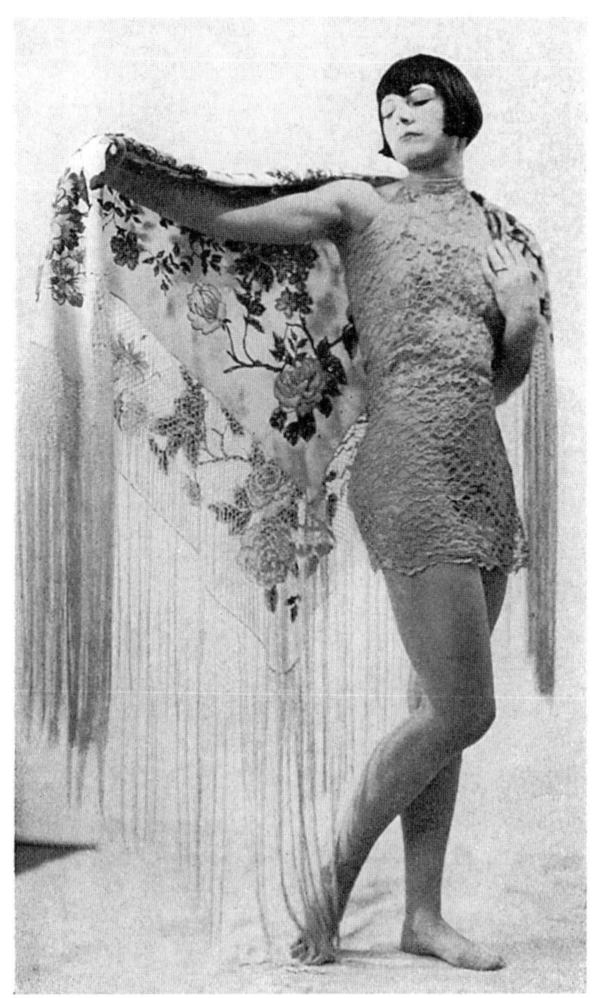

(*b*)

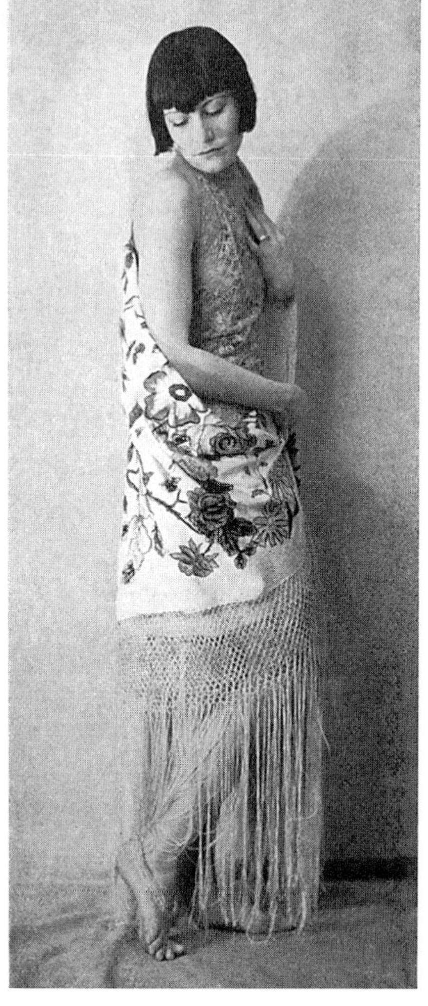

(*a*) Swinging around.

(*b*) Wrapping the shawl closely.

There are innumerable ways of displaying this beautiful type of shawl. These studies constitute two further suggestions.

(*a*)

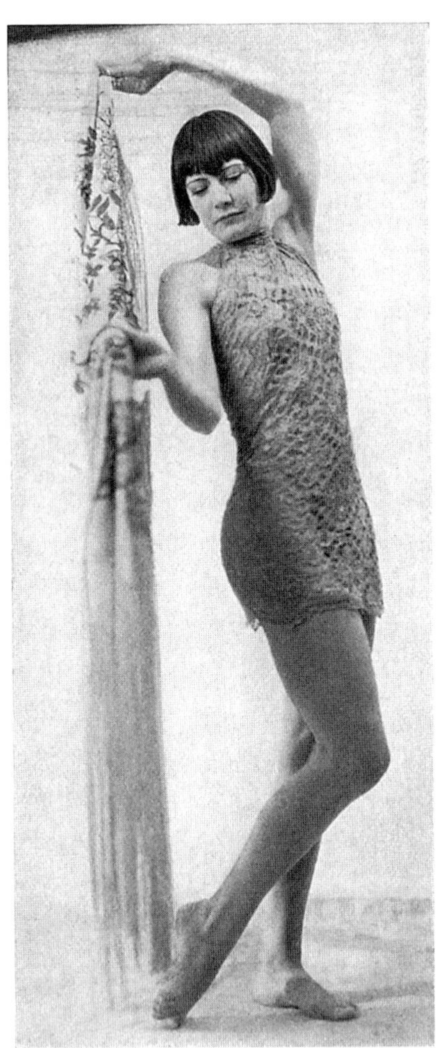

(*b*)

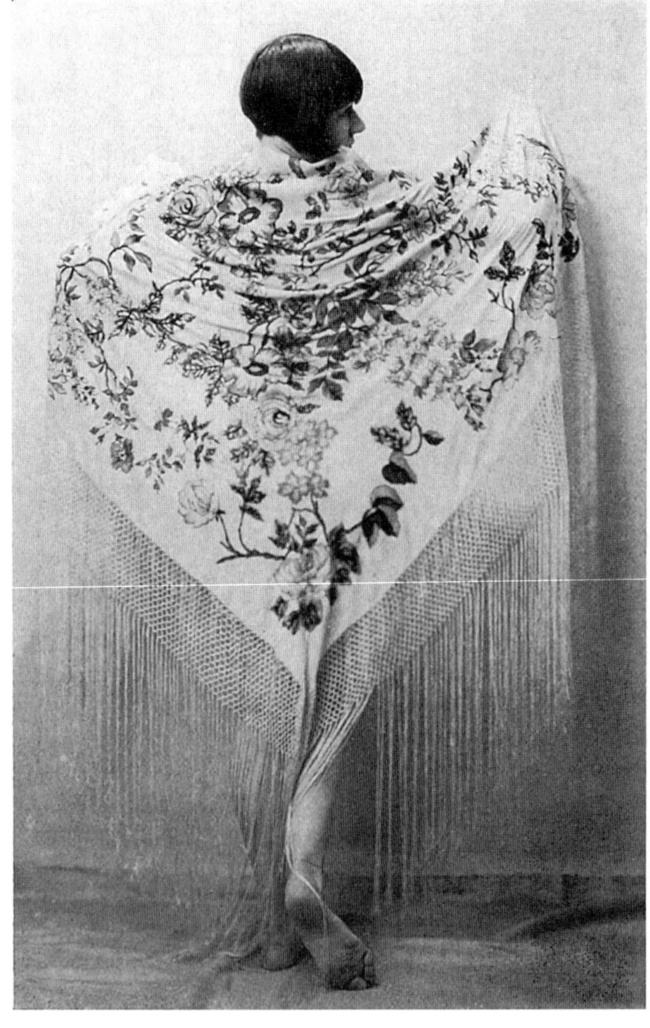

(*a*) Draping the shawl.

(*b*) Back view.

Interesting studies in drapery which could be adapted for many purposes in graphic art.

(*a*)

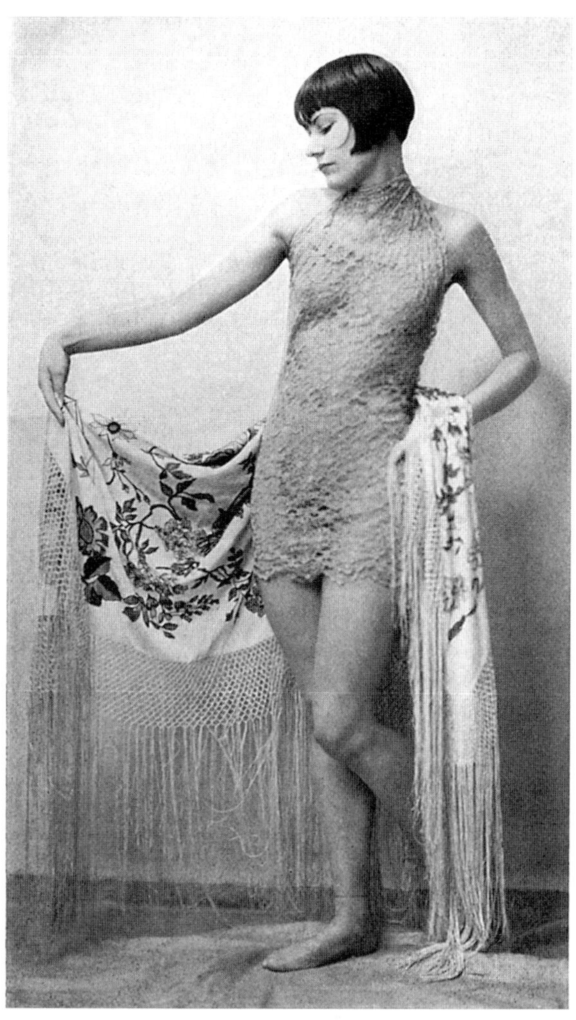

(*b*)

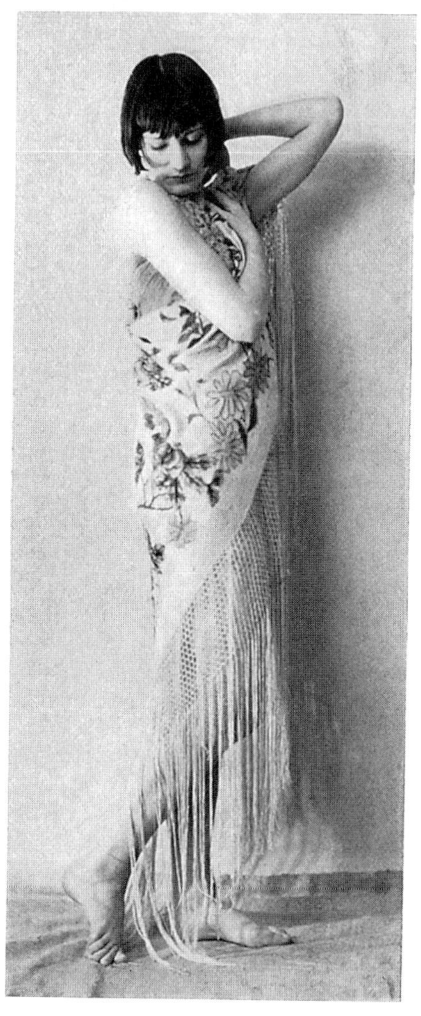

(*a*) The fallen Drapery.

(*b*) The complete Drapery.

Two more suggestions for Draping studies, of special interest to the fashion artist.

(*a*)

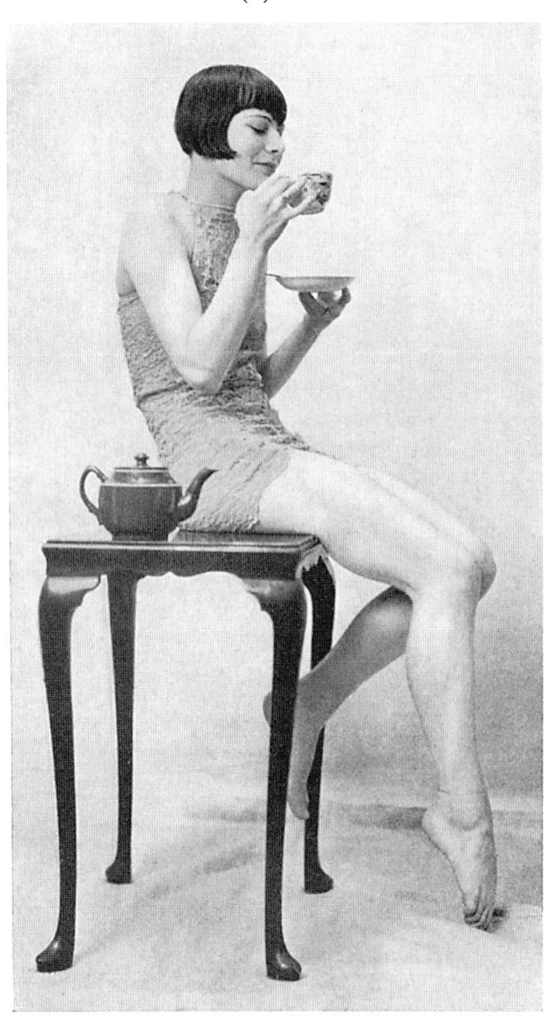

(*b*)

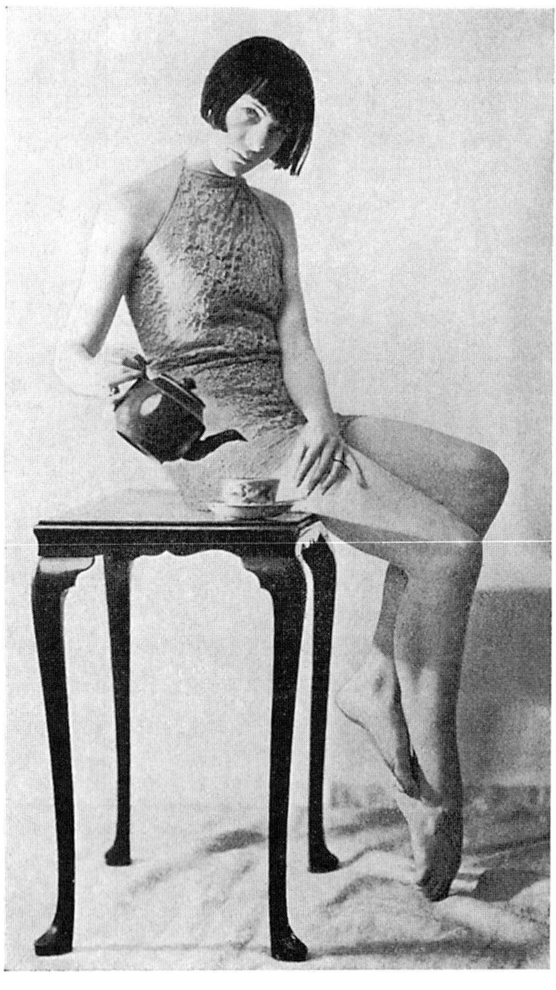

(*a*) A Cup of Tea.

(*b*) Pouring out Tea.

Two graceful and absolutely natural poses, particularly adaptable to the purposes of commercial art.

(*a*)

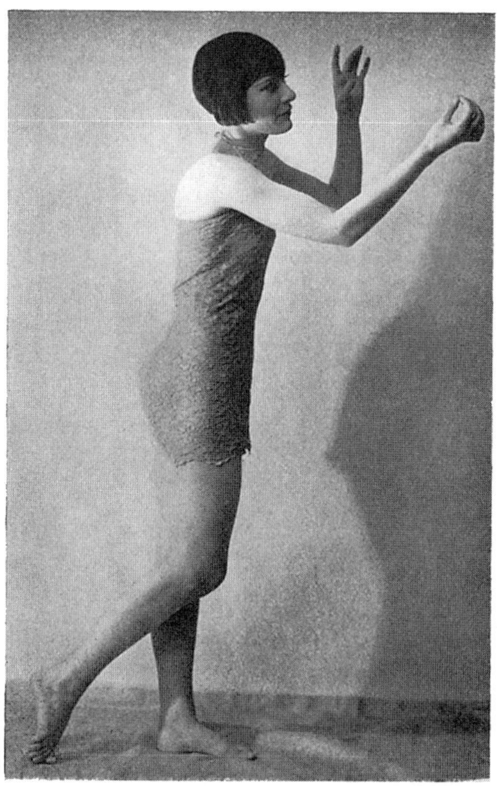

(*b*)

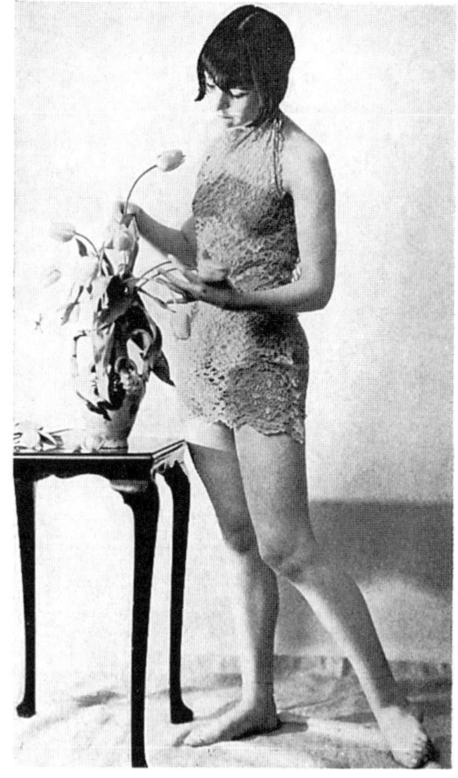

(*c*)

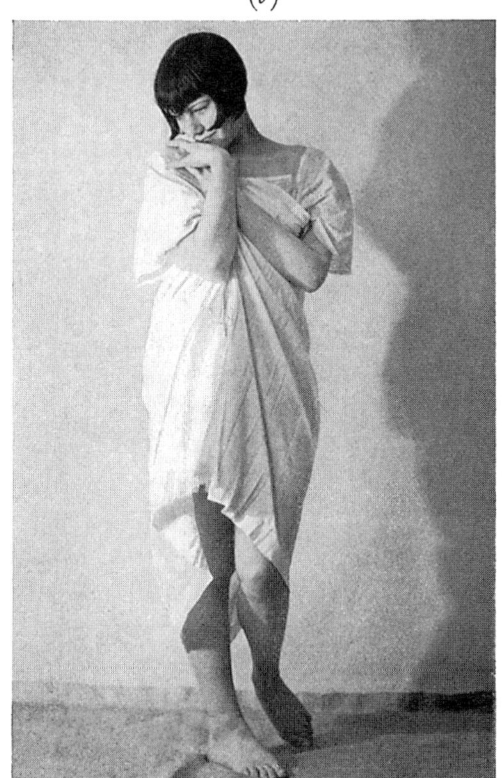

(*d*)

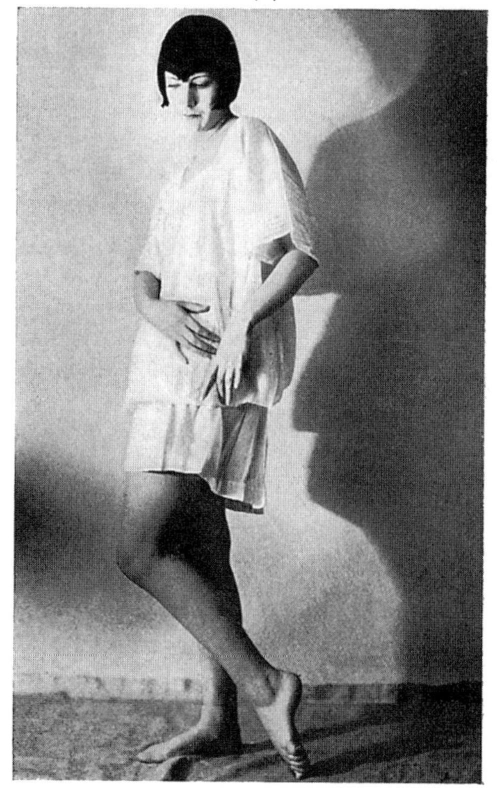

(*a*) Feeding a bird.
(*b*) Arranging flowers.
(*c*) A thoughtful attitude.
(*d*) Posing the hands.

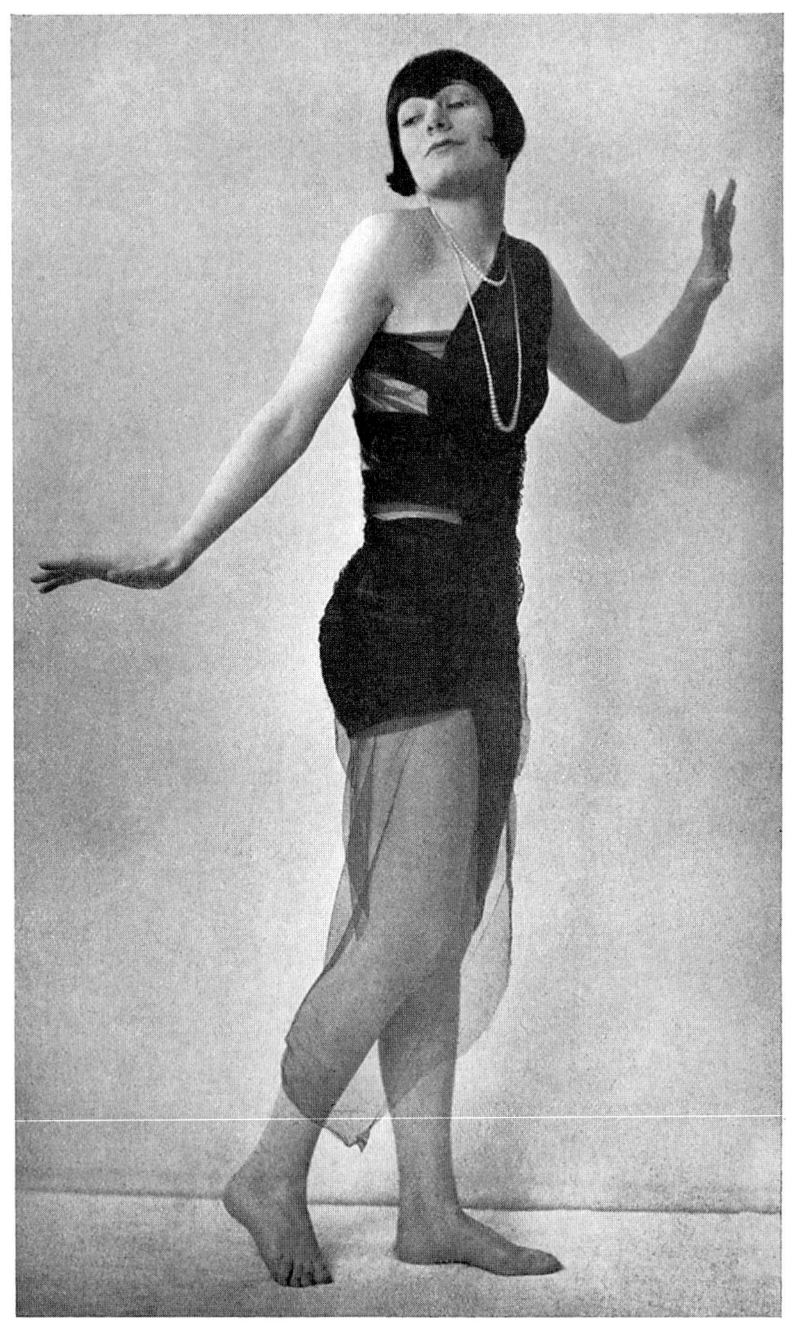

This should be found an excellent pose of the body for displaying a beautiful dress.

(*a*)

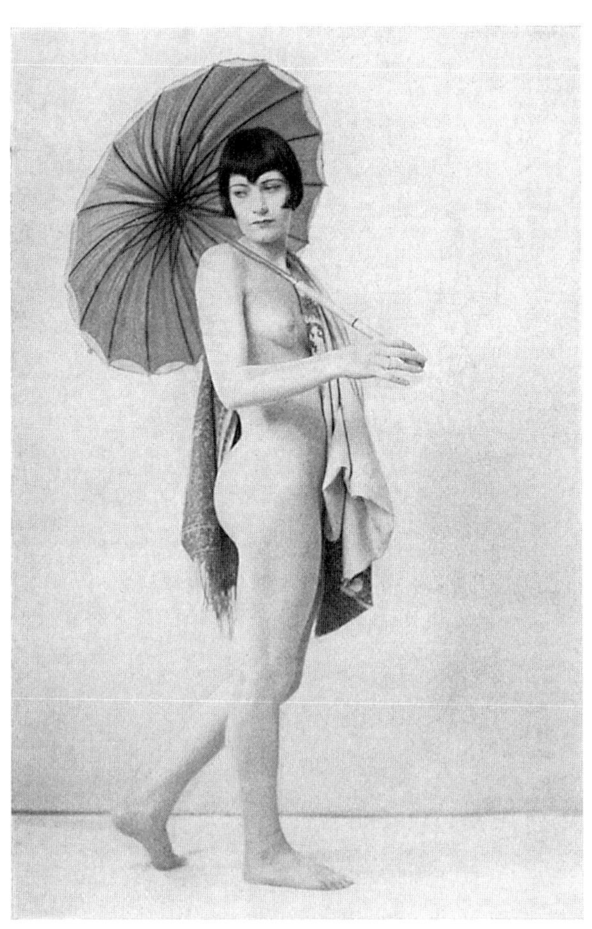

(*b*)

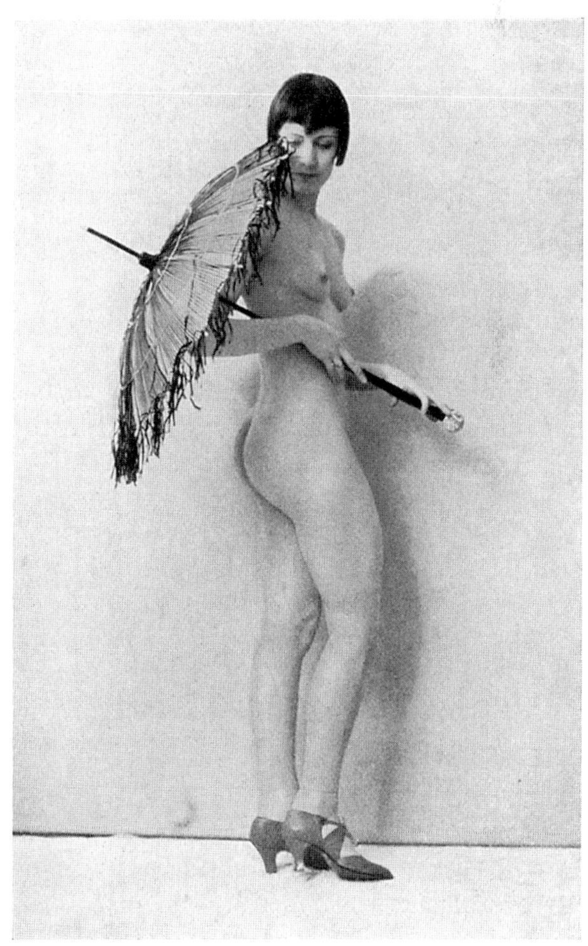

(*a*) A graceful Walking Pose.

(*b*) Light and Shadow.

Two suggestions for displaying a beautiful sunshade.

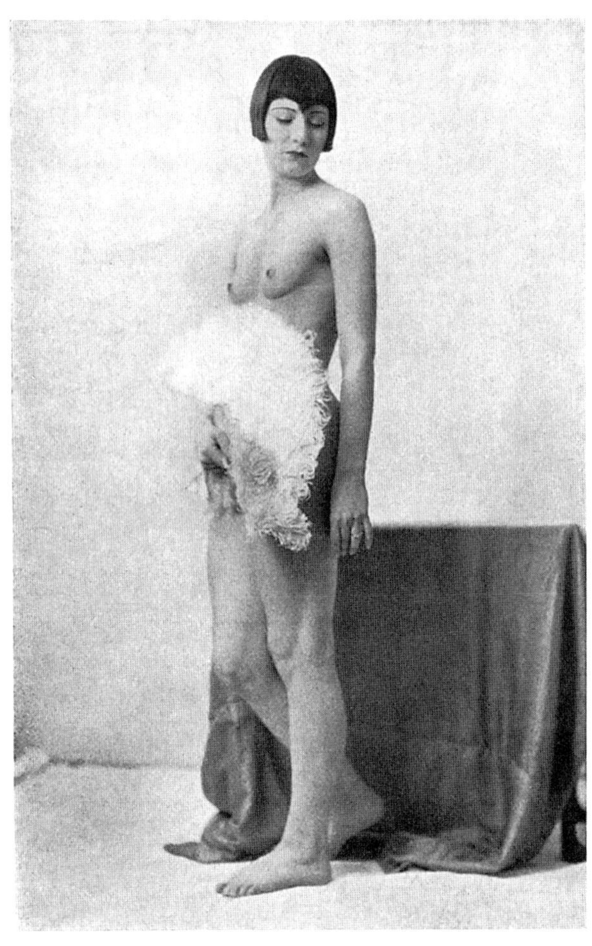

Two interesting and dignified poses with a Feather Fan, excellent suggestions for the portraitist or commercial artist.

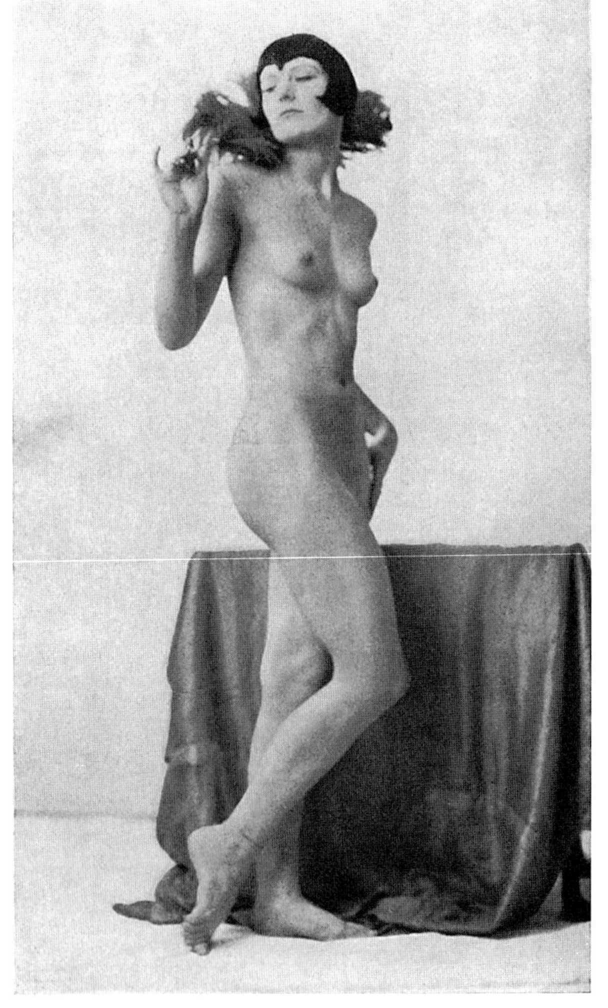

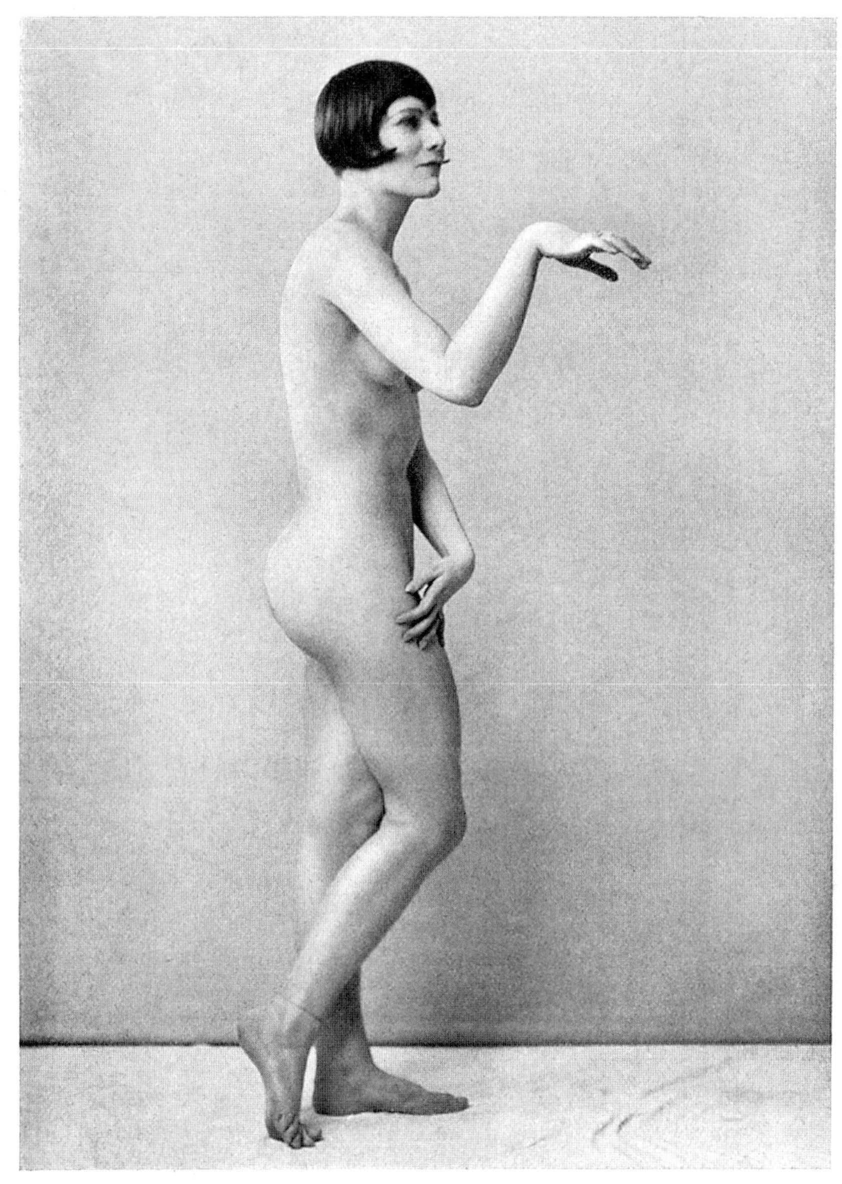

An attitude reminiscent of Greek sculpture.

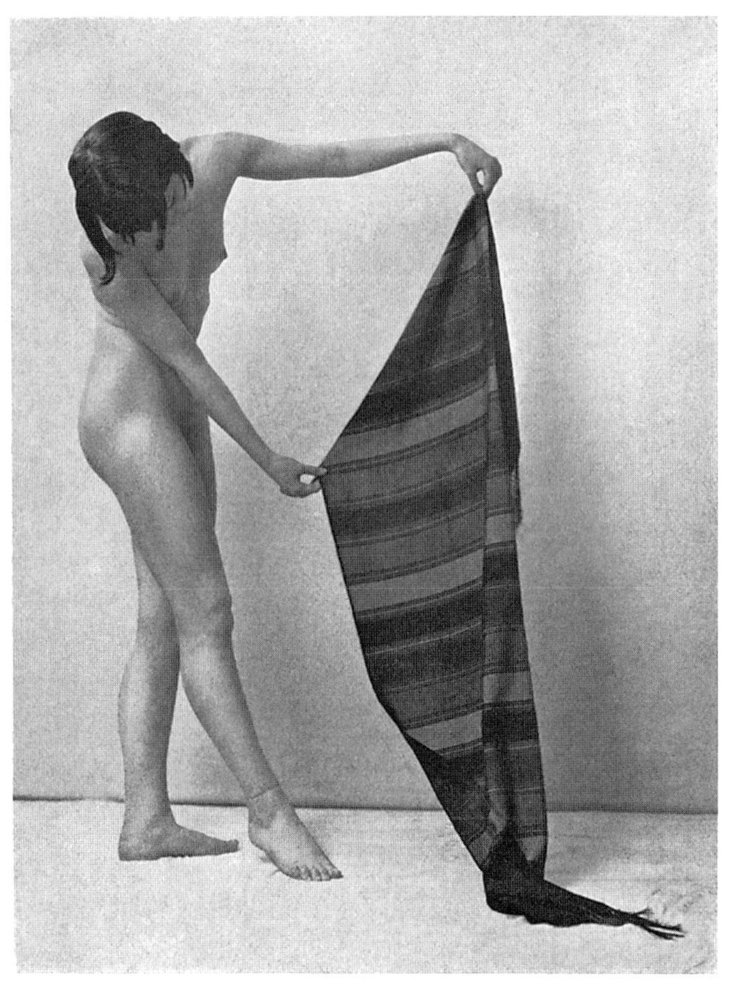

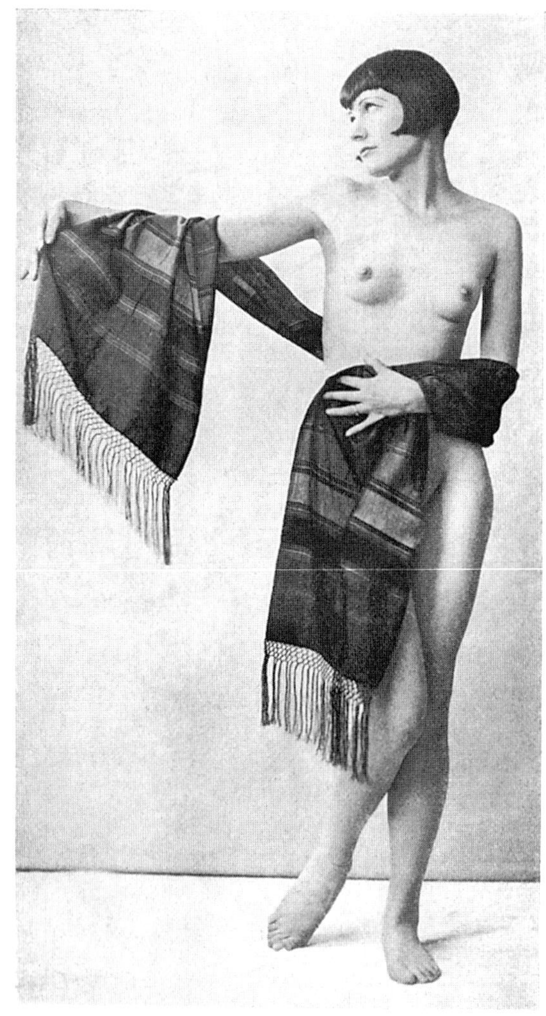

(*a*) Displaying the scarf.

(*b*) Wrapping it round.

Easily adaptable suggestions for displaying a beautiful scarf.

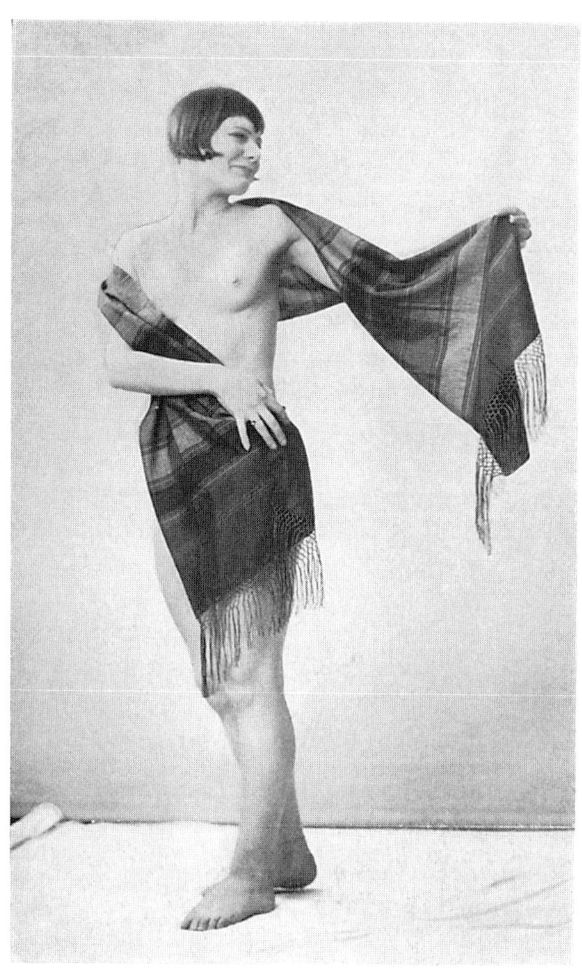

Two more suggestions for displaying the scarf. Both pictures are interesting anatomical studies.

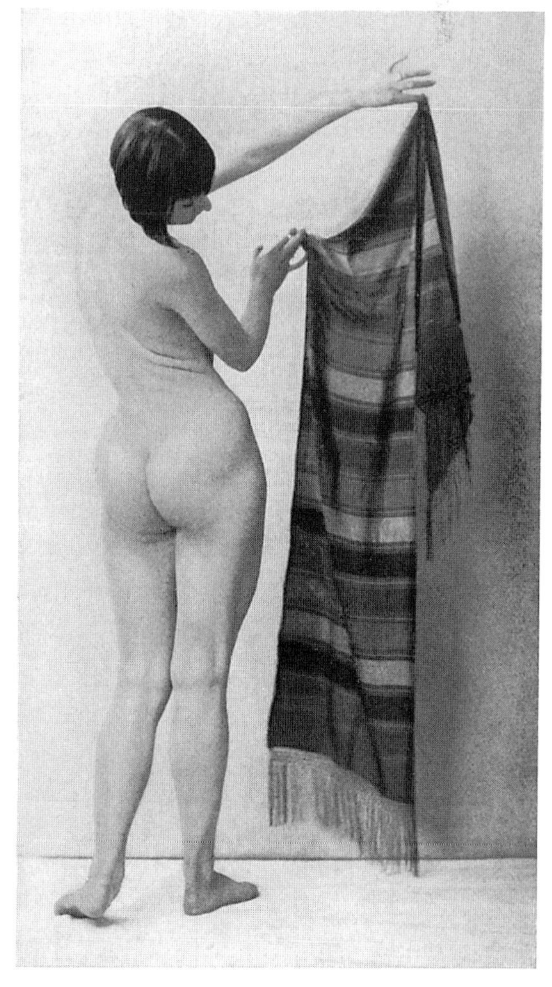

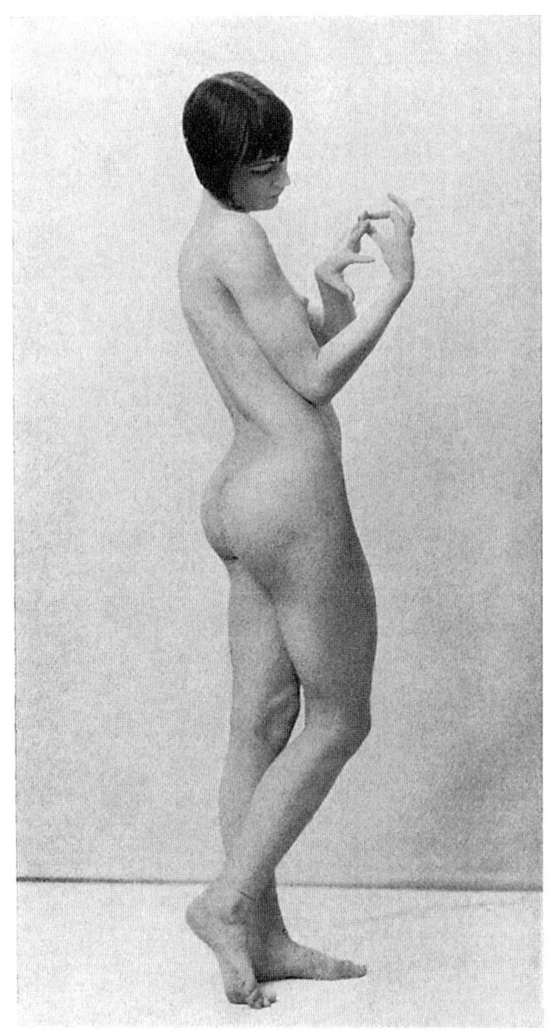

Another pose reminiscent of antique sculpture, shown from two angles.

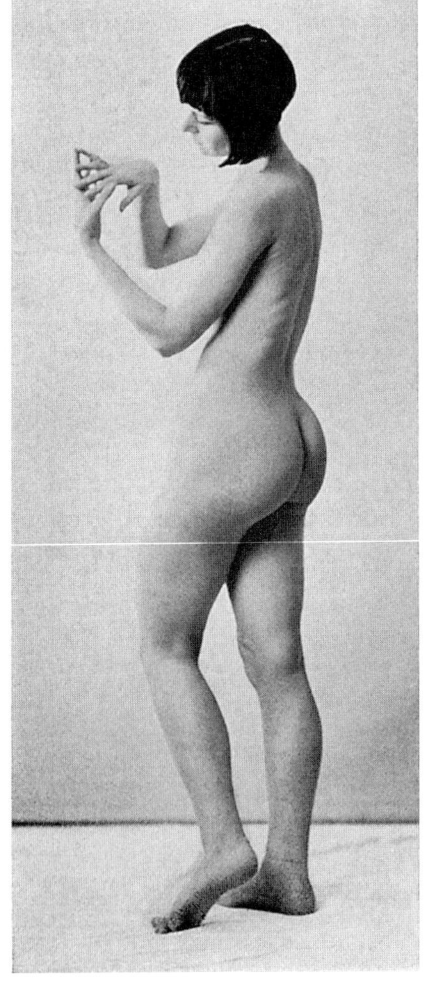

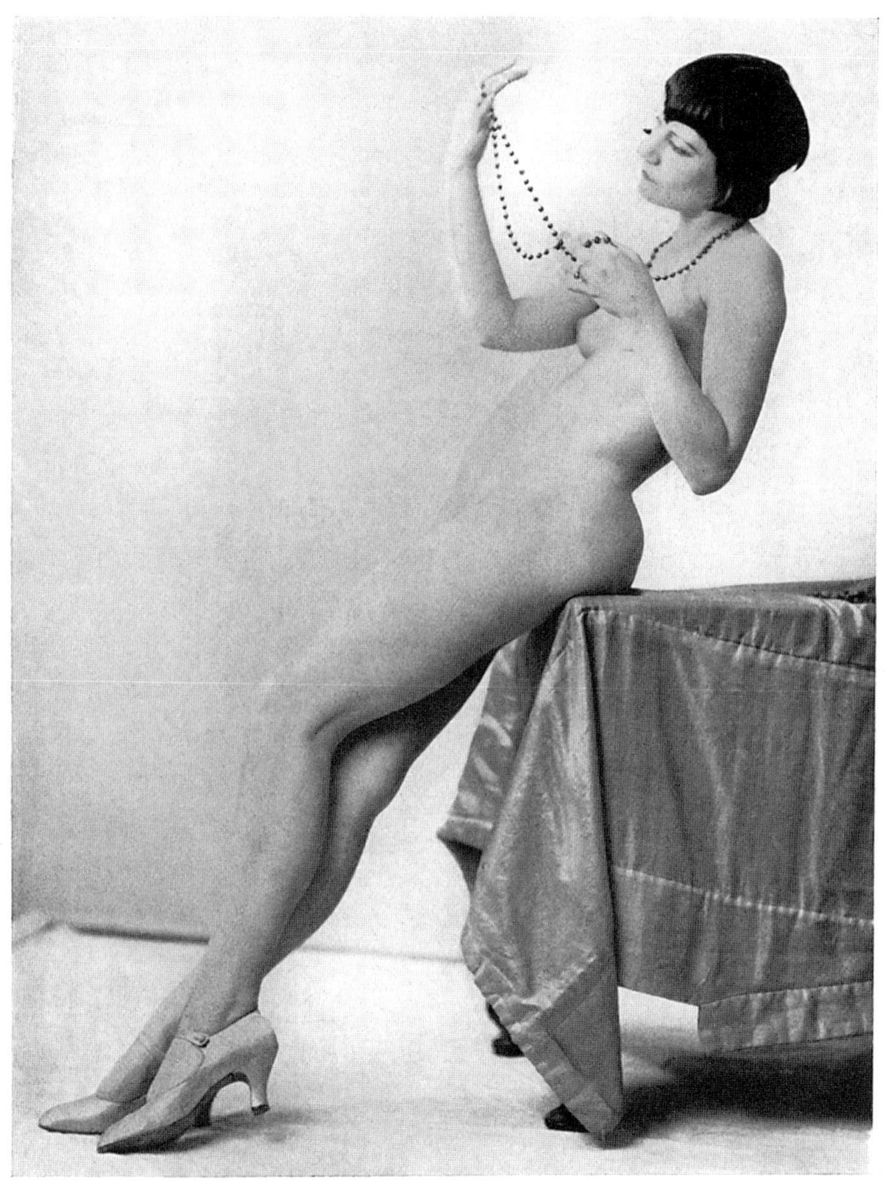

Admiring the necklace.
An easy natural attitude of much charm and interest.

(*a*)

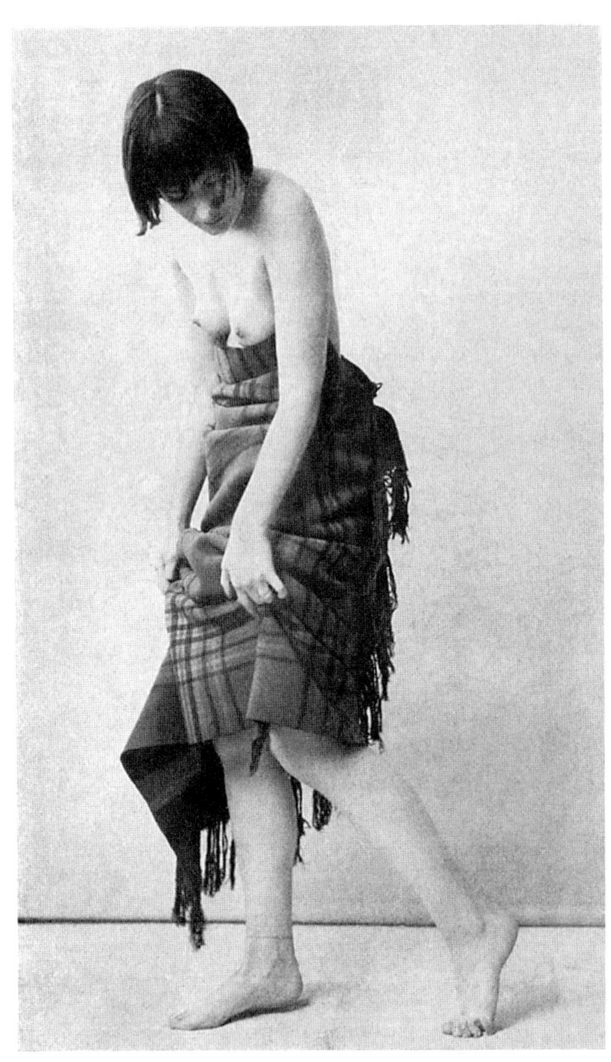

(*b*)

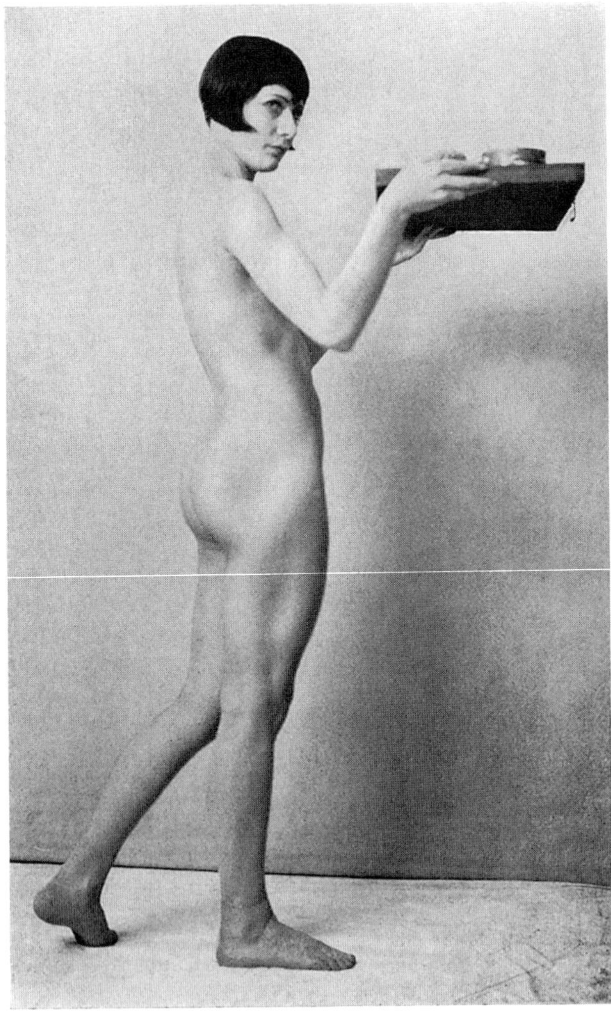

(*a*) Wading in shallow waters.

(*b*) Bringing in the tray.

Two graceful action poses which could be very usefully adapted.

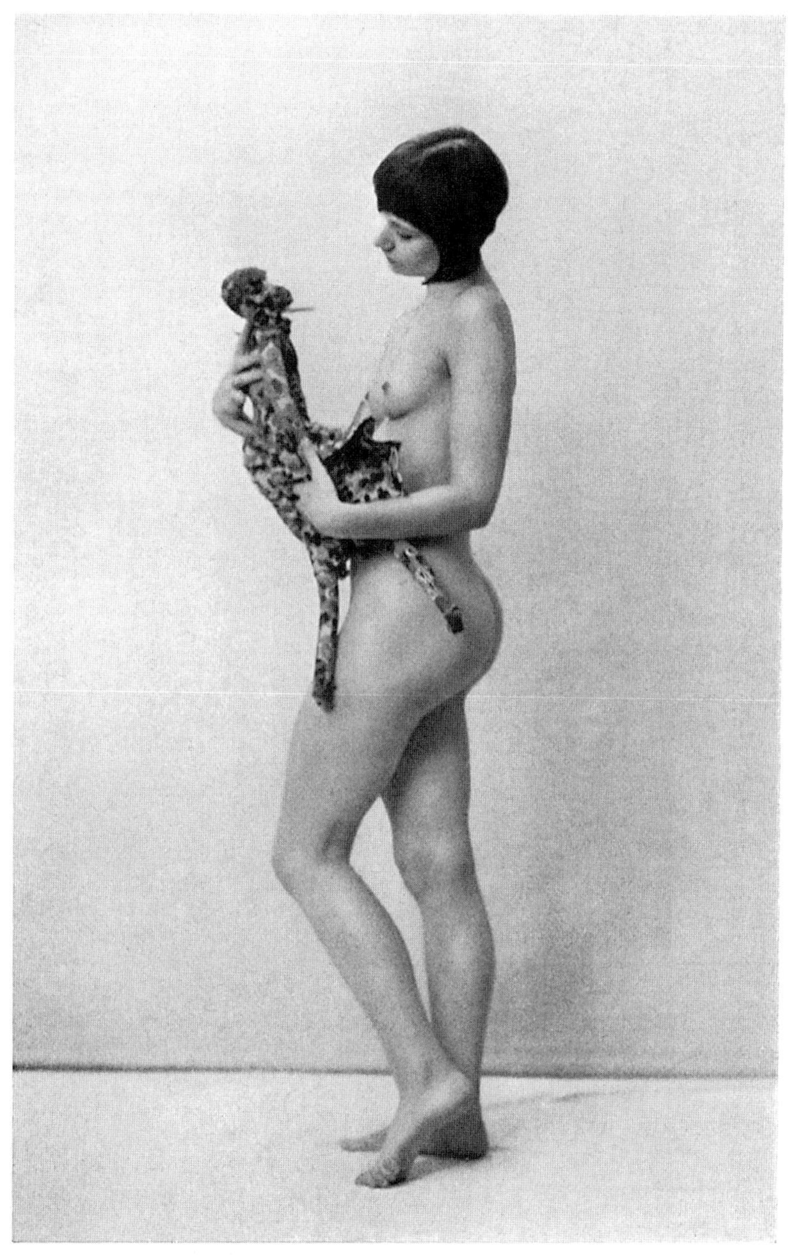

A charming pose, with an amusing doll.

(*a*)

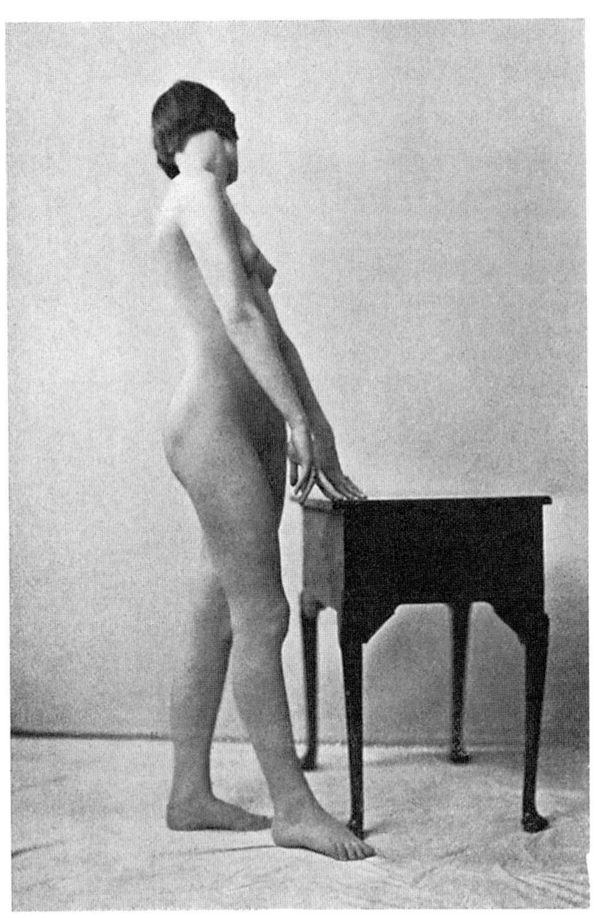

Two interesting poses in which the table plays an important part.

(*b*)

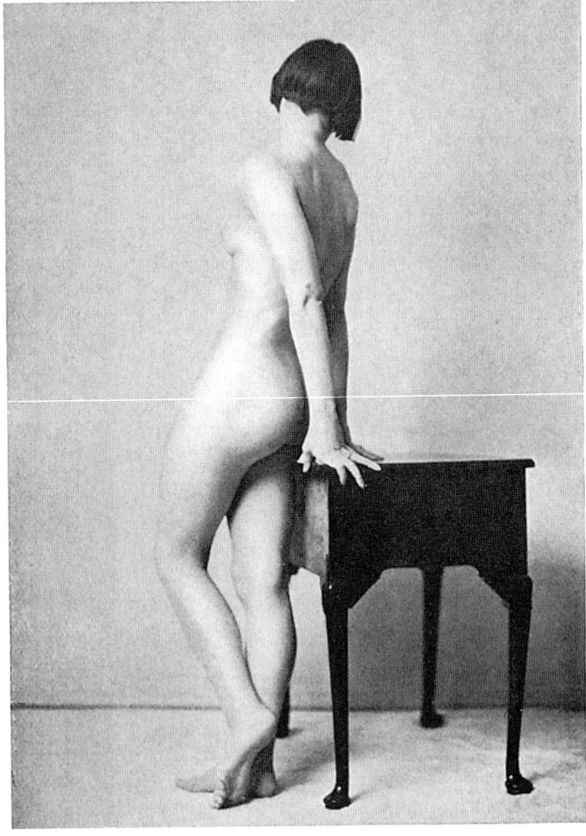

(*a*)

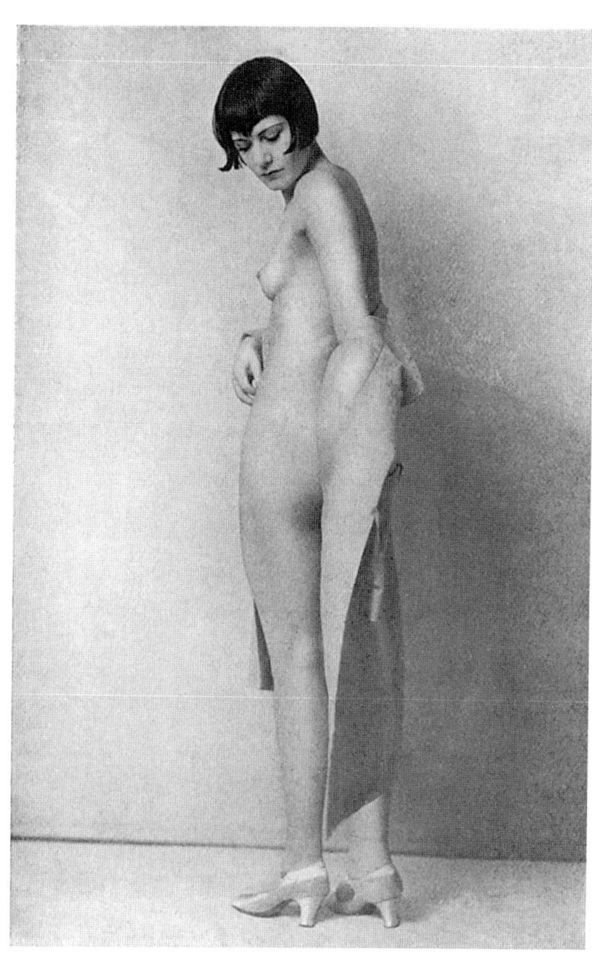

(*a*) Slipping off a coat.

(*b*) Examining a new frock.

Suggestions for fashion drawing or dress advertisement.

(*b*)

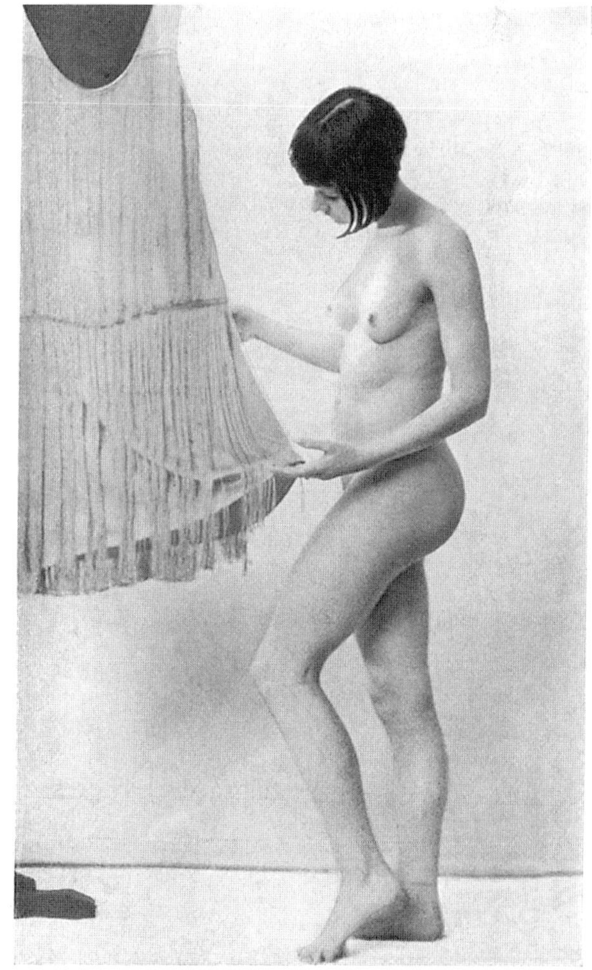

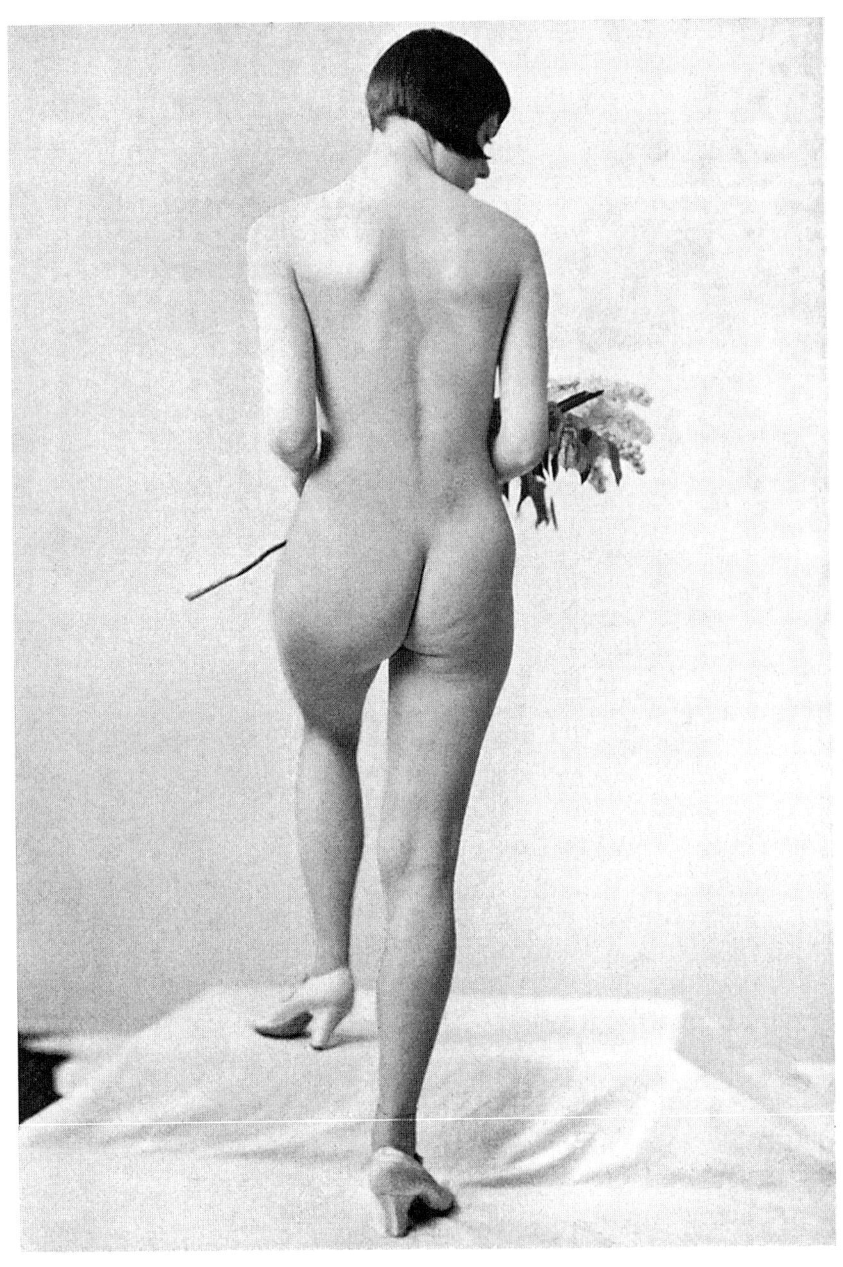

A graceful interesting study of much charm.

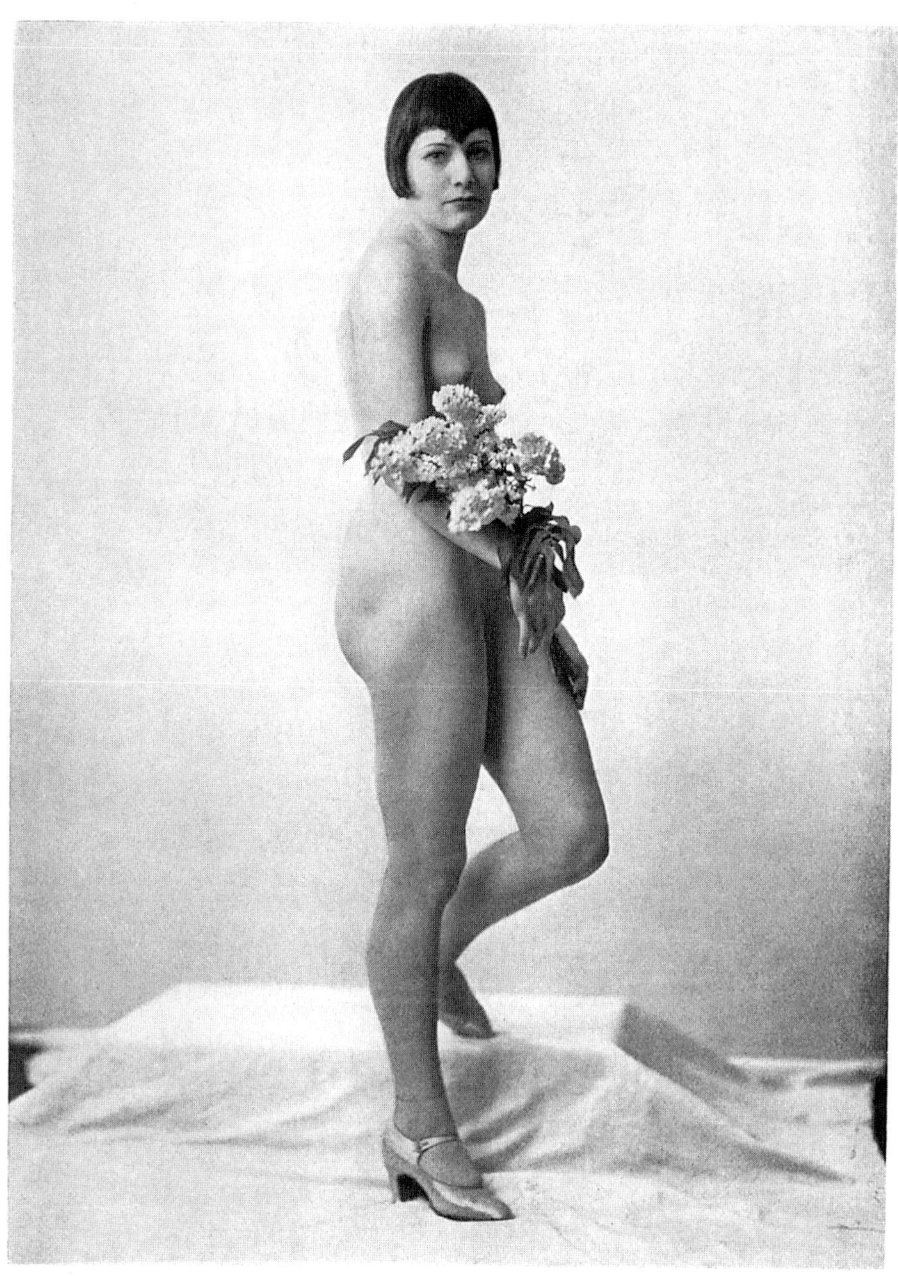

A charming study which should interest the portraitist. The flowers play an important part in the general scheme of composition.

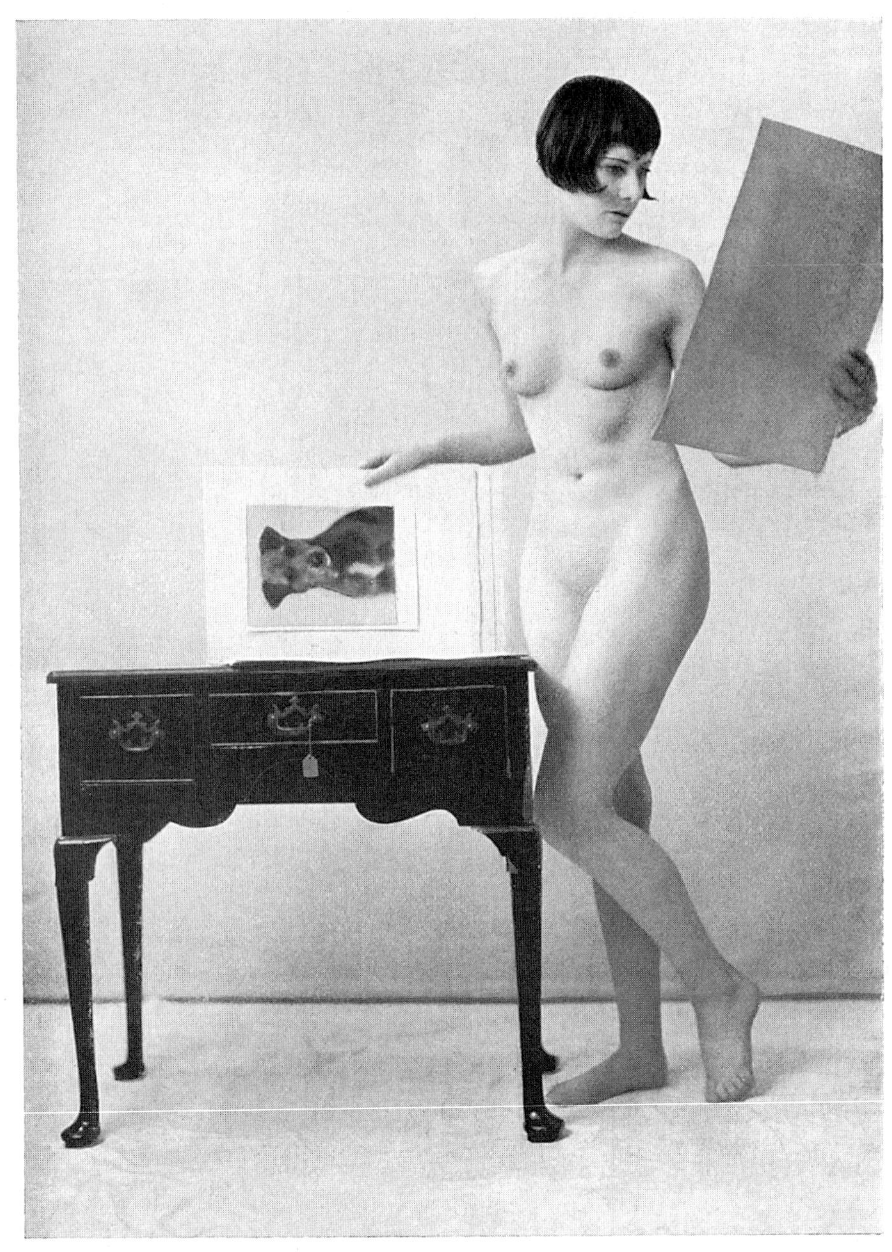

A natural attitude of much ease and grace.

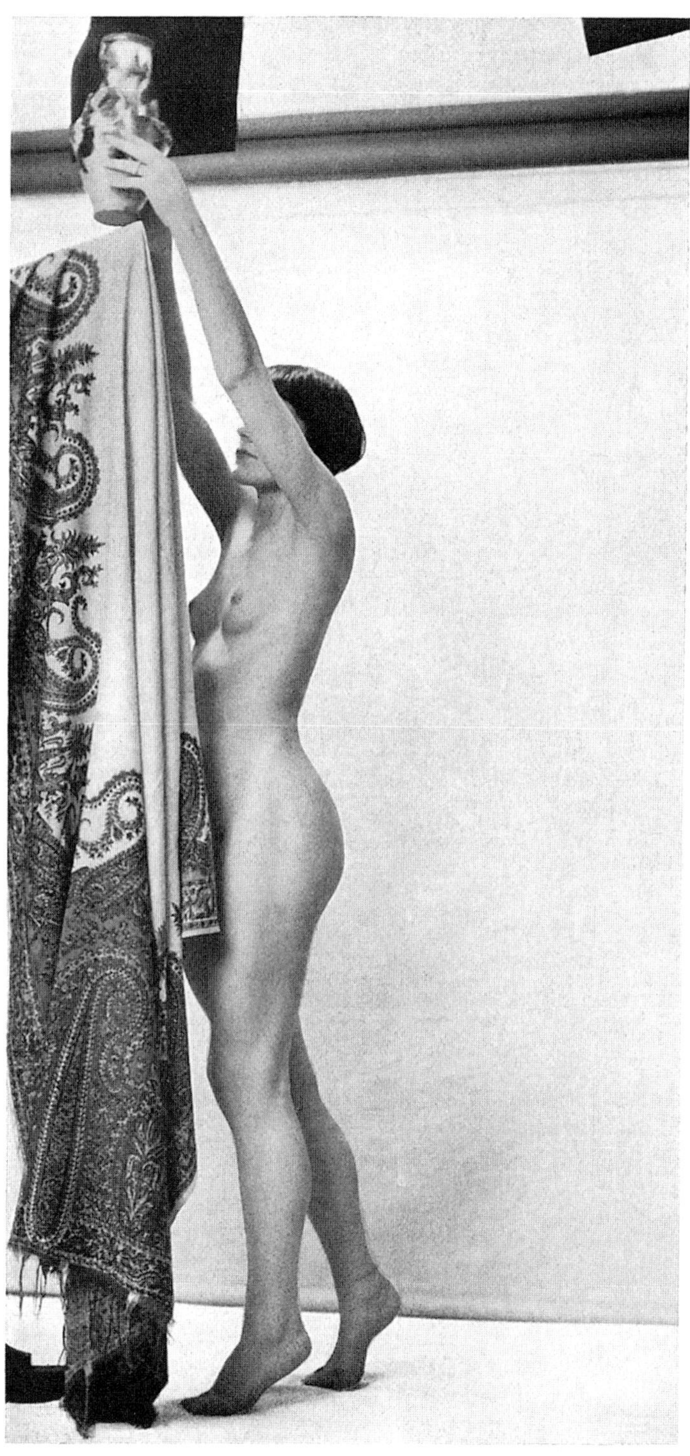

Note the tense line of the body contrasted with the severe folds of the falling drapery.

(*a*)

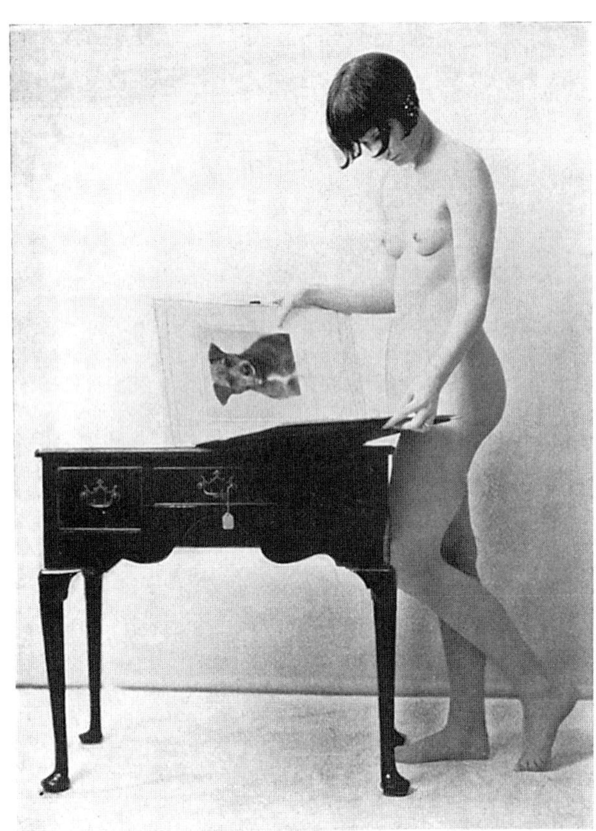

(*b*)

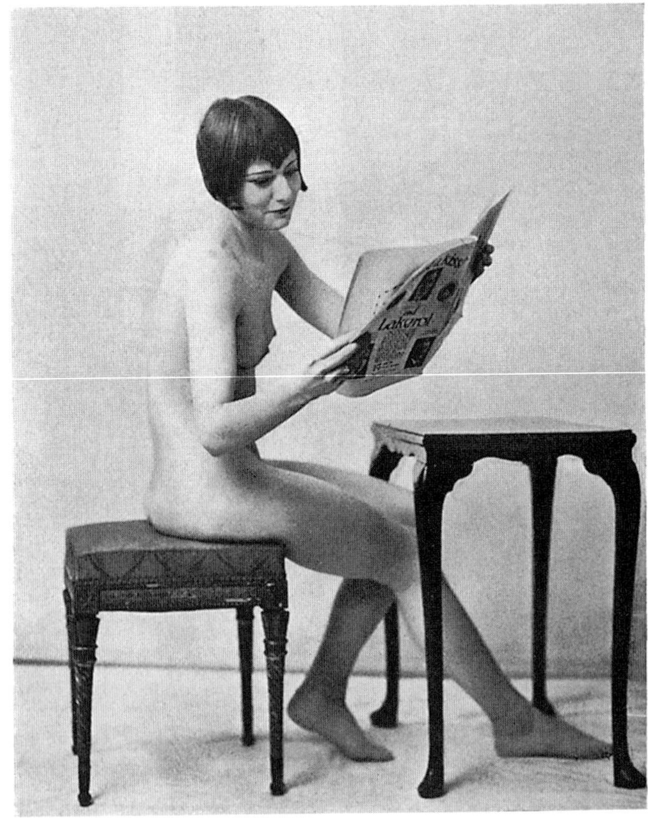

(*a*) Looking at pictures.

(*b*) Glancing through a magazine.

These two pictures suggest respectively contemplative interest and passing amusement.

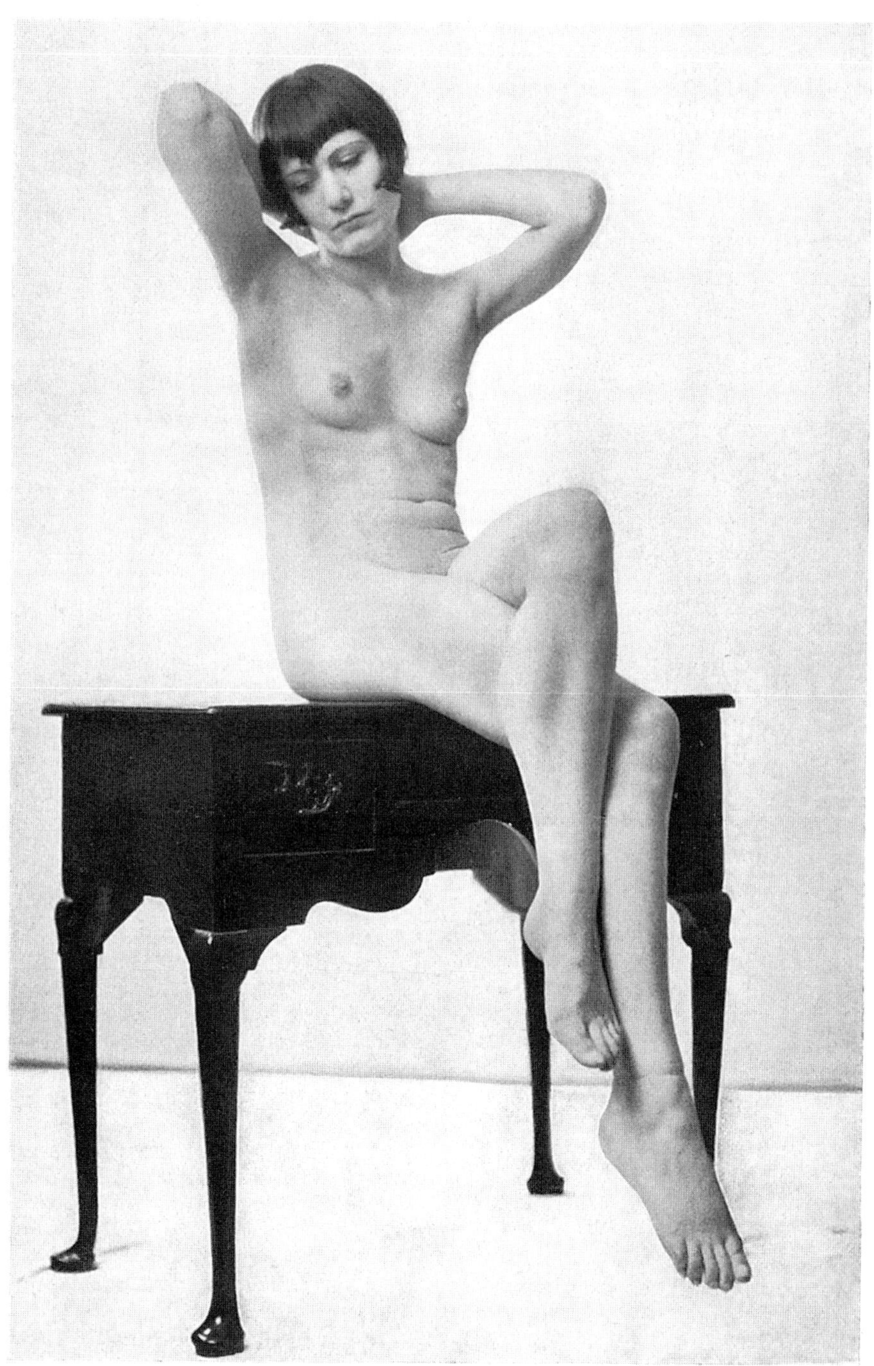

A sitting study that suggests contemplative relaxation. The body is perfectly poised and balanced, yet the whole effect is easy and natural.

(*a*)

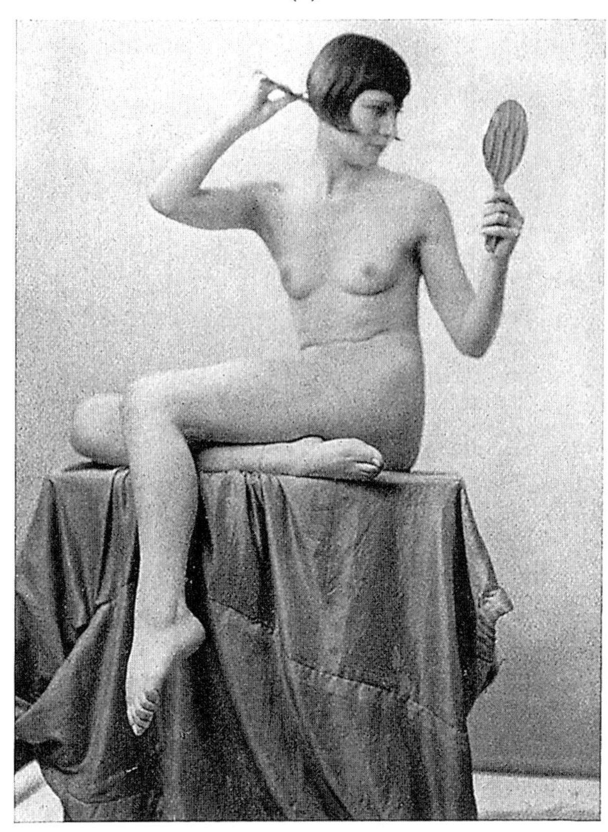

(*b*)

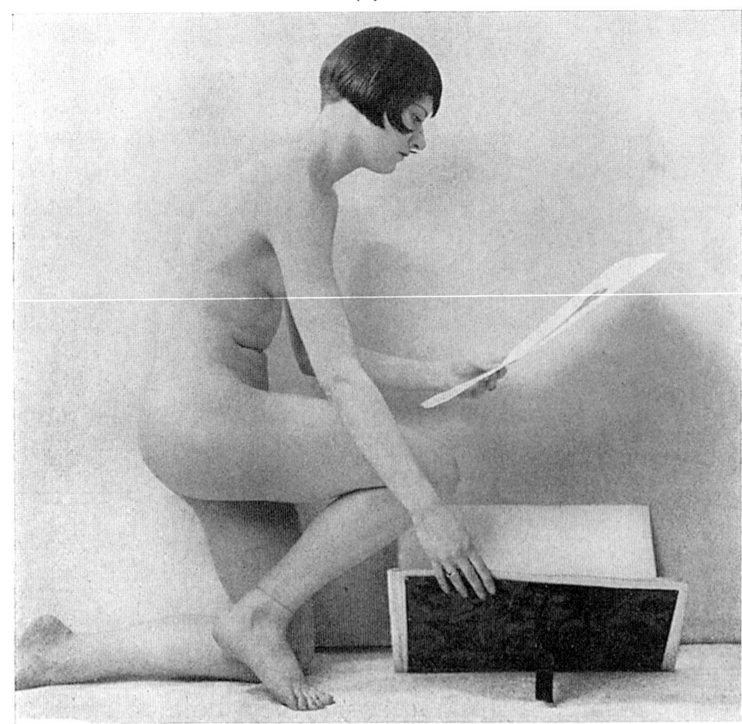

(*a*) At the mirror. (*b*) Glancing through pictures.

(*a*)

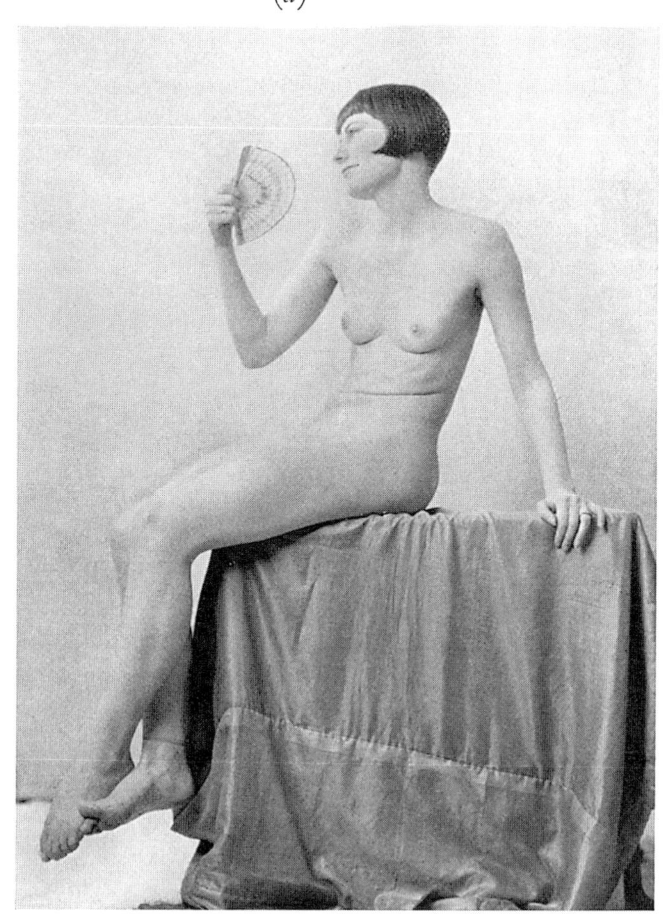

(*b*)

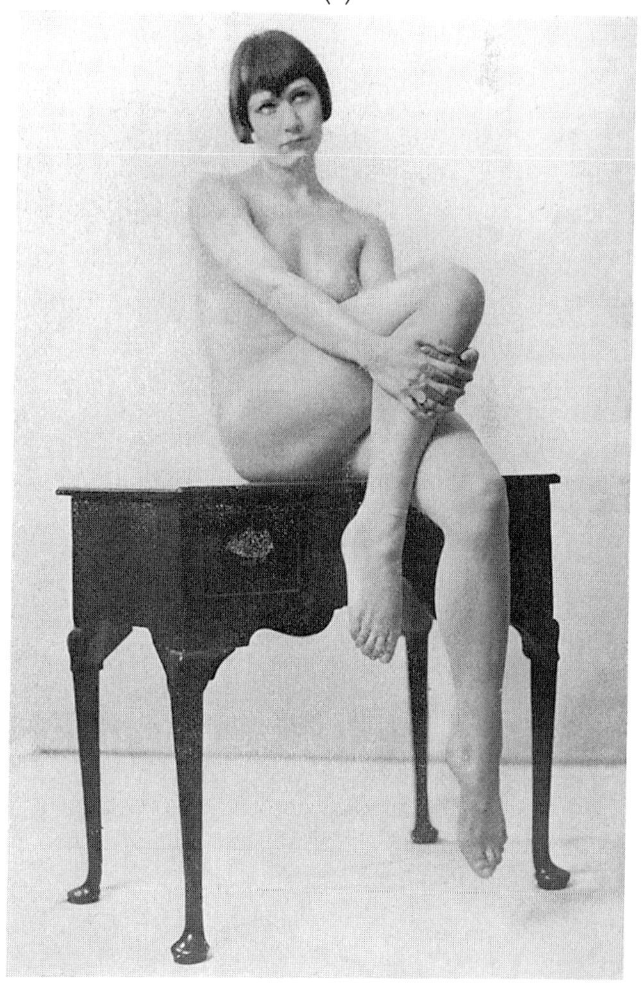

(*a*) The small fan.

(*b*) Contemplation.

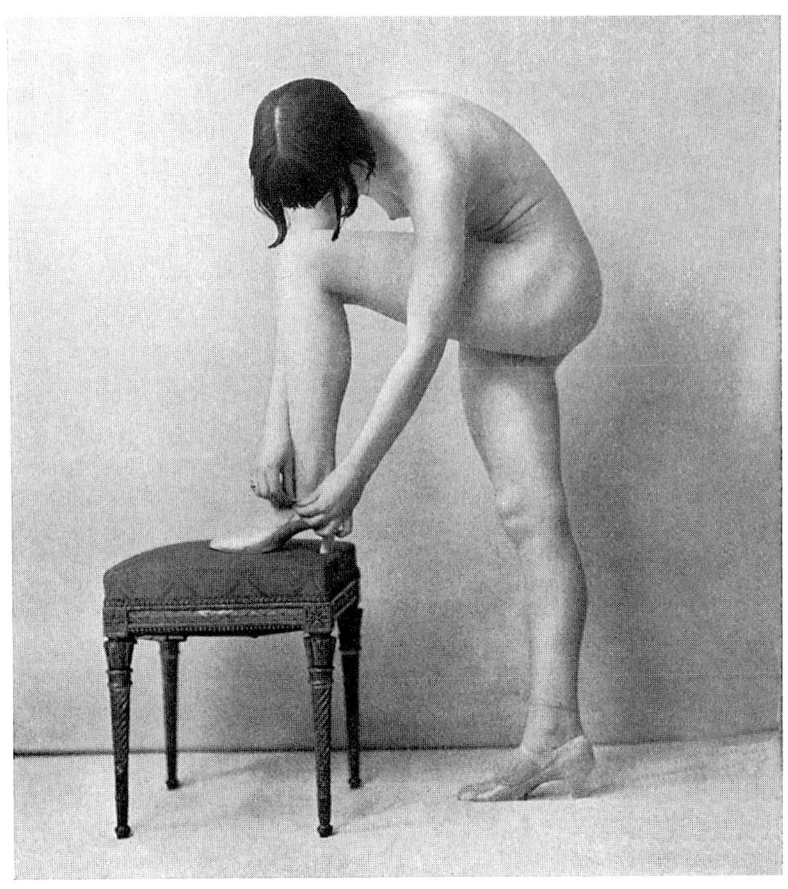

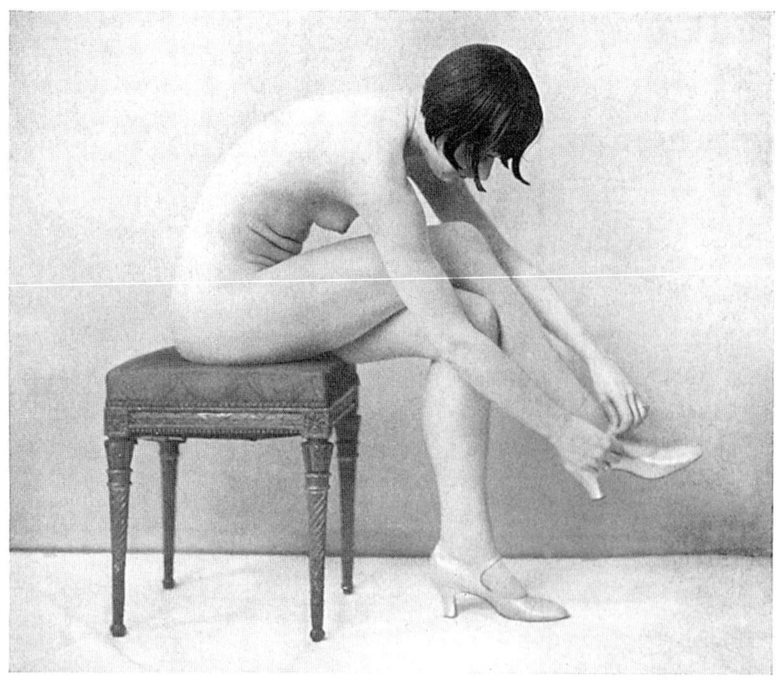

Two methods of fastening a shoe, each forming an interesting natural composition.

HANDS AND GLOVES

(*pages* 140 *to* 146)

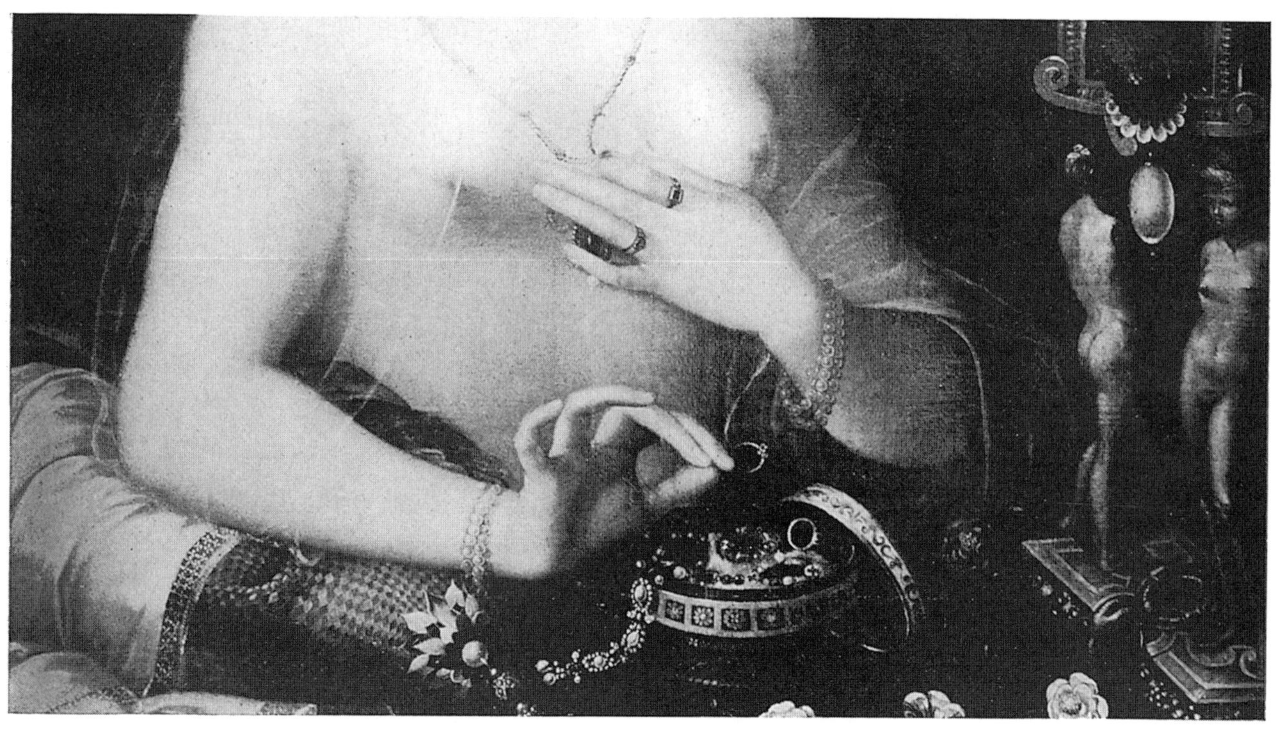

WITH SOME ENLARGED ANATOMICAL DETAILS FROM THE STANDARD POSES

(*pages* 148 *to* 152)

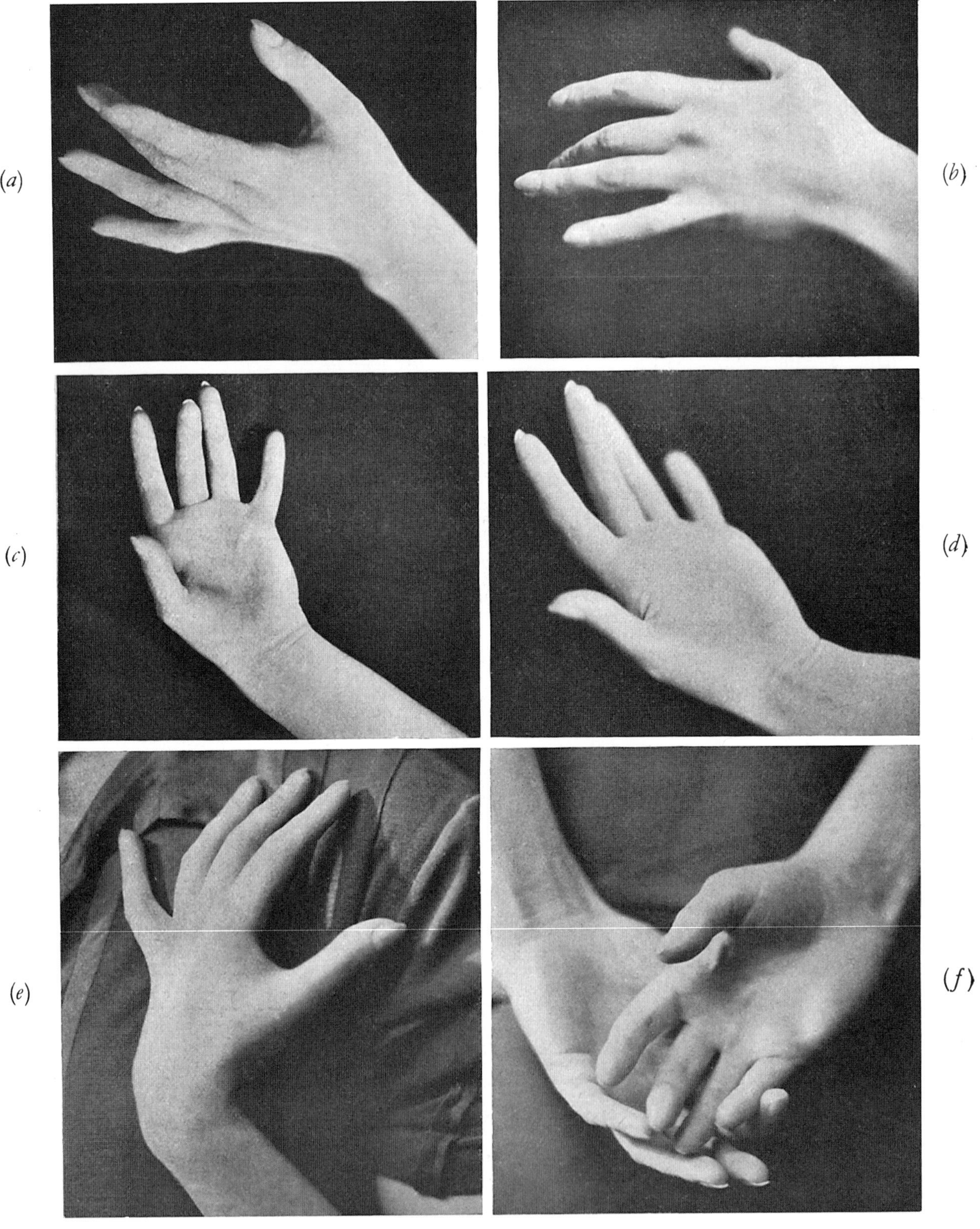

(*a*) The raised hand, sinuous and beautiful. (*b*) A delicate, bird-like poise. (*c*) The delicate modelling of the palm. (*d*) The balance between thumb and fingers is well shown in this pose. (*e*) Note the curve flowing through the wrist to the finger-tips. (*f*) A light, open touch The hands are behind the figure.

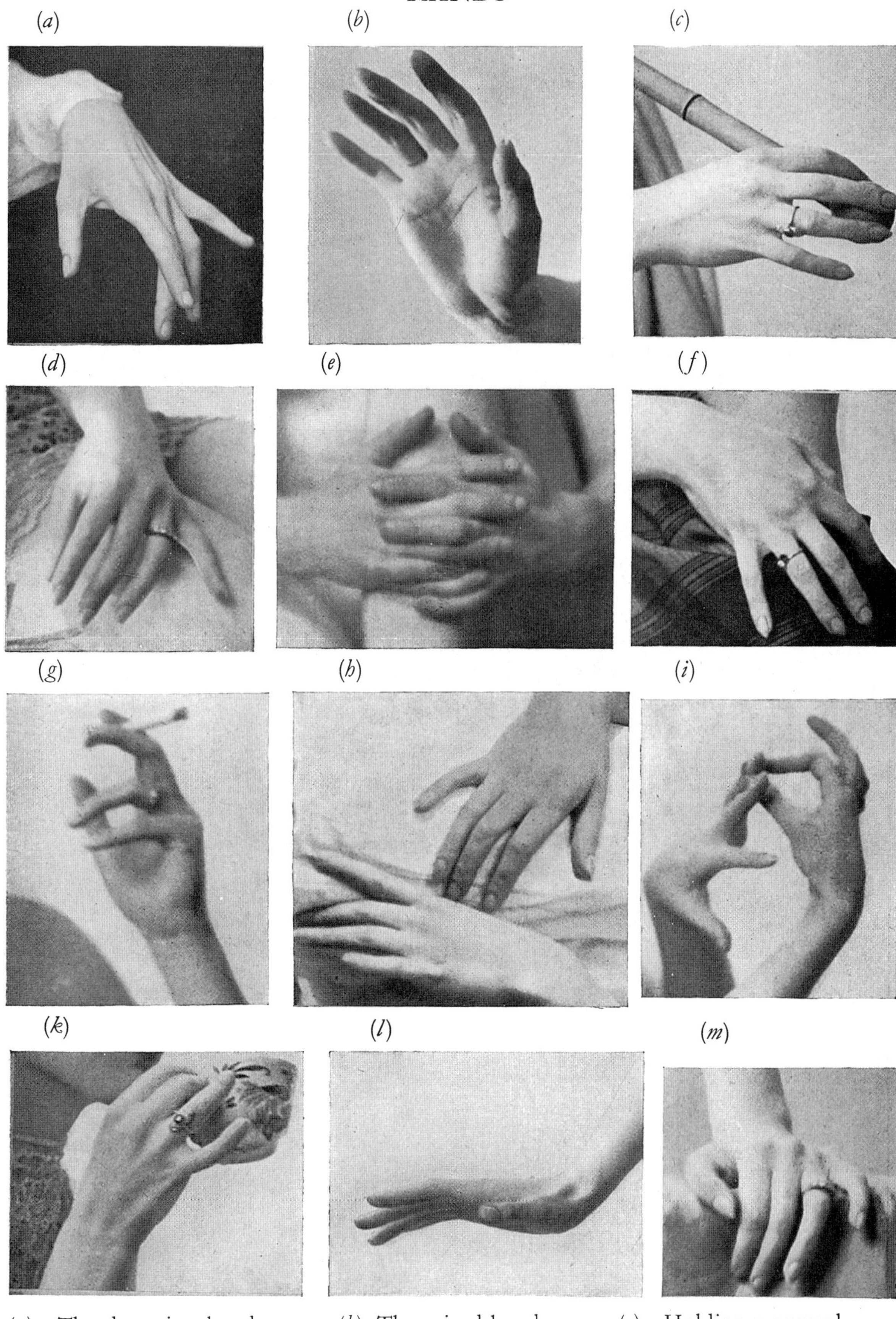

(*a*) The drooping hand. (*b*) The raised hand. (*c*) Holding a parasol.
(*d*) Resting on the thigh. (*e*) Clasping the knee. (*f*) Lightly holding a scarf.
(*g*) Holding a cigarette. (*h*) An interesting pose. (*i*) Slipping on a ring.
(*k*) Holding a cup to drink. (*l*) Half raised. (*m*) Resting on a ledge.

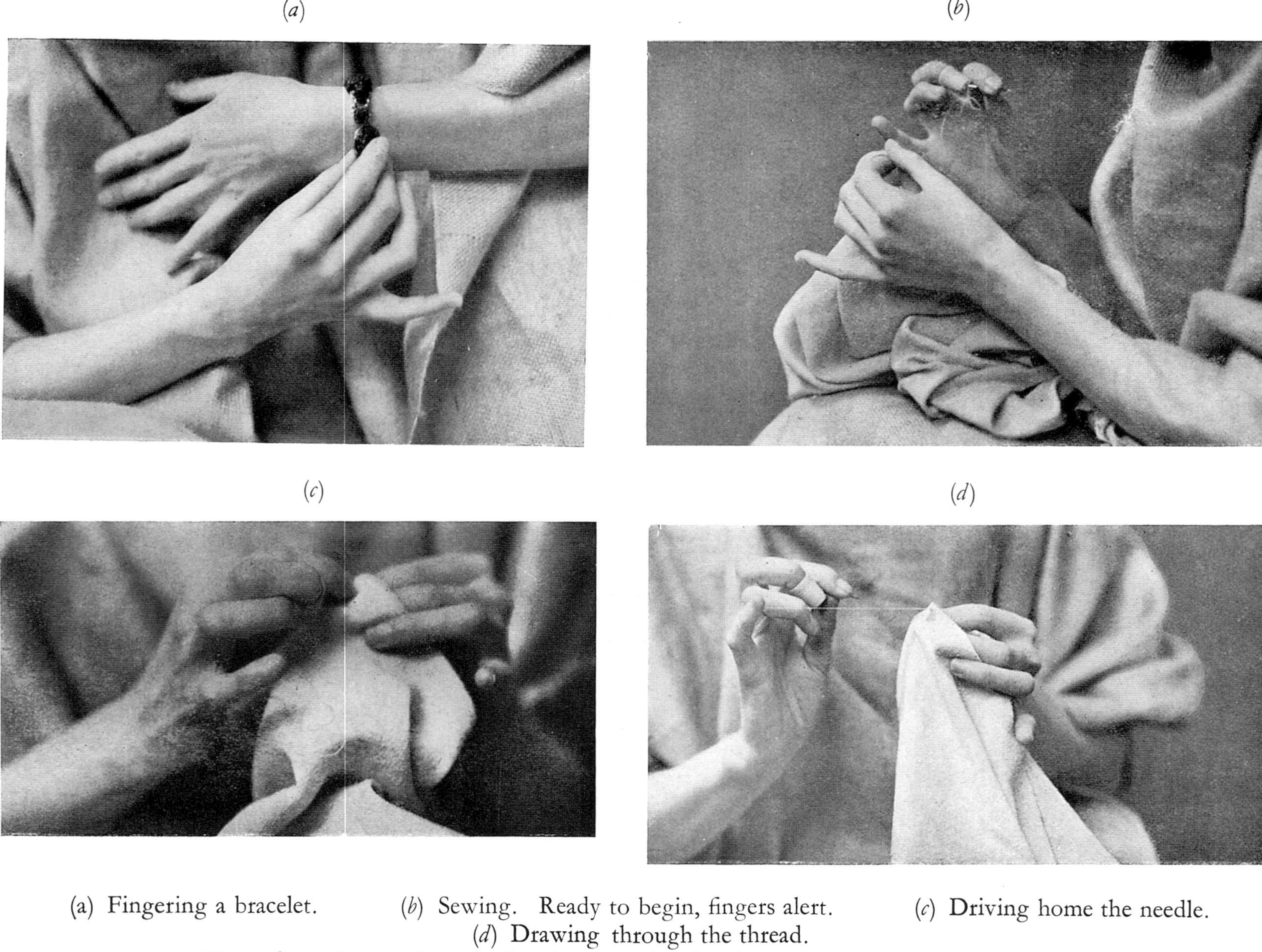

(a) Fingering a bracelet. (*b*) Sewing. Ready to begin, fingers alert. (*c*) Driving home the needle. (*d*) Drawing through the thread.

These four pictures show the hands "in action," wrists tense, fingers nimble and active.

(*a*)

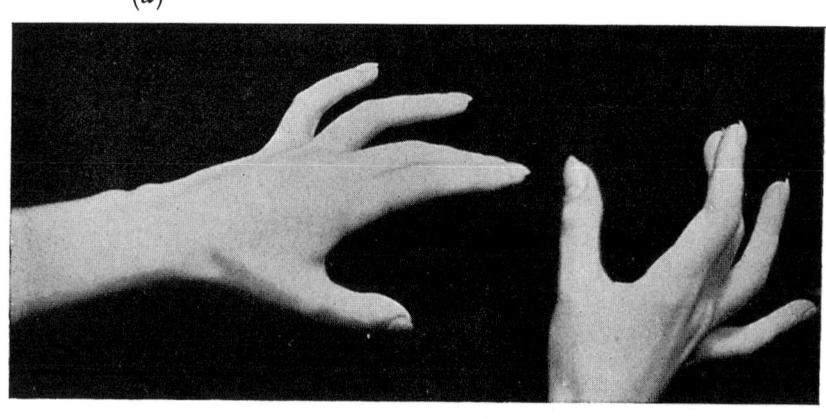

(*b*)

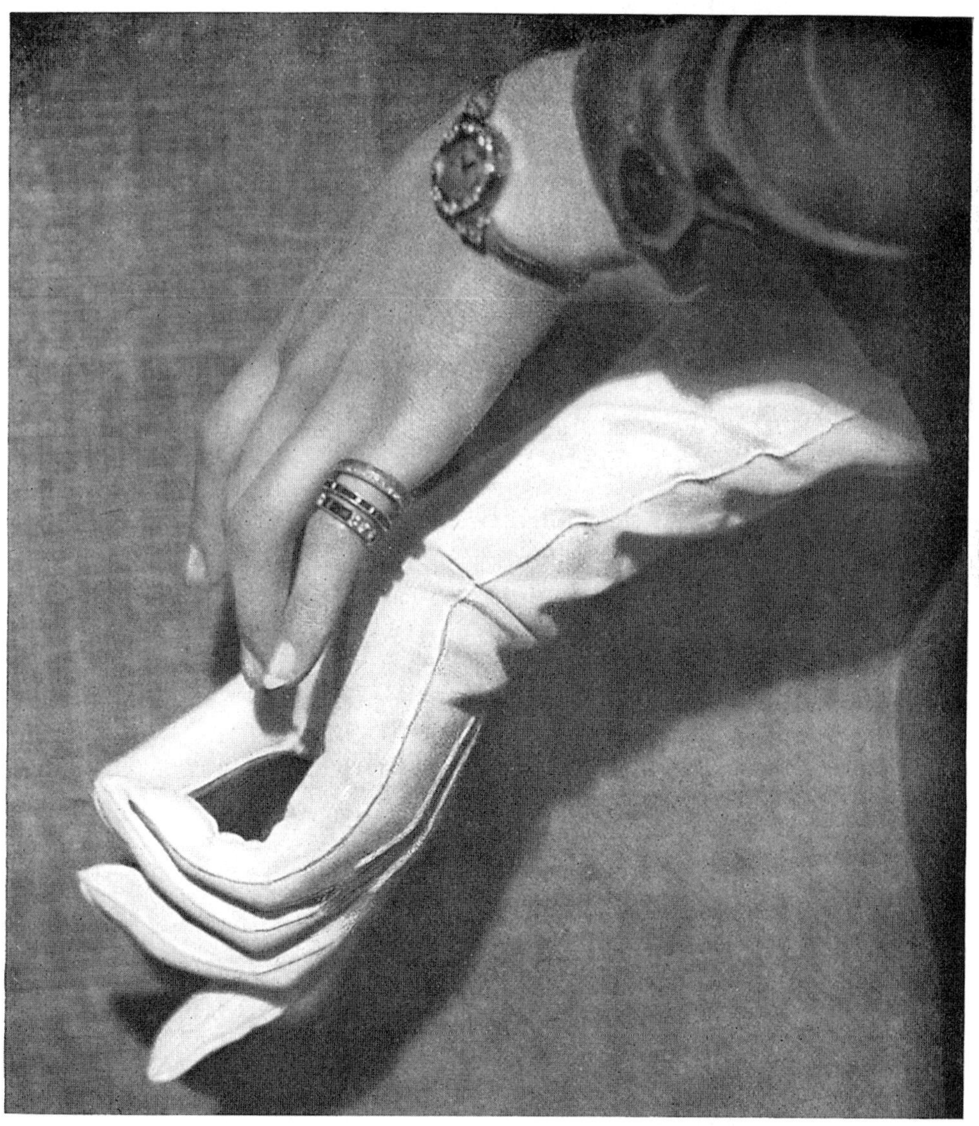

(*a*) Curved, shell-like hands. (*b*) Fitting on a glove. A beautiful composition which displays the shapely fingers with their loose rings to the fullest advantage against the elegantly gloved right hand.

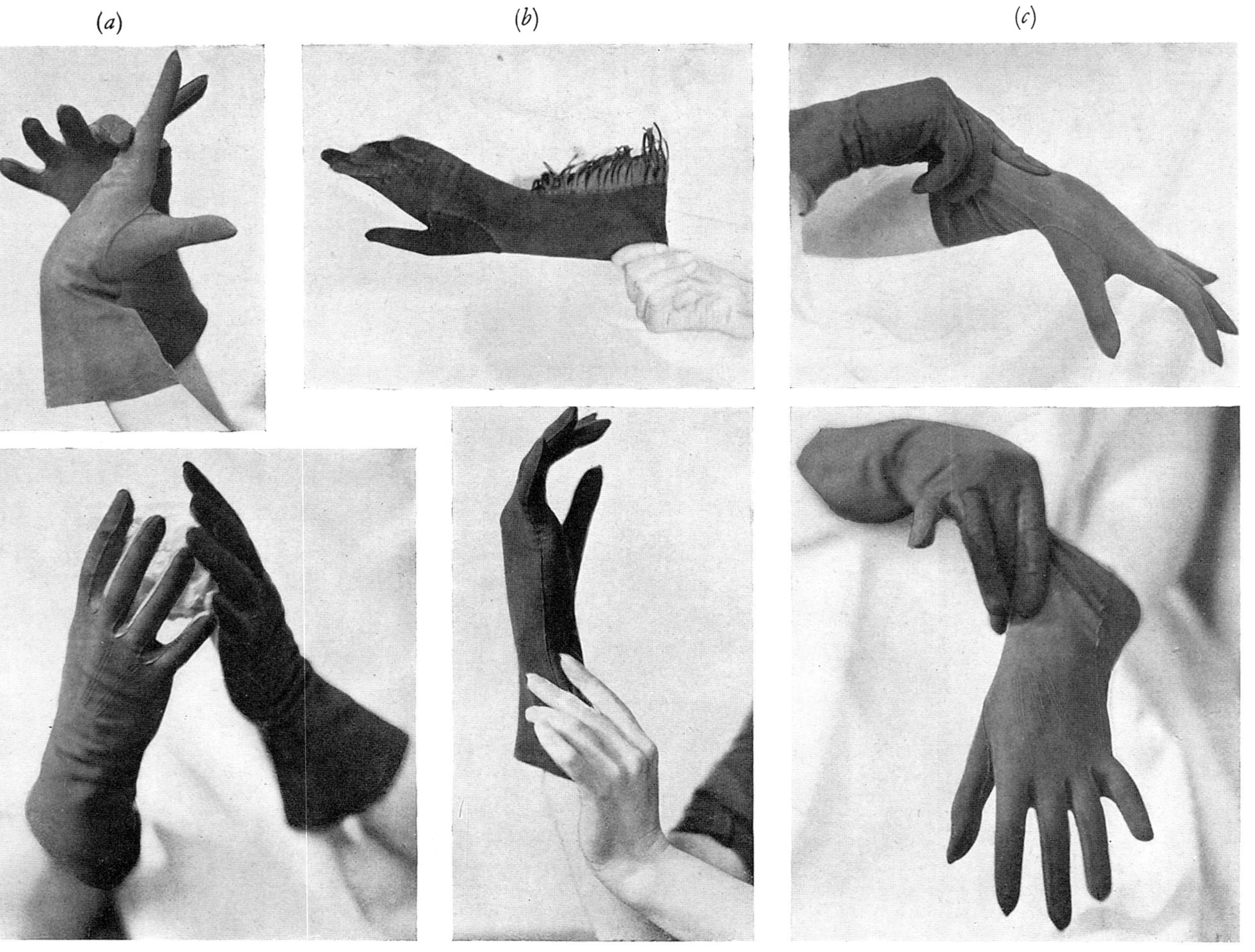

(*a*) Settling the fingers. (*b*) Pulling on the glove. (*c*) Second hand in. (*d*) Catch! (*e*) Settling the wrist. (*f*) The final tug.

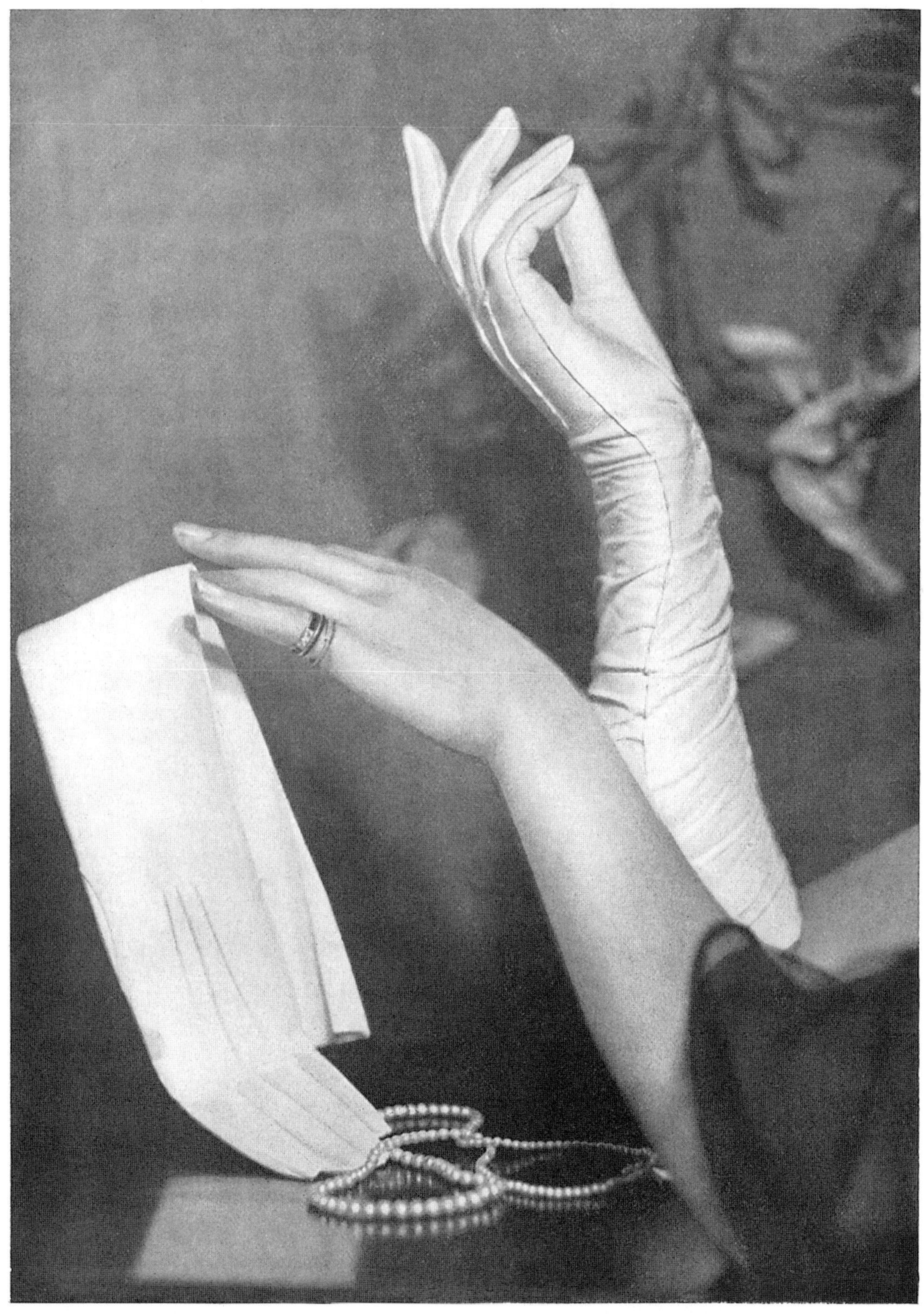

Beautiful hands displaying beautiful gloves.

(*a*) (*b*)

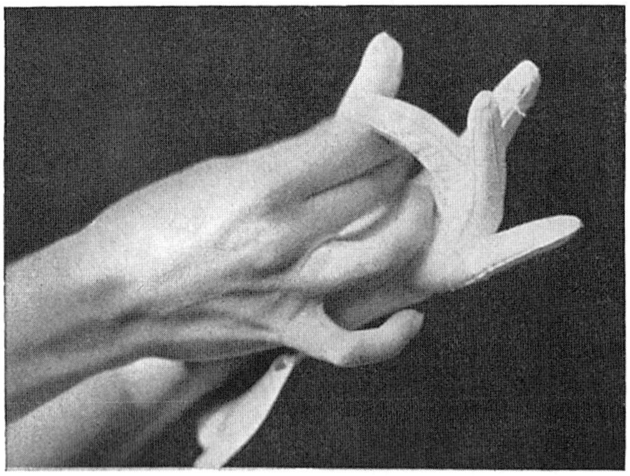

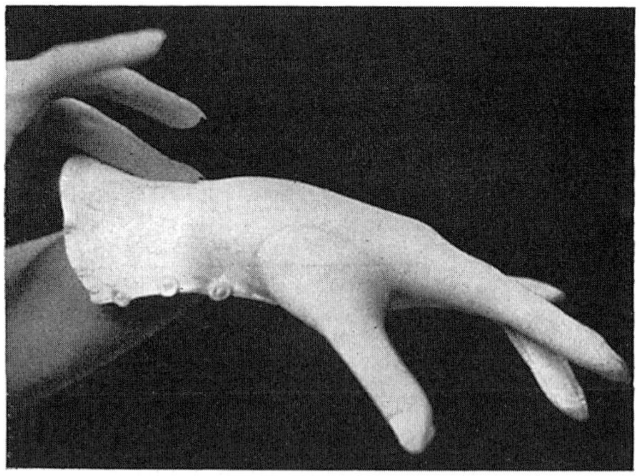

(*c*) 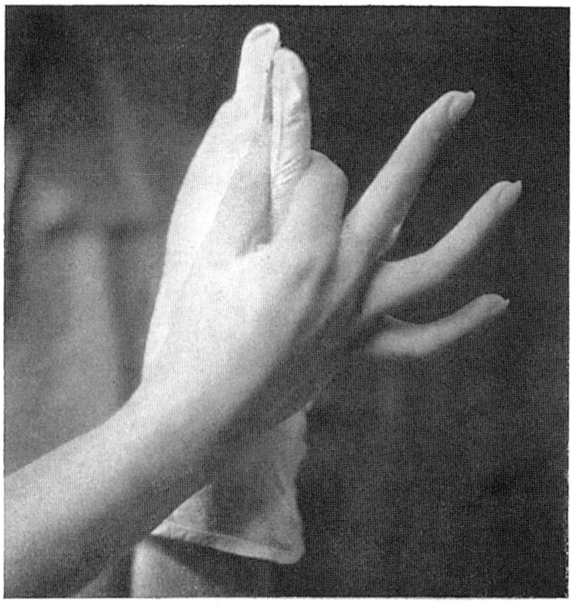 (*d*)

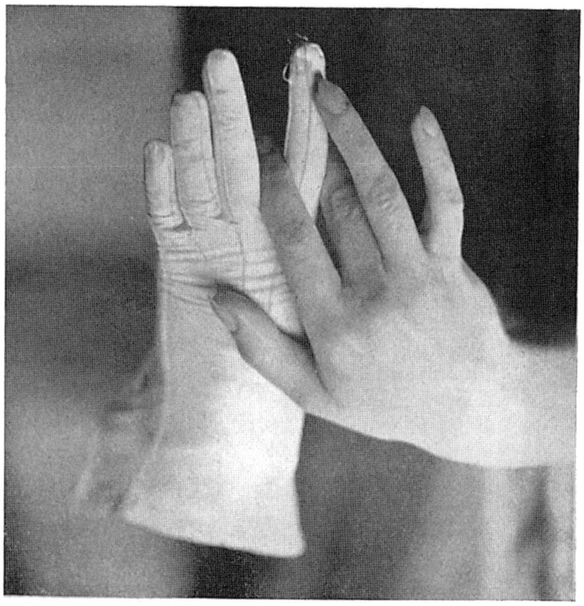

(*e*) 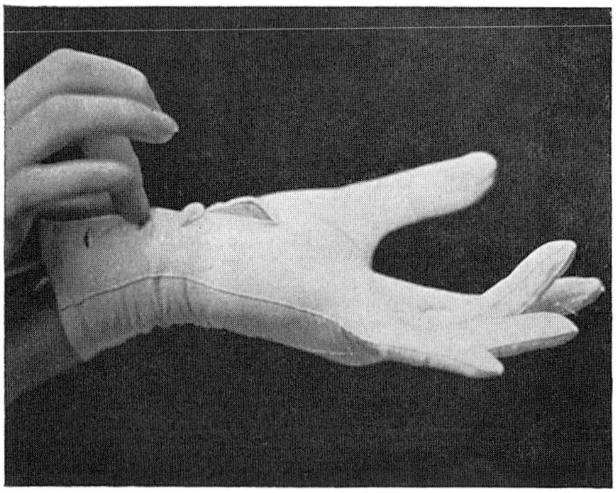 (*f*)

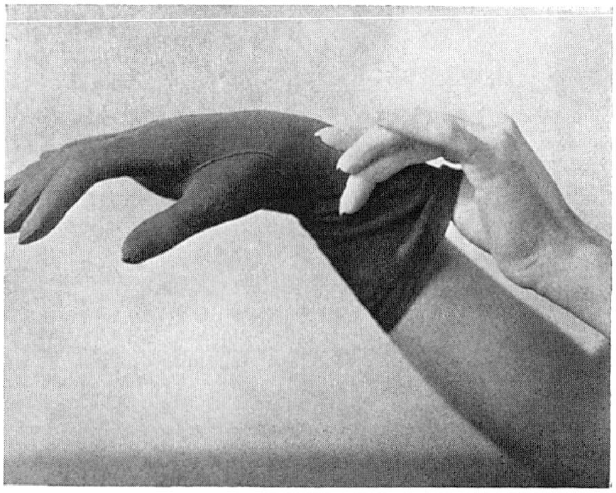

(*a*) Thumb first. (*b*) A gentle pull. (*c*) Down to the finger-tips.
(*d*) Between the fingers. (*e*) Buttoning the wrist. (*f*) Well down at the back.

HANDS AND GLOVES

IT has been said that some artists have given themselves away by their disregard of hands or ineffectual rendering of them. In some cases it is a question of shallowness of knowledge, but just as often of neglect and disrespect. It is often assumed that no importance need be paid to the drawing or study of hands, and that the public pays little attention to their faithful or careful representation.

Hands are as vitally part of the personality as the face, and almost as difficult to portray; and yet with a certain amount of practice and perspicuity the artist can soon distinguish between the bony or fleshy, plump or muscular hand, the capable, the fastidious, or the fussy hand, the demonstrative or reticent hand. By a study of these types his draughtsmanship will soon be able to evolve the essential character of each.

In drawing a pair of hands effectively the first essential is to analyse their construction and then to measure their proportions with care. But to render them effectively the artist must also make a careful study of their natural movements and attitudes. An attempt has been made in this section to aid him to this end and to assemble for his benefit a series of photographs of graceful hands in a variety of natural positions, at work and at rest. The gloved hand has also been included for the usefulness of its application in fashion-drawing and commercial art.

ENLARGED DETAILS FROM THE STANDARD POSES

THESE have been included for their utility to artists and students. The first page (148) is devoted to feet, which are perhaps as difficult as hands to represent successfully, and just as often hastily and inaccurately sketched in. Following this are details of neck, shoulders, and torso (pages 149 to 151) which show to a large scale how bones and muscles respond to various movements. They should be studied carefully in conjunction with the actual poses from which they are enlarged. The last page (152) is of knees and legs. The knees again suffer severely at the hands of careless or inexperienced artists who neglect their really quite simple system of joint and muscle.

We would advise the student to make a careful study of these examples in conjunction with the skeletons on pages 73 and 74. A good knowledge of the skeleton is half the battle in obtaining anatomical exactitude. The important principles to be understood from these pages, however, are the disposition of the muscles in the more complicated portions of the human mechanism when subjected to varying movements. Their study, it is hoped, will go some way towards driving this home, though it can never wholly be absorbed without actual sketching experience from the living model.

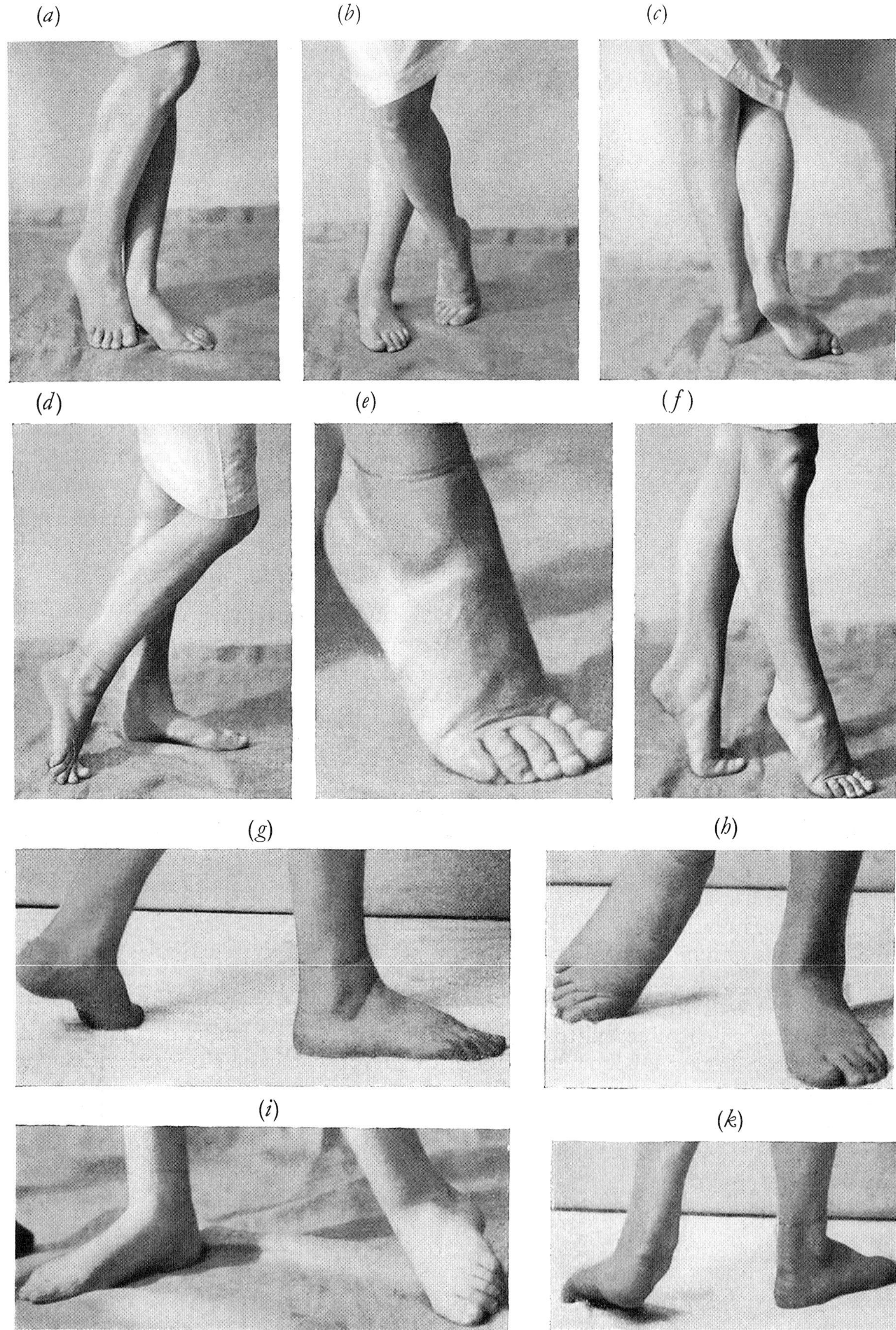

(*a*) Right knee flexed. (*b*) Feet crossed. (*c*) Back view of (*a*). (*d*) A walking movement. (*e*) Tip-toes. (*f*) Tip-toes, both feet. (*g*), (*h*), (*i*), and (*k*). Walking movements.

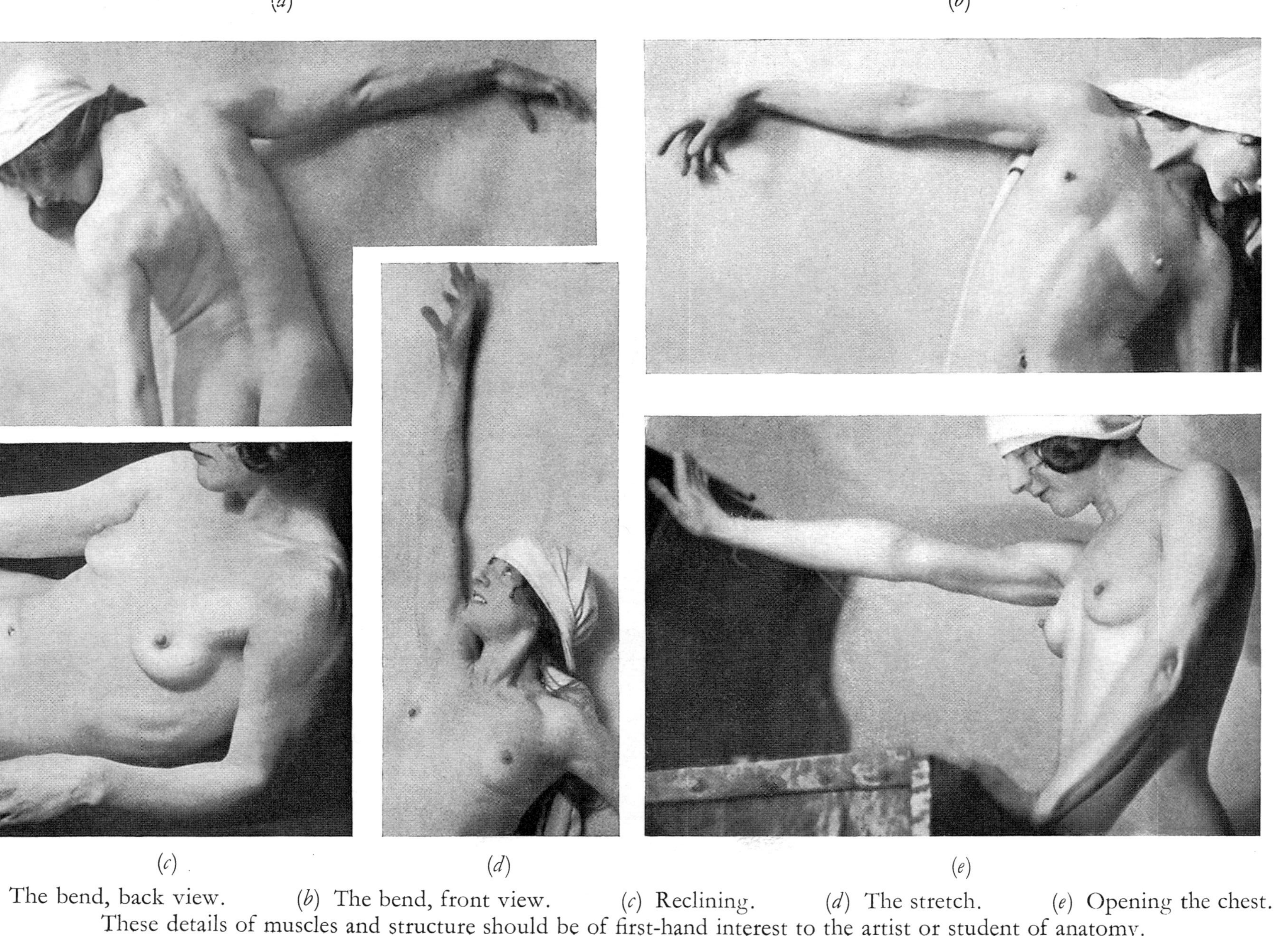

(*a*) The bend, back view. (*b*) The bend, front view. (*c*) Reclining. (*d*) The stretch. (*e*) Opening the chest. These details of muscles and structure should be of first-hand interest to the artist or student of anatomy.

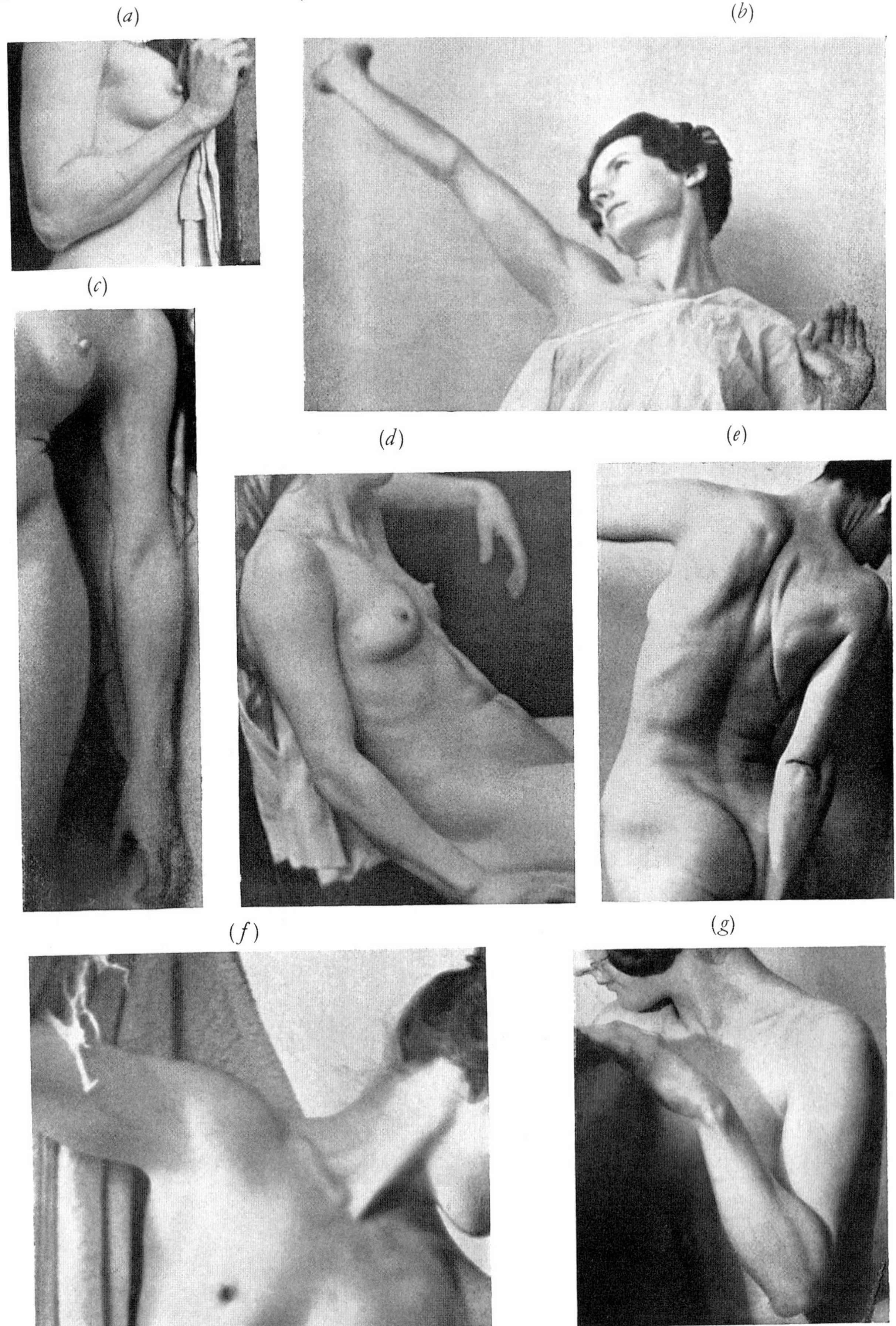

(*a*) Gripping a parasol. (*b*) Stretching after sleep. (*c*) A droop to the left. (*d*) Reclining, muscles relaxed. (*e*) A swing to the right, shoulder-blades drawn together. (*f*) A towelling movement. (*g*) A leaning pose.

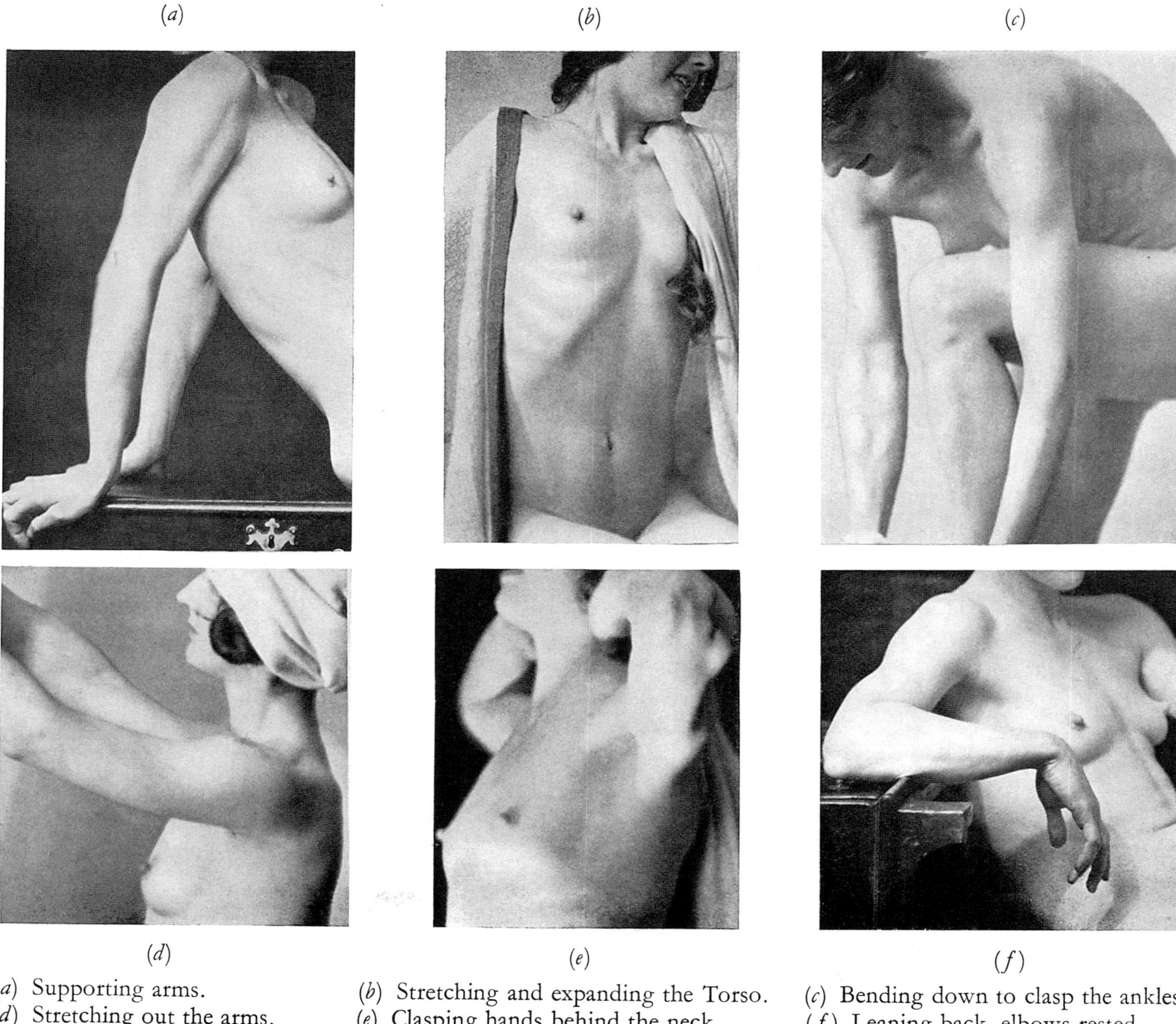

(a) Supporting arms.
(d) Stretching out the arms.

(b) Stretching and expanding the Torso.
(e) Clasping hands behind the neck.

(c) Bending down to clasp the ankles.
(f) Leaning back, elbows rested.

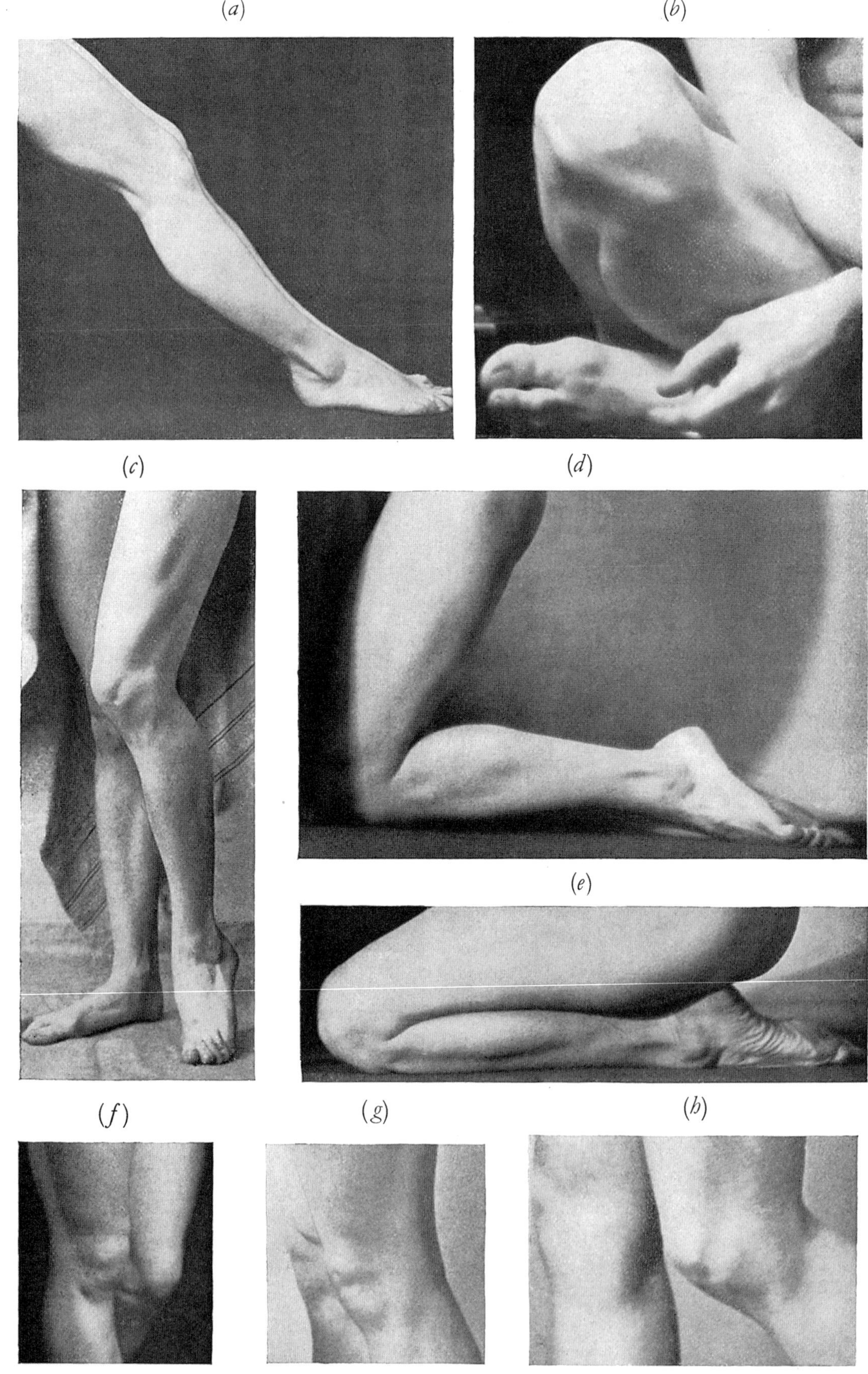

(*a*) The sitting position, legs outstretched. (*b*) Squatting, with arms crossed over knees. (*c*) Standing, left knee flexed. (*d*) Kneeling upright. (*e*) Kneeling backwards. (*f*), (*g*), and (*h*) Some walking movements of the knees.